Reward Management

Human Resource Management in Action Series

Edited by Brian Towers

Successful Training Practice   Alan Anderson

Managing Performance Appraisal Systems   Gordon Anderson

Employee Relations in Europe   Jeff Bridgford and John Stirling

Practical Employment Law   Paul Lewis

The Successful Management of Redundancy   Paul Lewis

Managing the Team   Mick Marchington

The Japanization of British Industry   Nick Oliver and
Barry Wilkinson

Managing Managers   Ed Snape, Tom Redman and Greg Bamber

Strategy and the Human Resource   Ken Starkey and
Alan McKinlay

Handbook of Human Resource Management   Brian Towers

Other HRM books from Blackwell Business

Successful Selection Interviewing   Neil Anderson and
Vivian Shackleton

The Equal Opportunities Handbook   Helen Collins

The EU Pregnancy Directive   Helen Collins

Industrial Relations   Edited by Paul Edwards

The Human Resources Management Handbook
Edited by Gerald R. Ferris, Sherman D. Rosen,
Darold T. Barnum

Personnel Management   Edited by Keith Sisson

Developments in the Management of Human Resources   John Storey

Handbook of Training and Development   Edited by Steve Truelove

Reward Management

Employee Performance, Motivation and Pay

David A. Hume

The right of David A. Hume to be identified as author of this work has been
asserted in accordance with the Copyright, Designs and Patents Act 1988.

First published 1995

Reprinted 1998

Blackwell Publishers Ltd
108 Cowley Road
Oxford OX4 1JF, UK

Blackwell Publishers Inc
350 Main Street
Malden, Massachusetts 02148, USA

British Library Cataloguing in Publication Data
A CIP catalogue record for this book is available from the British Library

*Library of Congress Cataloging in Publication Data*has been applied for.

ISBN 0–631–19623–4 (Pbk)

Typeset in 11 on 13pt Plantin
by Best-set Typesetter Ltd, Hong Kong
Printed and bound in Great Britain
by Athenæum Press Ltd, Gateshead, Tyne & Wear

This book is printed on acid-free paper

Contents

Figures

Tables

Acknowledgements

I would like to thank my students, colleagues and friends at SAC for their support and patience when I was 'locked away' writing this book. I would also like to thank the many individuals and organizations who have made valuable contributions to this book by providing information for the text.

A special thank you to my wife Karlyn, and children Ross, Nicola and Ryan for their love, patience and support.

1
Employee and Organizational Performance

Introduction

MORE MONEY = HIGHER EMPLOYEE PERFORMANCE LEVELS? – Is this the answer to employee motivation within the modern business world? Throughout the 1980s and 1990s the topic of financial rewards for employees has become a very important, at times controversial, topic on the agenda of most human resource management professionals. New payment structures and the increasing use of performance related remuneration (PRR) have resulted in reward management becoming a very complicated and specialized area within the human resource management profession. The aim of this book is to discuss the main issues surrounding the process of rewarding employees in return for their contribution to the organization. Whilst the book is primarily concerned with extrinsic financial or remunerative rewards, it also discusses the importance of non-financial intrinsic rewards. Although financial rewards can have a very dramatic effect, both positive and negative, on the work performance of employees, the effect of non-financial rewards should never be underestimated.

Organization Performance

Prior to the industrial revolution of the eighteenth century, the organization of work, and therefore of labour, tended to be on a small scale. Such organization was primarily based on the cottage industries with networks of widely dispersed workers. The advent of the industrial revolution initiated the movement of workers from rural settings to large industrial organizations in urban towns and cities. The managers of these new, large organizations were required to develop new managerial skills to be able to organize and co-ordinate the management of resources on a large scale. One such skill which these managers had to acquire was the ability to manage human resources on a large scale. Further development of large industrial organizations continued uninterrupted for more than one hundred years, until the second half of the nineteenth century. By this time, organizations were faced with new business pressures from the industrialized world:

- increasing competition;
- trade restrictions;
- new technologies;
- the rapid growth of organized labour.

As a result of such pressures, organizations were required to evaluate their overall performance and effectiveness, such evaluations becoming a prerequisite for organizational success. As part of these evaluations, organizations had to consider how the following factors influenced their overall performance:

- the organizational structure;
- the quality of product/service;
- the demands of the customer/consumer;
- the competitive position;
- forward planning;
- technology;
- human resources (employees).

This book focuses on the contribution of employees to the overall performance of organizations. It examines how employers attempt to improve employee performance through reward policies, in particular, by forming a correlation between such performance and subsequent remuneration – performance related remuneration (PRR). The underlying assumption is that if employee performance can be improved as a result of remunerative incentives, this in turn will improve the performance of the organization.

Employee Performance

Within modern organizations, whilst labour is one of the most important assets, it is often one of the major operating costs. Therefore, it is essential that in return for expenditure on salaries, wages and other remunerative benefits, employers are assured a high level of performance from their employees. In other words, to be able to run efficient and productive organizations, employers must receive value for money from their employees.

To be able to improve the performance of employees, the motivation of individuals or groups of individuals requires careful consideration. Whilst the topic of motivation will be discussed fully in chapter 2, any successful motivation policy will involve stimulating the employees to behave in a manner which is appropriate to the business strategy of the organization and will result in the fulfilment of the organizational objectives. The primary objectives of most organizations tend to relate to increased efficiency/productivity, the strategy required to achieve such objectives being based on a number of performance management techniques. Whilst the topic of performance management is discussed fully in chapter 3, some of the techniques which are likely to be components of a performance management system include:

1 *Reducing worker fatigue* This approach involves manipulating ergonomic factors within the working environment such as rest pauses, temperature, humidity, lighting intensity and the design of the work station in an attempt to reduce worker fatigue and improve performance.
2 *Human relations management* The theory behind this approach is that by smoothing out employment relationships between managers and staff, and between the staff themselves, improved levels of performance can be gained.
3 *Management systems* This approach suggests that different organizations require different management systems in order to obtain high levels of performance from their employees, such requirements depending on the type of business or industry. Some organizations require 'organic' management systems reflected in high levels of employee commitment achieved through loosely defined responsibilities and relationships, free communication, and co-operation across hierarchical and divisional

boundaries. Other organizations require 'mechanistic' management systems characterized by high levels of control over employees gained through clearly defined duties, responsibility and
authority, specified chains of command, and structured channels
of communication.

4   *Job enrichment*   The aim of this approach is to improve employee performance by increasing employee motivation through
various aspects of work design such as increasing individual
responsibility, recognition and achievement through management techniques such as job rotation, job enlargement, and
the use of work groups. Horizontal job enrichment involves
increasing employee control over the immediate job. Vertical
job enrichment involves increasing employee involvement in
the organization and/or their jobs. This may be achieved by
increased involvement in the organization's policy making,
increased job responsibility, and increased opportunities for
training and advancement. Overall, job enrichment involves
increased employee participation in organizational activities/
processes.

5   *Work study*   The principles of work study are: (a) to find a better
way of doing a job, and (b) to establish how long that job should
take. By combining these two principles, the aim of work study is
to improve the performance and effective use of human (and
other) resources.

6   *Performance related remuneration*   This approach aims at improving   employee   performance   by   increasing   employee
motivation through financial incentives directly related to the
work performance of the employee. This approach will be
referred to throughout the book and is discussed in detail in
chapter 11.

Whilst it is clear that there are many approaches to improving
employee performance, those mentioned above being some examples, there are several important points to note:

1   Each approach may be used on its own but is likely to be more effective
when used in conjunction with one or more other approaches.
2   What may be successful in one organization may be unsuccessful in
another organization – each attempt at managing employee performance must be considered in relation to the culture and objectives of the
organization concerned.

3   Each approach can be used in an attempt to improve the performance of individuals *or* the performance of work groups (departments, sections, workplaces, organizations).

Employee Performance and Remuneration

Whilst the principle of remunerating employees for service to their employer is not new, the past 20 years have been dominated by an increasing trend in the development and use of systems of performance related remuneration. The primary aim of performance related remuneration is to improve the performance of the organization by improving the performance of the employees. Such performance improvement is dependent on the successful fulfilment of a series of objectives identified in a research paper by Angela M. Bowey, *et al.* (1982) 'Effects of incentive payment systems, United Kingdom 1977–1980'. From a series of 15 possible objectives of incentive schemes, Bowey, *et al.* (in Smith 1989) found that managers and supervisors considered those in the list below to be the most important. Performance related remuneration is therefore concerned with improving organizational performance by improving employee performance through a remuneration system which will help to guarantee the recruitment, retention and effective deployment of a highly motivated workforce.

Objectives	Percentage of respondents
To increase earnings	69
To increase output	75
To improve quality	29
To improve labour flexibility	31
To reduce labour turnover	25
To reduce overtime	27
To improve recruitment	26
To motivate	48
To increase profits	43

The use of performance related remuneration is based on the assumption that the motivation of employees will be increased, and performance improved, by the attraction and receipt of financial incentives. Whilst remuneration is a major inducement and can improve employee performance, it is dangerously simplistic to consider this as the only motivator. Motivation is a complex process with individuals having different needs and goals. Consequently, there are various employment and organizational factors which can act as employee motivators. The application and effect of such factors must be considered when examining the use of performance related remuneration. It should be noted at this stage that remuneration does not simply refer to money in the form of salary, bonus and commission, for example. Remuneration is normally a reward package involving such aspects as:

- salary
- bonus
- commission
- profit sharing
- pension scheme
- sick pay
- holidays
- cars
- housing assistance
- medical benefits
- low interest loans
- subsidized catering
- crèches

Remuneration can therefore be considered to be a total package involving all aspects of pay and employee benefits.

As a consequence of the complexity of motivation and the diverse nature of remuneration, there are many methods of relating the performance of employees directly to their remuneration. Some of these methods are outlined below and will be examined in more detail in chapter 11.

1   *Payment by results*   Such systems take many forms but essentially involve relating the pay or part of the pay of an employee or group of employees to the number of items they produce or the time they take to do a certain amount of work. Examples of payment by results systems include piecework, measured day work, productivity agreements and gainsharing.

2   *Value added strategy*   This is an organizational application where the workforce is financially rewarded for their contribution to the improved performance, profitability and overall effectiveness of the organization. Such contribution can be achieved through

increased manufacturing productivity, improved utilization of assets, improved quality and reduced costs.

3 *Commission* The use of commission as a performance motivator is primarily used within jobs involving the sale of products or services. The employee or group of employees are financially rewarded in a way which is related to the number or volume of sales. Some sales positions are based solely on commission whilst others involve a basic salary with a bonus or commission in addition.

4 *Merit pay* This is a method which involves the assessment of employee performance against a predetermined performance standard and the provision or non-provision of appropriate financial rewards. Such financial rewards may be provided in the form of a financial bonus or a salary increase. Merit pay often involves performance appraisal as the method of assessing employee performance.

5 *Profit sharing* The main principle behind profit sharing is that employees will be financially rewarded on the basis of the financial performance and profitability of the organization. Such financial reward is based on a predetermined proportion of pre-tax profits and can take the form of cash, shares or share trusts.

6 *Profit related pay* This is a system of remuneration where a proportion of the employee's earnings is directly related to the financial performance and profitability of the organization.

Structure of Book

This book has been structured to provide the reader with a discussion of the main issues relating to reward management. The first part of the book, chapters 2–4, examines the area of employee motivation and discusses the role which remuneration may have in motivating employees to behave in a manner which is supportive of the business objectives of the organization. The second part of the book, chapters 5–8, concentrates on the practicalities of remunerating employees – the development of payment systems, the types of payment systems which can be used (and factors affecting their design), job evaluation and equal pay. The third part of the book, chapters 9 and 10, discusses the provision of non-cash remunerative benefits whilst chapter 11 examines the issue of performance related remuneration. The penultimate chapter of the book discusses the issues relating to remunerating expatriate employees and the book concludes with chapter 13 which considers how employers should manage the reward system.

2

Theories of Motivation

Introduction

Motivation is essentially an area of psychology which attempts to explain why people, or animals, behave in a certain manner. The study of motivation involves the examination of two aspects of behaviour. Firstly, motivation is concerned with the influences which cause specific actions in humans – the direction of behaviour. Secondly, motivation also involves consideration of the intensity or strength of behaviour. Although humans can be motivated to act in a similar fashion, the degree of effort or commitment can vary enormously. For example, two students can be motivated to study by the prospect of impending exams, but the degree or intensity of the behaviour can differ between the two students. Similarly, whilst employees will normally attend work in return for an agreed wage or salary, the level of effort or work rate of employees receiving the same wage or salary is likely to be significantly different. Motivation is therefore concerned with both the direction and intensity of behaviour – what causes specific actions, and what determines the intensity of such action.

Throughout the twentieth century, there has been much written by social scientists on the subject of motivation. The theories which have emerged are many and varied, and often conflicting if not contradictory. Several names are prominent in the field of psychological theories of motivation: Maslow, Herzberg, McGregor, Tolman, Vroom, Locke, Watson and Pavlov. The objective of this chapter is to examine and evaluate some of the theories of motivation and relate them to the application of the basic principles of motivation to workplace situations, this area of motivation being known as employee motivation. Employee motivation is essential in any workplace if the goals and objectives of the organization are to be fulfilled. The senior managers within organizations must therefore ensure that the overall business strategy of their organization takes adequate account of employee motivation and utilizes appropriate management policies to guarantee high levels of employee performance and commitment. At a basic level, a well-motivated workforce will contribute more to, and help to guarantee, the profitability and success of the organization. However, it is not only the organization which will benefit; a well-motivated employee is more likely to be satisfied and fulfilled within their organizational role. The responsibility for employee motivation lies with group or team leaders, often the supervisor or manager. Whilst some methods of motivation may be outwith their control, supervisors and managers are in the best position to motivate their staff on a day-to-day basis.

In order to examine some of the motivation theories, it is useful to categorize the various theories into three schools of thought, namely, physiological theories, cognitive theories and social/behaviourist theories.

The *physiological theories* are based on the assumption that humans have a set of innate needs or drives and that these needs or drives constitute the biological determinants of our behaviour. Such theories suggest that humans are motivated to act in a specific way in an attempt to satisfy or fulfil a series of innate needs. These needs are with us when we are born and remain with us throughout life. The suggestion from the physiological theorists, therefore, is that human beings merely react to their innate needs and will act in such a way that these needs will be satisfied. Such an approach can be described as passive-reaction, reacting in an automatic fashion to the innate drives which are present at any point in time. Social scientists associated with physiological motivation theories include Maslow, Herzberg, McGregor, Alderfer and McClelland.

In contrast to the physiological theories, the *cognitive theories* suggest that motivation is an active response by humans to factors both inside and outside the individual. The cognitive theories stress that motivation results from a conscious assessment of the effort and subsequent implications of certain actions. Cognitive theories propose that individuals will only perform specific actions once they have undergone a rational process of reasoned judgements of such actions, so there is therefore an emphasis on the conscious and purposive nature of behaviour. The social science theorists identified with cognitive theories of motivation include Vroom, Lewin, Locke, Heider, Kelly and Tolman.

Social/behaviourist theories form the third school of thought and draw together two approaches to motivation: social theory and behaviourist theory. The base for these theories is the assumption that humans are motivated by external factors, that is, the environment. The suggestion is that our actions are reflexive and instinctive and are the response to a specific stimulus or group of stimuli from the outside environment. The behaviourist theory places great emphasis on the effect of learning and reinforcement, and as a result the behaviourist theory of motivation is closely connected to the psychological theories of learning and reinforcement. The social theorists are primarily concerned with the effect of society on the behaviour and actions of individuals. As a result, the social theorists are especially interested in the interaction between individuals and groups and the effect of society on behaviour. Bringing both approaches together, the social/behaviourist theories of motivation are concerned with the effect of the environment on the behaviour of individuals and place a specific emphasis on the effect of social interaction. Social scientists associated with the social/behaviourist theories of motivation include Lawler, Watson, Taylor, Thorndike, Pavlov and Skinner.

To be able to draw some conclusions regarding the importance and effect of motivation, especially in the workplace, it is necessary to examine each approach to the subject of motivation and assess their value and worth.

Physiological Theories

A. H. Maslow

Perhaps the best known physiological theory of motivation is the hierarchy of needs theory developed by Abraham H. Maslow. The theory suggests that each individual has a series of innate needs. If such needs are unfulfilled then the individual will be motivated to act in a specific manner in an attempt to gratify these unfulfilled needs. It should be noted that Maslow is concerned with needs and not wants. He advocates that all individuals have a set of human needs which are prioritized on an ascending scale, primary needs dealing with physiology and safety, and secondary needs dealing with the psychological aspects of human existence – Maslow's hierarchy of

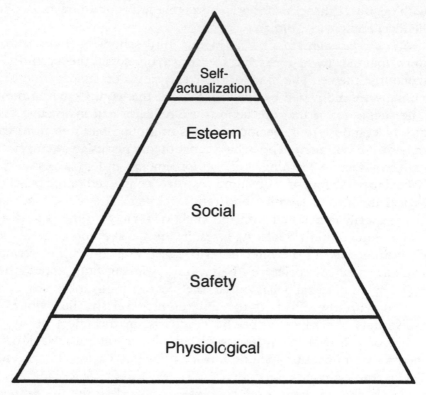

Figure 2.1　*Maslow's hierarchy of needs*

needs. These needs in ascending order are: physiological, safety, social/love, esteem, and self-actualization, see figure 2.1.

Physiological needs　These are primary biological needs related to survival, such as hunger, thirst, sleep and sex. Maslow suggests, however, that it is pointless trying to categorize *all* of the physiological needs because the list could be endless depending on how one defines the necessary requirements for survival. As Maslow (1954) states: 'It seems impossible as well as useless to make any list of fundamental physiological needs, for they can come to almost any number one might wish, depending on the degree of specificity of description.' Maslow views the physiological needs as the most important group of needs since an individual who is 'missing everything in life in an extreme fashion' (Maslow, 1954) is likely to be motivated by the physiological needs, such as hunger and thirst, more than any other need. Once the physiological needs are fulfilled, motivation for the individual comes from safety needs.

Safety needs These needs are concerned with physical and psychological freedom from danger. Maslow (1954) categorizes the safety needs as 'The need for . . . security; stability; dependency; protection; freedom from fear, from anxiety and chaos; need for structure, order, law limits; strength in the protector; and so on.'

Maslow (1954) does, however, suggest that in a 'smoothly running, stable, good society' the average individual does not have any real safety needs as motivators since the safety needs would only become apparent when there was a societal breakdown or where an individual had a mental problem or was an economic or social underdog. When the physiological and safety needs are satisfied, in whatever manner, motivation comes from social needs.

Social needs These needs, sometimes known as love needs or belongingness needs, refer to the needs for friendship, love, and acceptance/belongingness to a group. Maslow (1954) suggests that when a person's social needs are not satisfied 'he will hunger for affectionate relations with people in general, namely, for a place in his group or family, and he will strive with great intensity to achieve this goal . . . he will feel sharply the pangs of loneliness, of ostracism, of rejection, of friendlessness or rootlessness.'

Esteem needs If the previous three sets of needs are satisfied, then the need for esteem emerges and forms the base for individual motivation. Esteem needs refer to the requirement to develop and maintain self-respect, respect from others, status and recognition. Maslow (1954) classifies the esteem needs into two subsidiary sets:

> First, the desire for strength, for achievement, for adequacy, for mastery and competence, for confidence in the face of the world, and for independence and freedom. Second, we have what we may call the desire for reputation or prestige, status, fame and glory, dominance, recognition, attention, importance, dignity or appreciation. Satisfaction of the self-esteem need leads to feelings of self-confidence, worth, strength, capability, and adequacy, of being useful and necessary in the world.

Self-actualization needs Assuming that the first four categories of needs are satisfied, the need for self-actualization surfaces. Self-actualization can be described as the need to fulfil one's potential. It is not concerned with the opinions or views of others but is only concerned with satisfying oneself that one is doing the best that they can – reaching what they believe to be their full potential. Maslow (1954) defines self-actualization as 'the desire to become more and more what one is, to become everything that one is idiosyncratically capable of becoming'.

Whilst many writers (such as Smith, 1989; Rawlins, 1992; Baird *et al.*, 1990) describe Maslow's hierarchy as having these five groups of needs, Maslow actually proposes that there are an additional two sets of needs which are 'immediate prerequisites' (Maslow, 1954) for the satisfaction of the other five sets of needs. These needs are the need for freedom of speech and inquiry, and the need to know and understand.

The need for freedom of speech and inquiry Maslow suggests that in order to satisfy the five groups of needs outlined above, it is necessary for the individual to have the freedom to express themselves, the freedom to investigate and seek information, and the freedom to encourage justice, fairness and honesty.

The need to know and understand Like the need for freedom of speech and inquiry, Maslow suggests that if the physiological, safety, social, esteem and self-actualization needs are to be fulfilled, the individual must have the freedom to gain knowledge and understanding. Maslow (1954) defines this as 'a desire to understand, to systemize, to organize, to analyse, to look for relations and meanings, to construct a system of values'. Maslow (1954) stresses the importance of such conditions 'since without them the basic satisfactions are quite impossible, or at least, severely endangered'.

With regards to the hierarchical structure of his theory, Maslow suggests that individuals begin by trying to fulfil the lower needs (physiological) and only once these needs are satisfied will the individual be motivated to fulfil the next set of needs (safety). Such a procedure continues up the hierarchical structure with the fulfilment of one set of needs opening up the desire to fulfil another set of needs. Maslow believed, however, that very few people manage to satisfy the highest set of needs (self-actualization).

It should be noted that the ascending scale is not a one-way process – if lower needs become unfulfilled, then the individual will revert back to being motivated by the lower set of needs. Maslow did not believe, however, that his hierarchy would apply rigidly to all individuals. He believed that some individuals would try to fulfil higher needs at the expense of not fulfilling lower needs. The struc-

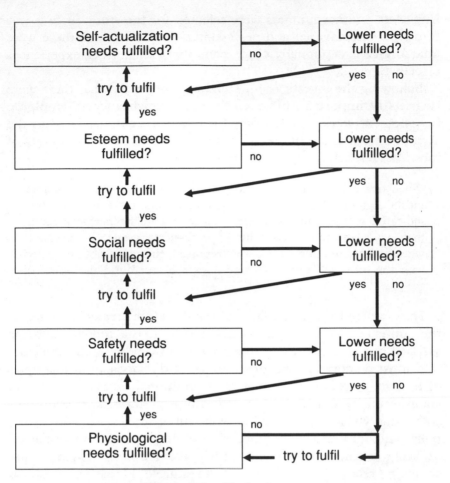

Figure 2.2 *Maslow's system*

ture and systems of Maslow's hierarchy of needs might be summarized as in figure 2.2.

F. W. Herzberg

The two factor model of motivation developed by Frederick W. Herzberg is essentially concerned with explaining motivation at work – employee motivation (Herzberg *et al.*, 1959). Herzberg and his colleagues performed a study in an attempt to develop a theory of employee motivation by determining what people want from their jobs. The investigation centred on approximately 200 accountants and engineers in the Pittsburgh area of the United States of America.

Engineers and accountants were selected for the study since it was found that managerial and professional people such as these were able to give exceptionally vivid accounts of their work experiences (Herzberg *et al.*, 1959).

Following the investigation, Herzberg concluded that there were two sets of important influencing factors which affected employee behaviour at work – dissatisfiers (or hygiene factors) related to the context of jobs and satisfiers (or motivators) related to the content of jobs. As Herzberg *et al.*, 1959 state:

> When our respondents reported feeling happy with their jobs, they most frequently described factors relating to their tasks, to events that indicated to them that they were successful in the performance of their work, and to the possibility of professional growth. Conversely, when feelings of unhappiness were reported, they were not associated with the job itself but with conditions that surround the doing of the job.

Dissatisfiers (or hygiene factors) are therefore elements related to the context of jobs which do not result in the individual being satisfied but merely prevent the individual from being dissatisfied – they must be correct/appropriate to avoid dissatisfaction. Examples of hygiene factors include working conditions, salary, supervision, status, security, personal life, relationships with peers, relationships with supervisors, relationships with subordinates, and company policy and administration. Since most of these factors can be classed as being extrinsic to the individual, avoidance of dissatisfaction should be relatively simple. A central feature of Herzberg's theory is that although an organization may have appropriate hygiene factors for each employee, such a situation will not motivate the employee but merely remove the barriers to motivation – the dissatisfiers. As Herzberg *et al.* (1959) state:

> Improvement in these factors of hygiene will serve to remove the impediments to positive job attitudes. When these factors deteriorate to a level below that which the employee considers acceptable, then job dissatisfaction ensues. However, the reverse does not hold true. When job context can be characterized as optimal, we will not get dissatisfaction, but neither will we get much in the way of positive attitudes.

It is therefore essential that the hygiene factors are correct before the motivators can have any effect; if there is any dissatisfaction then the individual cannot be motivated. Herzberg's hygiene factors tend to reflect stages one, two and three of Maslow's hierarchy of needs.

The satisfiers (or motivators) are those factors within the workplace which resulted in the individuals being satisfied at work. The workers are therefore motivated by such factors since they lead to satisfaction. Examples of motivators could be achievement, recognition, responsibility, advancement, growth and the work itself. Such factors are essentially intrinsic to the individual and can therefore be difficult to satisfy. Herzberg views the satisfiers as elements related to the content of jobs which allow the individual employee to develop their occupation as a source of personal growth. He therefore suggests that employees will be motivated by such factors as they allow them to satisfy the need for self-actualization. The satisfiers or motivators reflect to a certain extent stages four and five of Maslow's hierarchy of needs, esteem and self-actualization.

D. McGregor

Douglas McGregor is perhaps best known for his analysis of motivation at work (McGregor, 1960). The base for McGregor's theory on motivation is the belief that there is a direct correlation between the way managers treat their workers and worker motivation. According to McGregor, managers tend to have two views on workers' attitudes to work – one which will result in low levels of motivation (Theory X), and one which will result in higher levels of motivation (Theory Y).

Theory X is an elitist management approach where workers are treated with little or no respect, with an emphasis on control, discipline, conformity, obedience and dependence. According to the theory, the attitude of managers towards workers is based on the following beliefs (Evans, 1990):

1　The average human being has an inherent dislike of work, and will avoid it if he or she can.
2　Because of this characteristic dislike of work, most people must be coerced, controlled, directed, threatened with punishment to get them to put forth adequate effort toward the achievement of organizational objectives.
3　The average human being prefers to be directed, wishes to avoid responsibility, has relatively little ambition and wants security above all.

Overall, McGregor's Theory X is patronizing and makes no allowance for worker individualism, ambition or autonomy. At this point, a cautionary note should be emphasized: if you treat people as if they are dumb, rebellious, easily led, lazy, and you feel the need to control them and force them into submission, they may come to believe that they are inferior, and, furthermore, they will almost certainly rebel against such treatment.

Theory Y approaches employee management from an entirely different viewpoint from that of Theory X. Indeed, where Theory X is based on aspects of management such as discipline and control, Theory Y emphasizes decentralization, delegation, participation and consultation. The main characteristics of the Theory Y approach to management can be summarized as follows (Evans, 1990):

1   The expenditure of physical and mental effort in work is as natural as play or rest.
2   External control and the threat of punishment are not the only means of bringing about effort towards organizational objectives. People will work and discipline themselves in the service of objectives to which they are committed.
3   People are committed to objectives in proportion to the rewards associated with achieving the objectives.
4   The average human being learns, under proper conditions, not only to accept but to seek responsibility.
5   The capacity to exercise a relatively high degree of imagination, ingenuity and creativity in the solution of organizational problems is widely, not narrowly, distributed in the population.
6   Under the conditions of modern industrial life, the intellectual capacity of the average human being is only partially utilized.

Overall, Theory Y advocates participative management and suggests that in order to motivate workers it is necessary to allow them to use their abilities and skills within the workplace, because by doing so, they will feel involved as an integral part of the organization.

C. P. Alderfer

The existence, relatedness, growth (ERG) approach to motivation adopted by Clayton P. Alderfer suggests that people are motivated to act in a specific manner in an attempt to bring about individual satisfaction. Alderfer (1972) defines satisfaction as 'the outcome of an event between a person and his environment. It refers to the internal state of a person who has obtained what he was seeking.'

Such satisfaction depends on the fulfilment of three sets of innate needs: existence, relatedness and growth. Whilst these needs are innate, the ERG theory adopts an 'open system' in that individuals are constantly interacting with the environment which in turn affects their behaviour.

Existence needs are essentially concerned with survival and hence are related to material and physiological factors. Examples of existence needs include hunger, thirst and, in the employment field, pay, fringe benefits and working conditions. Relatedness needs recognize that people do not live in a self-contained vacuum but engage in relationships with other people and groups within society. Accordingly, individuals are motivated to seek satisfaction in their social relationships and will behave in such a manner that their relatedness needs will be fulfilled. Relatedness needs are therefore concerned with social processes such as sharing, acceptance, confirmation, understanding and influence. Growth needs essentially refer to creating the optimum use of existing capacities, and the development of new capacities. Satisfaction of growth needs depends on the individual developing to their full potential, as Alderfer (1972) suggests, 'satisfaction ... depends on a person finding the opportunities to be what he is most fully and to become what he can.'

The ERG theory developed by Alderfer has some similarities with Maslow's hierarchy of needs: the existence needs correspond closely with Maslow's physiological and safety needs, the relatedness needs correspond to the social/love needs, and the growth needs correspond with Maslow's esteem and self-actualization needs. Although these similarities exist, Alderfer, unlike Maslow, does not suggest a rigid hierarchical structure and does not propose that an individual will try to satisfy one set of needs at a time.

Overall, Alderfer's ERG theory of motivation is based on the satisfaction of three sets of needs, existence, relatedness and growth, these needs being able to exist simultaneously and to be satisfied in a flexible order. Alderfer explains the relationship between the three sets of needs by providing seven propositions:

1 The less existence needs are satisfied, the more they will be desired.
2 The less relatedness needs are satisfied, the more existence needs will be desired.
3 The more existence needs are satisfied, the more relatedness needs will be desired.

4   The less relatedness needs are satisfied, the more they will be desired.
5   The less growth needs are satisfied, the more relatedness needs will be desired.
6   The more relatedness needs are satisfied, the more growth needs will be desired.
7   The more growth needs are satisfied, the more they will be desired. (Alderfer, 1972)

D. C. McClelland

The theory of motivation developed by David C. McClelland is based on the assumption that individuals have three innate needs which are of primary importance (McClelland, 1961):

1   The need for achievement (n.ach), described as the need for competitive success and high standards of personal excellence.
2   The need for affiliation (n.aff), described as the need for warm, friendly and compassionate relationships with other individuals/groups.
3   The need for power (n.pwr), described as the need to control or influence others.

According to McClelland, all individuals have each of these needs although the level or intensity of the needs varies between each person. Some people can therefore have a high level of n.ach and low levels of n.aff and n.pwr, whilst others have a high level of n.aff and low levels of n.ach and n.pwr. McClelland applies his theory to the field of management and suggests that a high n.ach is important for junior and middle management jobs whilst senior management jobs require a high n.pwr. According to McClelland, a high n.aff is not helpful at any level of management.

Overall, the motivation theory developed by McClelland is based on the desire to fulfil three innate needs (n.ach, n.aff and n.pwr) which are present to differing extents in all individuals. The relationship between the three needs has important implications for management careers.

Evaluation of Physiological Theories

The central feature and main strength of the physiological theories of motivation is that they identify a basic motivational influence on every individual – their innate needs. It is clear that the behaviour of all human beings, irrespective of their age, sex or cultural background, is influenced by the presence of innate needs – they are motivated to satisfy or fulfil their natural physiological needs. The set of needs present in any individual at any point in time is unique to that person and depends on such factors as their physiological state, age and their rate of growth. Physiological needs could include hunger, thirst, safety, belongingness and self-fulfilment.

The main criticism of the physiological theories is that they rely entirely on passive-reaction to innate needs and make no allowance for the influence of rational cognitive decisions or the effect of societal and environmental factors. There is no suggestion that individuals can be motivated by any other factor apart from physiological needs, such as societal pressure or the value judgements taken when arriving at a decision.

When examining the motivation of employees, the physiological theories of motivation can have important implications. Since the behaviour of employees can be influenced by many different factors, the management of human resources is a very complicated issue. If, however, it can be demonstrated that a particular management style or policy can assist with satisfying the innate needs of employees, it may be possible to encourage specific forms of behaviour by providing the means by which particular innate needs can be satisfied. For example, if an employee has an unfulfilled need for esteem and it is shown that particular forms of behaviour will result in praise, encouragement and recognition, the employee is likely to behave in a manner which will result in the satisfaction of their esteem needs.

Physiological Theories and Remuneration

Since the physiological theories of motivation are based on the presence of a set of innate needs within each individual, remuneration could only serve to improve or increase employee motivation if the provision of additional aspects of remuneration would assist in the satisfaction of these innate needs. With reference to Maslow's hierarchy of needs, for example, remuneration could help to satisfy needs in each level of the hierarchy. At the lowest level, remuneration in the form of cash could help to satisfy the hunger needs. At the second level, remuneration again in the form of cash could help to satisfy safety needs by purchasing safety equipment such as a burglar alarm. In each level of the hierarchy, it is therefore possible that remuneration could assist in the fulfilment of certain needs.

In Herzberg's two factor model of motivation, remuneration is not considered to be a motivating factor, indeed it is a factor which requires to be appropriate in order to avoid dissatisfaction. Herzberg does, however, agree that remuneration can play a role in successful motivational schemes. As Herzberg *et al.* (1959) comment:

> Reports on the Lincoln Electric Company of Cleveland, Ohio and the George A. Hormel meat-packing plant at Austin, Minnesota, suggest good examples of the efficacy of money incentives for increasing production, job satisfaction, and company loyalty. [In such systems] money earned as a direct reward for outstanding individual performance is a reinforcement of the motivators of recognition and achievement.

As stated earlier, Alderfer's ERG theory of motivation has many similarities with Maslow's hierarchy of needs in that people are motivated to fulfil a series of innate needs. In the same way as remuneration applies to Maslow's theory, it also applies to Alderfer's theory in that remuneration could help to satisfy needs in each of the three sets of needs proposed by Alderfer – existence, relatedness and growth.

McClelland's theory of motivation suggests the presence of three innate needs which are of primary importance: the need for achievement, the need for affiliation, and the need for power. The relationship between remuneration and motivation in this theory is not as clear as it is in Maslow's and Alderfer's theories. However, if remuneration could be shown to assist an individual in the fulfilment of any of the above three innate needs, its use could be of significant importance.

The Theory X/Theory Y approach of McGregor stresses the importance of factors such as worker involvement, recognition and achievement in much the same way as Herzberg. As a result, it is unlikely that remuneration has a significant role to play since the emphasis is on participative management.

Overall, if it can be shown that an aspect of remuneration could assist in the fulfilment of any of the innate needs emphasized in the above theories, a well-designed remuneration strategy could be an important factor in the motivation of employees. The assumption would be that the employee will behave in a manner which will result in a remunerative reward which in turn will assist in the fulfilment of an innate need. The difficult aspect in attempting to motivate employees through remuneration policies is establishing a method by which remuneration can actually result in satisfying the innate needs of the individual.

Cognitive Theories

As stated earlier, the cognitive theories of motivation are based on the assumption that the behaviour of individuals is determined by a process of conscious and rational evaluations of the outcome and value of such behaviour. The cognitive theorists therefore emphasize the thinking, judging and rational processes which take place prior to action.

E. C. Tolman

One of the earliest cognitive theories to emerge was formulated by Edward C. Tolman, an American psychologist. Tolman proposed an expectancy theory of motivation. This theory suggests that the behaviour of individuals is not based on needs or drives but is determined by the presence of goals and the probability or expectancy that their behaviour will lead to the attainment or achievement of these goals. Tolman's expectancy theory of motivation is therefore based on the assumption that people are not driven by deprivations and needs but rather are guided to important goals by perceptions and cognitions.

Tolman argues that the behaviour of individuals is determined by their expectations of the consequences of such behaviour. Individuals will behave in a specific manner once they have established that there is a high expectancy that such behaviour will have desired results such as the attainment of goals. According to Tolman, therefore, individuals form a mental association between behaviour and the outcome of behaviour. Such associations generate expectancies that certain behaviour will result in certain outcomes. In contrast to the physiological theories of motivation which adopt a universalistic approach where the assumptions of the theories apply to everyone, the expectancy theory developed by Tolman allows for individual motivation and the influence of society.

V. H. Vroom

Victor H. Vroom supported the Expectancy Theory approach of Tolman but developed the idea further, and, in addition to the concept of expectancy, introduced the notions of valence and instrumentality. The base for Vroom's theory is analogous to Tolman's expectancy theory – that individuals will behave in a specific way when there is a high expectancy that such behaviour will result in a desired outcome. As Vroom (1964) states: 'an expectancy is defined as a momentary belief concerning the likelihood that a particular act will be followed by a particular outcome.'

The second aspect which Vroom introduces to his theory is the concept of valence. Valence essentially refers to the value of outcomes or goals. According to Vroom, outcomes can be positively or negatively valent. We can value some outcomes highly and hence desire them (positive), or we can value outcomes lowly and try to avoid them (negative). The valence of outcomes or goals have potential value – we believe that certain behaviour will result in certain outcomes with a specific value even although the reality may be different. We now therefore have the concepts of expectancy and valence as being part of a cognitive process affecting motivation – we are motivated by the fact that we expect specific behaviour to result in specific outcomes and that such outcomes will have a degree of valence. The work of Vroom therefore suggests that behaviour depends firstly on the outcomes that an individual values, and secondly on the expectation that a particular type of behaviour will lead to those outcomes.

The third aspect to be introduced by Vroom is the concept of instrumentality. Vroom suggests that in addition to expectancy and valence, the behaviour of individuals is influenced by the degree to which additional desired goals can be attained as the direct result of such behaviour. Whilst expectancy and valence are concerned with how behaviour results in one specific outcome or goal, instrumentality is concerned with how additional goals are attained as the result of such behaviour, as a by-product or bonus. Vroom therefore proposes that the behaviour (or motivation) of an individual depends on a cognitive process which evaluates:

1   the expectancy that specific behaviour will result in the attainment of a specific goal,
2   the value of the desired goal, and

3 the degree to which such behaviour is instrumental in the attainment of other additional goals.

F. Heider and H. Kelly

The attribution theory of motivation was developed by Harold Kelly, who drew upon the pioneering work of Fritz Heider. Kelly suggests that our behaviour is influenced by a cognitive process which tries to relate the past behaviour of ourselves and others to specific causes – what were the causes behind specific behaviour? The attribution theory is therefore concerned with how we attribute explanations, or causes, to specific events or behaviours. Kelly argues that it is such attributions which influence or motivate our future behaviour. Attributions refer to the perceived causes of the outcomes of behaviour, with implications for the motivation of future behaviours.

Kelly believes that we can explain behaviour by internal attributions or external attributions. The internal attributions involve explaining actions or behaviour as the result of something inside the actor such as personality, mood, intelligence or disposition. External attributions involve explaining actions or behaviour as the result of something external to the actor such as the weather or society. Our attributions of behaviour also depend on three sources of information.

1 *Consensus* This information tells us whether or not the behaviour is characteristic of the immediate social group. Do most people behave this way (the situation causes the action) or is the behaviour uncharacteristic of the immediate social group (something inside the actor causing the behaviour).
2 *Consistency* Such information can tell us whether or not the behaviour is characteristic of the person. Do they normally behave like that or is there something causing uncharacteristic behaviour.
3 *Distinctiveness* This information makes it possible to assign certain factors (people/situations/things) as being the specific causes of behaviour. If an individual behaves in a similar manner in most situations or towards most people/things, then the action is not distinct. If, however, an individual acts in a specific manner in certain situations or towards certain people/things, then the behaviour can be described as being distinctive.

Kelly's attribution theory therefore suggests that behaviour is motivated by the reasons/causes we attribute to previous forms of behaviour.

K. A. Lewin

The phenomenal field theory of motivation owes much of its development to Kurt A. Lewin. Lewin suggests that each individual has a phenomenal field where everything of which we are conscious at any time (every thought, feeling, percept, memory) falls into a pattern of consistent organization, and whenever anything disrupts the organization of the field, a state of tension is set up inside the person, and this tension prods the person into taking action to restore organization.

Lewin therefore believes that the sum of our consciousness makes up our phenomenal field and that we are motivated at all times to keep this field as consistent as possible. If there is any tension or irregularities in the field then we will be motivated to seek goals which reduce and resolve the tension. Such goals therefore have to be attainable and consistent with our phenomenal field.

E. A. Locke

The goal theory of motivation developed by Edwin A. Locke suggests that individuals are motivated when they are set specific goals (Locke & Latham, 1984). The goal theory is therefore primarily concerned with employee motivation. Participation in goal setting is essential, as is feedback on performance. Locke proposes that motivation, and corresponding performance, is best when goals are difficult but based on agreement. Overall, the important aspects of Locke's goal theory are:

1 the setting of difficult goals,
2 participation in goal setting and
3 feedback on performance with guidance and advice.

The goal theory of motivation is similar to the concept of management by objectives where the assumption is that employees can be motivated by managers setting specific objectives.

Evaluation of Cognitive Theories

The main strength of the cognitive theories of motivation is that they identify the importance of conscious rational decision making as a factor which influences behaviour. The suggestion is that before individuals behave in a certain manner, they make a conscious decision as to the likely outcome and perceived value of such behaviour. Before buying a car, for example, the individual will make a decision based on their requirements of the car, the cost, the availability of alternatives, and so on. It is only after such a rational process that the individual will behave in a specific manner – to buy or not buy the car. The cognitive theories suggest that all human behaviour follows such a cognitive process; this is where the weakness of the cognitive theories can be identified. The cognitive theories take no account of reflexive or impulsive actions and therefore do not allow for the presence of innate needs. Cognitive theories must therefore explain reflexive/instinctive actions such as falling asleep.

With regards to employee motivation, the cognitive theories of motivation can have an important role to play if it can be established that the result or expected outcome of behaving in a particular manner has a high positive value to the individual. If an employee has a particular expectancy from a certain form of behaviour, and this has a positive value, the employee will be likely to behave in such a manner. For example, if an employee places a high value on recognition and expects to get a certificate of merit from maintaining a quality standard at work, they will be motivated to behave in a manner which guarantees the quality standard and subsequently results in the award of a certificate of merit.

Cognitive Theories and Remuneration

Since the central feature of the cognitive theories is a rational and conscious process which evaluates the outcome of actions, remuneration will only be useful if the provision of remuneration is valued highly. Each of the cognitive theories, for example, Tolman's expectancy theory of motivation and Vroom's expectancy, valence and instrumentality theory of motivation, suggest that individuals are motivated by the outcome of specific actions – such outcomes being assessed by a rational and conscious process. If the outcome of an action is considered to be valuable, such behaviour will be repeated. If, however, the outcome of an action is not considered to be valuable, or not valuable enough, the behaviour will tend not to be repeated.

The significant aspect of cognitive theories in relation to the use of systems of remuneration is the value of remuneration to the individual. If the individual values remuneration highly, be it in the form of cash or some other remunerative benefit such as a company car, they will be motivated to behave in a way that remunerative benefits will be received. If, however, the individual does not value remuneration highly, they will not be motivated by the offer or lure of remunerative benefits.

Social/Behaviourist Theories

The social/behaviourist theories explain motivation by referring to factors outside the individual. This is in sharp contrast to the physiological theories which are based on innate or internal needs, and the cognitive theories which emphasize the cognitive process of rational thinking and reasoning internal to the individual. The social/behaviourist theories suggest that the causes of behaviour (motivation) are outside the organism, in the environment, and that all human behaviour is therefore determined by, and is solely a product of, external factors in the environment.

The behaviourist approach to motivation cites reinforcement of behaviour as being the external influence determining motivation whilst the social approach specifies social interaction and social demands as being the source of human motives.

J. B. Watson, E. L. Thorndike, I. Pavlov, B. F. Skinner

The behaviourist approach to psychology, including motivation, owes much of its development to the influence of John B. Watson. Watson believed that the behaviour of humans, and animals, was directly determined by their interaction with the external environment. According to Watson, behaviourism can be defined as 'that division of natural science which takes human behaviour – the doings and sayings, both learned and unlearned, of people as its subject matter [and] attempts to formulate, through systematic observation and experimentation, the generalizations, laws and principles which underline man's behaviour' (Gillham, 1981).

Behaviourism therefore attempts to explain human behaviour by reference to influences in the external environment. One of the earliest psychologists to formulate a behaviourist theory was Edward L. Thorndike who studied the relationship between animal behaviour and the environment. Although his research was based on the behaviour of animals, his conclusions have subsequently been applied to human behaviour.

The principle developed by Thorndike was the law of effect. Thorndike proposed that the behaviour of animals was directly affected by the consequences of such action. In particular, he argued that if specific behaviour was followed by reward then the actions are more likely to be repeated. Conversely, behaviour which was followed by punishment tended not to recur. Rewards therefore have a positive effect, encouraging specific behaviour, whilst punishments have a negative effect, discouraging specific behaviour. Such a conclusion reflects the doctrine of hedonism which suggests that our behaviour is determined by the search for pleasure and the avoidance of pain. Thorndike's law of effect lays a heavy emphasis on the concept of reinforcement – maintaining specific forms of behaviour by reinforcing consequences, be they positive or negative. It is this concept of reinforcement which remains central to the behaviourist theory of motivation. Further work on reinforcement will be examined later.

The work of Thorndike also plays an important part in the psychology of learning, in that future behaviour is influenced to a great extent by what we have learned from previous experience will be the likely consequences of specific behaviour. A central feature of Thorndike's law of effect is his belief that the relationship between behaviour and the environment is a simple one. He suggests that animals, or humans, react in an automatic fashion to the consequences of behaviour. 'Thorndike saw the effects of rewards and punishments not as something his subjects thought about, but as an automatic strengthening or weakening of responses by their consequences – that is by the environment' (Mook, 1987).

Overall, Thorndike proposes that human behaviour is motivated by the extent to which past actions have been rewarded or punished. The law of effect therefore laid the foundations for a stimulus–response framework within the psychology of learning/motivation. Such a framework was developed by Watson and is based on the assumption that behaviour is regarded as a series of responses to specific stimuli and that the relationship between a stimulus and response can either be strengthened (by reward) or weakened (by punishment).

The stimulus–response concept has been examined further by two psychologists within the behaviourist tradition, Ivan P. Pavlov and Burrhus F. Skinner. These two psychologists differentiated between two types of responses: respondents and operants.

Respondents can be described as responses which are elicited by a specific stimulus. Such responses are therefore reflexive and are caused by identifiable stimuli. Whilst inbuilt reflexes can be classed as respondents, such as leg withdrawal from a pinprick, additional respondents were identified by Pavlov in his experiments of classical conditioning. As a result of his experiments, Pavlov could, in certain situations, attach a specific response to a particular stimulus. His most famous experiment was with dogs. Essentially, Pavlov conditioned the dogs into associating the ringing of a bell with the provision of food. At first he fed the dogs as normal but subsequently introduced the ringing of a bell prior to the provision of food. Eventually, the dogs formed an association between the bell and the food and consequently started to salivate (expecting food) at the sound of the bell. Such an experiment illustrated that behaviour can be influenced by the presence of a specific stimulus (classical conditioning).

The second type of response, *operants*, were investigated by Skinner. An operant can be described as a response which is not elicited by a stimulus. Such behaviour can therefore be described as voluntary rather than reflexive – responses which have no association with stimuli and hence are emitted by the organism. Such responses can, however, be reinforced by the presence of a positive reinforcing stimulus (operant conditioning). As Mook (1987) suggests, the heart of Skinner's system is his restatement of the law of effect. He presents his law of conditioning for operants: if the occurrence of an operant is followed by the presentation of a reinforcing stimulus, the strength (of the operant) is increased. And there is the converse law of extinction: if the occurrence of an operant already strengthened through conditioning is not followed by the reinforcing stimulus, the strength is decreased.

Both classical and operant conditioning are important contributions to the psychology of learning and reinforcement (motivation). In the first, an animal or human learns an association between two external stimuli – for example, a bell and food – whereas in the second, the animal or human learns an association between a piece of behaviour and an external reinforcing stimulus. Overall, the behaviourist approach to motivation emphasizes the concept of behavioural reinforcement – whether behaviour is rewarded or punished.

The social theory of motivation, like the behaviourist approach, is based on the influence of external factors on behaviour. Central to the social theory is the belief that our behaviour, and motivation, is determined by our interaction with individuals and social groups. The social theory of motivation is therefore concerned with interpersonal behaviour and with group processes. According to the social theorists, examples of human motives resulting from social interaction and social demands include aggression, altruism and affiliation. The conclusion from the social theorists is that our behaviour is largely determined by our comprehension of the behaviour, attitudes and opinions of our fellow human beings.

Evaluation of Social/Behaviourist Theories

The strength of the social/behaviourist theories of motivation is that they recognize the importance of societal and environmental factors as influences upon behaviour. The suggestion is that the behaviour of individuals can be influenced either by societal pressure or by the manipulation of each person's environment. Aspects central to the social/behaviourist theories are learning, reinforcement and conformity. The main weakness of these theories is that they, like the physiological theories, tend to rely on a passive-reaction assumption of human behaviour, suggesting that individuals react to the environment/society in a reflexive and instinctive manner – there is no account taken of cognitive processes.

In the area of employee motivation, the working environment of the employee, including the provision of rewards and punishments, can have a significant effect on the work performance of the individual. In certain circumstances, if the working environment of employees is manipulated, a corresponding effect on performance can often be found, either negative or positive. If the social/behaviourist theory of motivation is to be applied to employee motivation, therefore, the effect of the manipulation of the working environment must result in positive changes in behaviour. For example, if a new employee is assigned to a team which is very committed to high levels of performance which is reinforced by rewards, it is likely that this will have a positive effect on the work rate of the individual. If, however, the new employee was asked to join a team characterized by apathy, lethargy, hostility and poor performance levels, this is likely to have a corresponding negative effect.

Social/Behaviourist Theories and Remuneration

At first glance, the social/behaviourist approach to motivation may be considered to be identical to the cognitive approach to motivation. Whilst both approaches refer to the outcome of behaviour as being the important aspect of motivation, the cognitive approach relies on a rational and conscious decision making process, whereas the social/behaviourist approach relies on an automatic stimulus–response framework.

The use of remuneration within the social/behaviourist theory of motivation depends on whether the employee considers remuneration to be a reward. The theory suggests that if specific forms of behaviour are reinforced with a remunerative reward which is highly valued, such behaviour will be repeated. On the other hand, if no remunerative reward is provided, or is not considered to be highly valued, such behaviour is unlikely to take place. It is therefore clear that if the social/behaviourist theory is accepted, and remuneration is the chosen way to motivate employees, specific forms of behaviour should be reinforced by a highly valued remunerative reward.

Conclusion

Each of the three approaches to motivation which have been examined – physiological, cognitive and social/behaviourist – appear to have both strengths and weaknesses. Ironically, however, what appear to be the weaknesses of one theory can be considered as strengths of an alternative theory.

The main strength of the physiological theories is that they identify a number of innate needs which are present within all humans no matter what age, nationality or cultural background. Such innate needs include hunger, thirst, safety and social acceptance. The main weakness or criticism of the physiological theories is that they rely purely on passive-reaction to the presence of innate needs. In other words, there is no consideration of motivation resulting from behavioural or environmental influences. In addition, the theories take no account of conscious evaluation of the likely outcome of behaviour. By taking a passive-reaction standpoint, there is no reference to the possibility of active cognitive processes relating to individuals and their behaviour.

The central feature of the cognitive theories is an active process involving the conscious assessment of the effort and subsequent implications of certain actions. This feature provides the base for both the strength and weakness of the cognitive approach. The strength relates to the identification that behaviour and motivation can be determined/influenced by conscious judgements of the outcome of specific behaviour. Cognitive theories, therefore, identify a process of reasoned judgements, which can take place prior to specific actions/behaviour. The criticism of the approach relates to the suggestion that all behaviour is preceded by a cognitive process of reasoned judgements. Such an approach does not allow for the possible presence of reflexive/instinctive actions or innate needs.

The strength of the social/behaviourist approach is that it takes account of behaviour modification and social interaction as aspects inherent to any theory of motivation. This approach, therefore, suggests that human action or motivation can be influenced firstly by behaviour modification through processes such as learning and reinforcement, and secondly through social interaction and the corresponding social pressure from individuals or groups. The main criticism of this approach is that it suggests that humans always react to social/behaviourist influences in a reflexive and instinctive manner. This suggestion leaves no room for the possibility of cognitive processes which can influence actions and behaviour.

Overall, it appears that each of the three approaches that have been examined have strengths which help to explain the motivational processes behind human behaviour. Individuals appear to be motivated partly by innate needs, partly by cognitive processes and partly by external influences. It seems that the degree to which these innate needs, cognitive processes and social/behaviourist influences can be used to explain motivation depends on two factors:

1 The stage of development of the individual, both physically and mentally, and
2 The external environmental circumstances.

For example, the motivation behind a baby crying is more likely to be innate needs rather than the result of a cognitive process. Similarly, the motivation behind a company executive changing jobs is more likely to be the result of a cognitive process or social/behaviourist influences than the result of innate needs.

In relation to employee motivation, employees will only be motivated to behave in a particular manner if the management policies of the organization facilitate the fulfilment of innate needs, the achievement of highly valued expectancies or the positive reinforcement of specific forms of behaviour. The use of remuneration as a motivating influence for employees largely depends upon the value which the individual places upon money. If the employee places a high value on money, or any associated benefits, then the attraction of increased remuneration is likely to assist in motivating the employee. On the other hand, if the employee places little value on money, or its associated benefits, then a system of remuneration is unlikely to motivate the employee or directly affect their performance.

In conclusion, therefore, motivation and the value of remuneration as a motivating factor can be explained by reference to the three approaches to motivation theory, the applicability of each approach depending on the development of the individual and the external environmental influences. If the provision of increased remuneration helps in satisfying innate needs, carries a high cognitive value or is considered to be a reward then it is likely that employees will be motivated through the use of remuneration.

3

Performance Management

Introduction

Developed throughout the 1980s, performance management has become yet another trendy management practice, joining other management initiatives such as performance related remuneration (PRR), management by objectives (MBO), quality circles, total quality management, team briefings, empowerment, and so on. A precise definition of performance management is found in Armstrong and Murlis (1991) where the authors state:

> Performance management therefore consists of a systematic approach to the management of people, using performance, goals, measurement, feedback and recognition as a means of motivating them to realize their maximum potential. It embraces all formal or informal methods adopted by an organization and its managers to increase commitment and individual and corporate effectiveness. It is a broader concept than performance appraisal or performance related remuneration (PRR). These can indeed be important elements in a performance management system (PMS). But they will be part of an integrated approach, which consists of an interlocking series of processes, attitudes and behaviours which together produce a coherent strategy for adding value and improving results.

The apparent increase in popularity of performance management as a management technique can be attributed to two main causes. Since the early 1980s, organizations within the United Kingdom and throughout the world have experienced a continually increasing level of market competition from organizations within their home country and from foreign competitors. As a result, it has become imperative that if organizations are to survive and prosper they must ensure high levels of individual, group and corporate performance. In order to generate and sustain such high levels of performance, the senior managers of many organizations have essentially become obsessed with introducing management policies which are likely to have a significant impact on all aspects of performance within their organization. With regards to the performance of employees, performance management is a management technique which brings together a variety of human resource management policies which together focus on the objectives of the organization and the corresponding performance targets of individuals and groups. The objective of performance management is initially to identify employee performance targets and then, by monitoring the work performance of employees towards these targets on a continuous basis, to manage the performance of employees by the use of any appropriate management policies. The second factor which has resulted in the increasing popularity of performance management relates to the changing management culture from a position of controlling workers towards a process of securing employee commitment. Within the organizations of the 1990s, the view is that the co-operation of employees towards corporate objectives is more likely to be secured if the employees are made to feel part of the organization and therefore committed to its success. This is in stark contrast to the mechanistic style of management based on a number of strict regimes aimed at having rigid control over the behaviour and subsequent work performance of employees. Within performance management, the aim is to secure employee commitment to corporate objectives and individual targets by utilizing a number of management policies to assist successful achievement of such targets and objectives.

Parallel to developments in performance management, there have been significant developments in performance related remuneration. Such developments are examined in detail in chapter 5, Developments in Payment Systems. The main objective of performance related remuneration is to establish a correlation between the work performance of employees and their subsequent remuneration. Therefore, a necessary factor within any system of performance related remuneration is the measurement of the work performance of an individual employee or group of employees. Since both performance management and performance related remuneration involve the measurement of employee work performance, there has been a close association between the development of the two initiatives.

Performance Management Systems

In order to be effective, performance management systems must be part of the philosophy, culture and values of the organization and should focus the attention of both employer and employee on one mission – improved individual and organizational performance. Whilst a performance management system should encompass all initiatives aimed at improving performance to meet organizational objectives, the focus should be on a holistic, systematic, continual and cyclical process involving the identification of corporate and individual goals and the subsequent review and evaluation of how far these targets have been achieved. The Institute of Personnel Management (IPM), in their survey *Performance Management in the UK: An Analysis of the Issues* (1992), identified five key features which are likely to be central to an effective performance management system:

- It should communicate a vision of its objectives to all its employees.
- It should set out departmental and individual performance targets which are related to the wider objectives.
- It should conduct a formal review of progress towards these targets.
- It should use the review process to identify training, development and reward outcomes.
- It should evaluate the effectiveness of the whole process in order to improve effectiveness.

The above five features of a performance management system can be incorporated into a performance management cycle such as that illustrated in figure 3.1. The emphasis should be on a continuous, systematic and cyclical process which encompasses a '365 days a year' approach to monitoring and developing employee performance which is located in the context of organizational objectives and group and individual targets. The different stages in the performance management cycle are outlined below.

(1) Corporate objectives established and communicated to all employees. The starting point for any performance management cycle should be the identification and communication of the mission statement of the organization. Before it is possible to identify performance targets for individual employees or groups of employees, it is necessary for the managers of the organization to be clear about

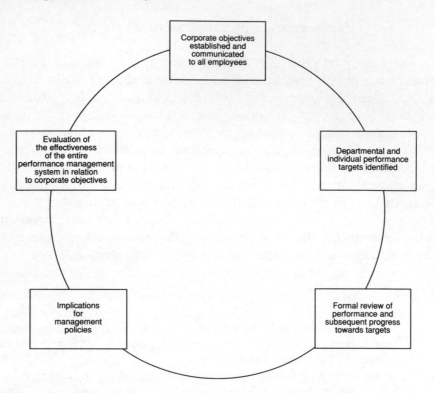

Figure 3.1   *The performance management cycle*

the direction and vision of the organization. Once the managers have a clear picture regarding the objectives of their organization and an appropriate corporate strategy, they must ensure that this vision is effectively communicated to all employees. Irrespective of whether or not the objectives and strategy of the organization changes, communication with employees must have a high profile and be sustained on a continuous basis.

(2)   Identification of group and individual performance targets. Once the corporate objectives have been established, it is necessary for these objectives to be translated into group and individual performance targets. In order to successfully achieve the corporate objectives, each individual employee, in addition to being aware of the mission of the organization, must know what the requirements or targets are for their own individual or group performance. This way, everyone within the organization will be aware of their potential

contribution to the success of the organization, and hopefully be committed to meeting their performance targets.

(3) Formal review of performance and progress towards targets. The next stage in the performance management cycle is to assess the performance of the employees and determine whether or not they are progressing towards, or indeed have achieved, their performance targets. This element of the cycle is essentially a performance appraisal whereby the work performance of the individual employee is assessed against the predetermined performance targets which they were given. At this stage, if it is established that the employee is performing satisfactorily and does not require any management guidance or intervention, the most appropriate course of action may be to praise the employee, give them recognition for high performance standards, and perhaps provide some form of reward. Should there be a problem in that there is little or no progress towards targets, it would be appropriate for the managers of the organization to consider possible management policies which would assist in improving performance levels in line with the corporate objectives and individual performance targets.

(4) Implications for management policies. As mentioned above, should the performance of employees not be in line with the corporate objectives of the organization, it will be necessary for the senior managers of the organization to review their management policies. The intention is that by introducing new management policies or amending existing ones, the performance of the human resources within the organization will be improved and result in the attainment of employee performance targets and the achievement of corporate objectives. The various management policies which may be amended or introduced are discussed later in this chapter.

(5) Evaluate the effectiveness of the performance management system in relation to corporate objectives. Once the performance management cycle has reached this stage, it will be necessary for the management of the organization to evaluate how effective the performance management system has been in contributing to or achieving corporate objectives. The intention is to highlight any problems in relation to the performance management system with the objective of amending it as necessary to ensure its success in the future.

Once the performance management system has been evaluated, reviewed and amended as necessary, the entire performance management cycle should by repeated in a systematic and continuous fashion.

The main purpose of introducing and operating a performance management system is to improve individual and organizational performance in line with business goals. As Stephen Williams writing in Neale (1991) states: 'When operated successfully, performance management will give the means for evaluating and improving both individual and company performance against predefined business strategies and objectives.' There are, however, a number of other related objectives including the following:

- the identification of training and development needs;
- increasing employee involvement and participation within the organization;
- establishing a foundation for the correlation between the performance of the individual and their remuneration;
- encouraging open communication between managers and employees;
- to act as a base for the assessment of potential career development and succession planning.

The Performance Management Organization

In the 1991 Institute of Personnel Management survey, *Performance Management in the UK: An Analysis of the Issues*, eight factors were highlighted as being characteristic of a performance management organization. Whilst there was no common definition of performance management found as a result of the survey, a number of factors were identified which differentiated between organizations with a performance management system and those pursuing other management policies to regulate employee performance. The eight factors considered to be characteristic of a performance management organization are outlined below.

(1)   Mission statements. Of those organizations responding to the Institute of Personnel Management survey, 83.8 per cent reported that they had a mission statement which expressed the organization's objectives and purpose. If the focus of the organization as a whole, each department, and each individual employee is to be on perform-

ance management, there must be a shared vision. Such a vision can be reflected though the mission statement of the organization and hence ensure that the performance management system is part of the overall organizational strategy aimed at fulfilling business objectives. In addition to having a mission statement, it is important for a performance management organization to publish its mission statement and communicate it to all employees.

(2)   Communication. In addition to communicating the mission statement to all employees, a performance management organization is likely to have a comprehensive communications network aimed at keeping employees informed of individual and organizational performance, and business developments. In particular, the performance management organization is likely to ensure that employees are kept informed of:

* any changes in business objectives and/or strategy;
* planned developments and initiatives;
* performance indicators;
* productivity/efficiency levels;
* financial results;
* performance reviews, and subsequent priorities for action (for example, training and development);
* any association between corporate, group or individual performance and employee remuneration;
* any developments relating to other performance improvement programmes.

(3)   Other management policies. Organizations which have a performance management system are likely to employ, as part of their overall strategy regarding the management of performance, a range of other programmes aimed at improving manpower utilization and performance. Some of these programmes are examined later in this chapter and include performance appraisal, scientific management, quality circles, performance related remuneration, work design and management systems.

(4)   Measurement of performance – employee categories. Whilst an organization which has a performance management system will monitor and evaluate the performance and effectiveness of all employees, the emphasis will be on the work performance of managers and white collar workers. The reason for this focus of attention is related to the fact that such employees are more likely to have a

direct influence on the performance and effectiveness of the organization. It is therefore essential that whilst all employees have an important role to play within the organization, close attention must be given to those employees with the biggest influence on end results.

(5)   Methods of measuring performance. Within a performance management system, the performance indicators for each employee are largely dependent on their role within the organization. With blue collar or manual employees, for example, there may be quantifiable outputs which can be measured and monitored. On the other hand, the performance of some white collar workers may be measured using training and learning targets or other established objectives, main job activities and tasks, and written job descriptions. For senior managers, however, the likely performance indicators will be related to clear and measurable accountabilities, objectives and targets, main job activities and tasks, and lists of competencies. Clearly, therefore, the performance indicators for each individual or group are likely to vary according to their job role and position within the organization.

(6)   Communicating employee performance requirements. Within a performance management system, the performance requirements or indicators for each employee are likely to be communicated to the individual in two main ways. Firstly, should the performance management system utilize a performance appraisal system, as is likely, the performance indicators for each individual will be communicated as part of the appraisal process (see the section on performance appraisal below). From the IPM survey, it would appear that in addition to the performance appraisal process, the performance indicators for employees are likely to be communicated via presentations by the Chief Executive Officer, or equivalent.

(7)   Performance management cycle. As highlighted in figure 3.1, performance management systems are based on a continuous and systematic cycle incorporating a series of stages. One of the key stages within such a cycle is the identification of individual performance targets. These performance targets must be set in a systematic fashion, be it annually, six monthly, monthly, weekly or daily. The frequency of such target setting appears to relate closely to the category of employee. Whilst senior managers and white collar employees tend to have their targets set annually or six monthly,

manual employees are more likely to have their targets set on a weekly or daily basis.

(8)   Link between performance management and performance related remuneration. As mentioned earlier in this chapter, the main objective of performance management is to maintain high levels of individual and organizational performance. Such management of performance is dependent on the setting and subsequent achievement of targets. One method of encouraging individual employees to achieve their targets is to praise and reward positive results. Should the managers of an organization decide to reward employees in a monetary fashion, they are likely to introduce a system of performance related remuneration. Any system of performance related remuneration requires a measurement of performance and, since a performance management system will involve such a measurement, it is common for organizations to establish a link between their performance management system and their remuneration strategy involving performance related remuneration.

Performance Management and Performance Appraisal

As mentioned above, one of the key aspects of a performance management system is an assessment of the work performance of employees in relation to their individual or group performance targets. One of the most common methods of assessing the performance level of employees is through the use of a system of performance appraisal. Most authors who write on the topic of performance appraisal usually offer, in some form, a definition of performance appraisal. Pratt (1985) suggests that whilst most good managers, as part of a continual process, regularly assess and develop their staff, performance appraisal places an emphasis on a formal system. He describes performance appraisal as: 'a formal and systematic method of staff assessment and development . . . The key is on the formal part of the definition. Systems are formalized in that there are usually set procedures, documentation, etc.' It should be noted that other terms for performance appraisal include staff reporting, staff assessment and performance review.

A central feature of any performance appraisal system is the establishment of objectives against which any assessment of the performance of the individual is based. At the beginning of the appraisal period, the individual is made aware of their performance objectives and reminded of the fact that their performance appraisal will be based on the accomplishment or otherwise of these objectives.

Within most performance appraisal systems, the appraisal of employees is normally carried out by each individual's immediate superior. The advantage of this is that the immediate superior usually has the best knowledge of the individual's job content, objectives and overall performance. The main disadvantage of appraisal by an immediate superior is the issue of friendship. With performance appraisal, it is quite possible for interpersonal relationships to bias performance ratings, either positively or negatively. It is often impossible to see a glaring deficiency in the performance of a friend, although it is easy to exaggerate such a deficiency in the performance of someone who is not liked. Whilst appraisal by immediate superior is the most commonly used method of appraisal, there are other methods which can be used to complement appraisal by immediate superior, or as an alternative. These methods of appraisal include:

* appraisal by superior's superior (the grandfather appraisal);
* appraisal by personnel staff;
* appraisal by peers;
* appraisal by subordinates;
* self-appraisal;
* appraisal by assessment centres.

In order to carry out performance appraisals effectively, most systems contain the following three components: documentation, interview and follow-up.

Documentation

Consists of forms for report and assessment together with relevant information and guidance. This component essentially serves as the focal point of most performance appraisal systems. Within report forms, different methods/techniques of assessment can be used such as:

Ranking This is often considered to be the simplest method of performance appraisal and basically consists of the appraiser placing the employees in order of merit – hence indicating the best performer through to the worst performer in a sequence of ranks. The main limitation of this method is that it assumes that in any group of employees there is a natural progression from good to poor and does not allow for all of the employees being of a similar high performance level.

Rating (alphabetical/numerical/graphical) This method of appraisal consists of the appraiser rating the employees on a series of personal and work qualities. The rating scales used allow for high and low scores to be given (for example, 1 to 5; A to E). The problems associated with this method include central tendency and misinterpretation. Central tendency is where appraisers looking for a simple, non-committal, non-controversial system of scoring use a central or middle score. Misinterpretation relates to the problem of each individual appraiser interpreting the scoring criteria differently.

Forced choice rating This method of appraisal is where the appraiser is provided with a series of adjectives or phrases and is asked to identify those adjectives or phrases which best and least describe the work performance of the employee. The problems associated with this method of appraisal include difficulty in analysing results and misinterpretation.

Free/controlled written report An alternative method of appraisal to those outlined above is to allow the appraiser to write a report, in their own words, regarding the work performance of employees. Such a report can either be free, in that the appraiser can write about any aspect of work performance, or alternatively can be controlled by giving the appraiser a number of headings under which they must comment.

Interview

Following the completion of a performance appraisal report, an interview is normally held which can be described as a formal discussion of performance assessment between the appraiser and the appraisee. Such interviews are normally carried out at regular intervals, generally every year. There are essentially three approaches·to appraisal interview and these are outlined below.

Tell and sell In this style of interviewing, the appraiser tells the appraisee what their strengths and weaknesses are, and suggests how the weaknesses could be rectified. The problem with this style of interviewing is that it allows little or no participation by the appraisee. As a result, when this style of appraisal interview is used, performance appraisal becomes a one-way dialogue rather than a two-way process of communication.

Tell and listen This style of appraisal interview is based on the appraiser telling the appraisee what their strengths and weaknesses are, and then listening to the comments of the appraisee. This style of appraisal, whilst being appropriate in some situations, can still be considered to be appraiser orientated.

Problem solving In the final style of appraisal interviewing, the appraiser and appraisee jointly identify strengths and weaknesses and tackle any problems together. This style of appraisal interviewing allows for the greatest level of appraisee participation in that they are involved with both identifying any problems and suggesting possible solutions.

Follow-up

Consists of some form of action resulting from the documentation and subsequent interview. Such action could involve training, regular problem solving sessions, promotion, remunerative benefits or even disciplinary action. Continuous assessment is also part of the follow-up, this involves continual, 365 days a year, communication between the appraiser and appraisee regarding the work process, highlighting problems or offering praise.

The objectives of performance appraisal were examined by Gill (1977), the main ones being identified as:

• to assess training and development needs;
• to help improve current performance;
• to assess past performance;
• to assess future potential/promotability;
• to assist career planning decisions;
• to set performance objectives;
• to assess increases or new levels of salary.

Overall, it would appear that the primary purpose of performance appraisal is to improve the efficiency of the organization by maximizing the utility of its human resources. In addition, performance appraisal systems should benefit the individual by outlining their role within the organization and by demonstrating the value of work done and the accomplishment of objectives.

Implications for Management Policies

Once the work performance of the employees has been assessed, there are likely to be important implications for a number of management policies. In particular, if performance levels have been identified as unsatisfactory and below target level, the management of the organization must introduce or amend existing management policies in an attempt to get employee performance to a satisfactory level. Overall, the management of performance should be considered as a holistic concept, and therefore organizations are likely to have a range of management policies in operation at any one time aimed at improving individual and organizational performance. Such policies are likely to include the following:

* scientific management;
* reducing worker fatigue;
* human relations management;
* management systems;
* work design;
* performance related remuneration.

Scientific management

This approach to performance management was developed in the late nineteenth/early twentieth century by Frederick W. Taylor (Taylor, 1911). The approach of Taylor advocated that the performance of employees, and hence organizations, could be improved by the introduction of scientific selection, education and development of workers. In addition, organizations should develop specific job descriptions, clearly established responsibilities, and systematic training programmes. Bilton *et al.* (1982), in explaining the principles of scientific management, suggest that left to their own devices workers will do as little as possible and engage in 'systematic soldiering' – working more slowly together in order to keep management ignorant of their potential. Similarly, left to plan their own work, workers' output is further lowered – they will do things in the customary way rather than the most efficient way. The solution according to Taylor was to 'relieve' the workers of the necessity of planning their own tasks – the separation of manual and mental work. He claimed that management should specialize in organizing work whilst the workers should specialize in doing the work. Taylor suggested that each job should be fragmented down into a series of tasks, and the best possible way of performing each task identified. The workers should then be scientifically selected, educated and trained to perform one specific task according to the way previously identified.

Scientific management therefore proposes that manual workers should become expert at performing one specific task within a job and that the whole job should be completed via a series of specialist 'task workers'.

Taylor essentially introduced what has become known as work study – the methodical study of work to devise the quickest and most efficient way of doing a job. Whilst scientific management can have beneficial results for the organization as a whole in terms of increased production rates, less expensive training and lower basic wage levels, the effects on the individual workers must be considered. Task fragmentation results in work which is tedious and boring and leads to apathy, dissatisfaction and carelessness among workers. In the long run, therefore, if scientific management is to result in the development of employee skills, improved employee commitment or high levels of performance, it must also take account of the feelings, attitudes, needs and desires of the employee.

Ergonomics

In the early 1920s, Elton Mayo and his colleagues from Harvard University focused on improving organizational performance by reducing employee fatigue. Mayo believed that if work fatigue was reduced, there would be a corresponding increase in employee performance. Accordingly, Mayo and his associates investigated the effect on employee performance resulting from changes in ergonomic factors such as rest periods, temperature, humidity, lighting and catering arrangements. Whilst it was found that employee performance was positively affected by changes in such ergonomic factors, the main finding of Mayo and his team was that employee job performance was affected more by the relationships between people than changes to any of the fatigue inducing factors that they had tested. Following on from the work of Mayo, there was considerable interest in 'human relations management' – the effect of human relationships on the performance of employees.

Human relations management

Fundamental to the whole approach of human relations management is the belief that conflict in the work situation is the basic cause of poor performance – it places an emphasis on people and their feelings and attitudes. Human relations management argues that in order to maintain high levels of performance, the relationships between management and workers should be harmonious and friendly. Central to the human relations theory is the belief that within the workplace there are group norms and values which influence the attitudes and behaviour of individuals. The aim of management should therefore be to use these group norms and values to their advantage by using them to fulfil the social needs of belongingness, involvement and commitment – this would assist in breaking down the barriers between the workers and the management.

To improve performance, therefore, managers should concentrate on management/worker communications aimed at smoothing out all conflicts and establishing sound, friendly and co-operative relationships between management and workers, and between the workers themselves. The emphasis, therefore, is on effective communications and harmonious relationships.

Management systems

This approach to performance management suggests that in order to establish high levels of performance within an organization, the management systems used within that organization must be appropriate to its industry, technology, culture, structure and environment. The management systems approach to the management of performance was investigated by Burns and Stalker (1961) in their studies of textile mills and electronics firms in Britain.

The belief is that whilst one management system may be successful in one organization, it may not be successful in another, hence the management systems adopted must be appropriate to the requirements and characteristics of each organization. For example, an organization which is required to cope with rapid change and uncertainty will dictate an 'organic' management system based on loosely defined responsibilities and relationships, free communication, and co-operation across hierarchical and divisional boundaries. Such a management system is appropriate since it allows the organization to have a flexible structure, capable of learning and adapting in response to information and knowledge arising at any point within the organization. On the other hand, some organizations require an alternative 'mechanistic' management system characterized by clearly defined duties, responsibilities and authority, specified chains of command, and structured channels of communication. Such management systems are often required in organizations which are 'static' in the sense that they do not need to cope with rapid change or uncertainty. In addition, organizations which rely on rules and procedures for functional efficiency will also require 'mechanistic' systems of management.

Baird *et al.* (1990), commenting on the work of Burns and Stalker, suggest that their proposal was that the success or otherwise of an organization depends on the nature of the organization's management system and the environment in which it is operating. They state:

> The mechanistic organization, characterized by rules, procedures, a clear hierarchy of authority and centralized decision making was more successful when the environment was predictable and stable, and less successful as the environment became unpredictable. The organic organization, characterized by flexibility, decentralized decision making, and the absence of rules and procedures, was more successful in rapidly changing environments.

The management systems approach to performance management therefore emphasizes the need for a management system appropriate to the demands and characteristics of the organization.

Work design

This is a wide-ranging approach which attempts to improve employee and organizational performance by altering the context of jobs. The main performance management techniques within the approach of work design are:

- job rotation;
- job enlargement;
- job enrichment;
- quality circles;
- work groups.

Job rotation If organizations adopt a scientific management approach to work design or are dependent on technological production lines, there is a high probability that employees will be performing routine, repetitive and mundane tasks for the majority of their working day. In such organizations, it is important that the problem of boredom and job dissatisfaction is overcome. One relatively simple solution to this problem is via the use of job rotation. Job rotation does not involve any changes to the job content or methods but involves the systematic movement of workers from one job to another at set intervals. For example, a worker employed on a car assembly line may spend a set interval such as an hour fitting doors, the next hour installing headlamps, the next hour fitting bumpers, and so on. Such an approach alleviates the problem of monotony and boredom and is likely to reduce dissatisfaction whilst increasing employee performance.

Job enlargement As the name suggests, job enlargement is concerned with increasing the number of tasks performed by an employee. The central point of job enlargement is that it involves the horizontal expansion of a worker's job. Instead of performing one task repeatedly day in, day out, the employee will have a series of two, three, four or more tasks to perform as part of their job. The use of this approach could mean that instead of performing a fragmented task in a sub-assembly operation, the employee actually completes the whole assembly operation, thus giving the employee some satisfaction in completing a job, rather than completing only a part of it. In addition to possibly overcoming boredom/monotony, job enlargement reduces the dependency a worker may have on others who may control the pace of a job and restrict an individual organizing a job to meet his or her own needs. For example, if the work involved assembling chairs, and the worker had previously only bolted the legs to the seat, job enlargement may involve the assembly of the whole chair including assembling the legs, attaching the back, and so on. Job enlargement may not only be used in situations which involve production lines but could also be used in any work area which is primarily monotonous and boring but will allow the expansion of job tasks. The effect of job enlargement on employee/organizational performance has been studied in several pieces of research. The use of job enlargement in the Endicott plant of IBM in 1944 was examined by Walker (1950). Walker concluded that where the jobs of machinists were enlarged to include machine set-up and inspection of finished quality, the result was improved product quality, less idle time for workers and machines, reduced scrap and a 95 per cent reduction in set-up and inspection times. Job enlargement therefore seeks to improve performance by horizontally expanding a job and by doing so giving the worker a sense of achievement and satisfaction.

Job enrichment   The aim of this technique is to improve employee performance by increasing employee motivation through responsibility, recognition and achievement. The belief is that by giving an employee more control over their work their job satisfaction will increase, they will be motivated and overall performance will improve. Job enrichment normally involves the vertical expansion of an individual's work, in that tasks or responsibilities which were formerly the responsibility of the individual's manager or supervisor are incorporated into the employee's job.

The phrase 'job enrichment' was coined by the psychologist Frederick Herzberg who proposed a two-factor theory of motivation based on a series of motivators (see chapter 2). Herzberg believed that in any job there are characteristics of work which lead to satisfaction and motivation; he labelled these characteristics 'motivators'. Herzberg's motivators include:

- achievement;
- recognition;
- responsibility;
- advancement;
- growth in competence;
- the work itself.

According to Herzberg, the above motivators can be encouraged by job enrichment which could involve:

- removing controls;
- increasing accountability;
- creating natural work units;
- granting additional authority;
- providing direct feedback;
- introducing new tasks;
- allocating special assignments.

Overall, job enrichment is concerned with increasing the amount of worker autonomy in an attempt to improve motivation and performance through an increased sense of achievement, recognition, challenge and accomplishment.

Quality circles   A quality circle (QC) is a group of around five to ten specially trained workers from the same department, or doing similar work, who voluntarily meet on a regular basis to identify, investigate, analyse and solve their own work related problems. As Evans (1990) suggests, QCs enable employees at the lowest levels in the organization not only to initiate ideas, but to communicate them upwards.

The basic aim of a quality circle is simple – a circle leader (perhaps a work-team supervisor) meets with their QC to tackle work problems with the objective of improving quality and productivity. The initial expense of setting up QCs may be large, and therefore a firm commitment by senior management to the introduction of QCs is required – this also gives validity to the operation of any QC. Dessler (1983) gives many examples of the successful use of QCs in America where the introduction of QCs has led to savings of tens of thousands of dollars in many companies. In addition, whilst the primary aim of QCs may be to improve quality and productivity, the use of QCs to deal with work related problems, and with problems with only remote connections to work, seems to improve morale, working relationships and overall job satisfaction.

Work groups   The principle behind the use of work groups is defined in Buchanan and McCalman (1989), in which they quote Pehr Gyllenhammar, the President of Volvo, who suggested that by 'replacing the mechanical line with the human work group . . . employees can act in co-operation, discussing more, deciding among themselves how to organize the work – and, as a result, doing much more.'

Many similarities can be drawn between the use of work groups to improve employee performance and the use of QCs. Both approaches are based on group interaction and communication, and the devolution of decision making and other responsibilities from supervisors or managers to individual work groups. The theory behind work groups is that by allowing groups of employees to discuss work related matters and make appropriate recommendations or decisions, their sense of achievement, job satisfaction and overall motivation will be improved.

Performance related remuneration

As mentioned above, many employers, in an attempt to improve the work performance of employees, establish a correlation between the performance of the individual and their subsequent remuneration. The topic of performance related remuneration is discussed fully in chapter 11.

Conclusion

Performance management can therefore be described as a human resource management strategy aimed at achieving business objectives through improved individual and organizational performance. It is likely to involve a systematic and cyclical process incorporating the establishment of performance objectives, a review of performance towards such targets, an examination of the implications for management policies and an evaluation of the effectiveness of the performance management system in relation to corporate objectives.

In response to several factors, the main one being market competition, many organizations are incorporating performance management into their overall business strategy aimed at improving business performance and effectiveness. In addition to managing individual and organizational performance, performance management can also assist with the achievement of other objectives such as the identification of training and development needs and improving organizational communication systems.

Whilst performance management may be an effective method of managing individual and organizational performance, it is common for performance management systems to be part of a holistic approach to the management of performance and may include other management practices such as performance appraisal, performance related pay and work design.

4

Remuneration and Motivation

Introduction

For many years behavioural psychologists have researched and produced motivation theories based on the reinforcement of behaviour. Whilst the concept of motivation has been discussed fully in chapter 2, the underlying assumption is that specific forms of behaviour can be encouraged or discouraged through the provision or withdrawal of rewards and punishments. Central to any remuneration system therefore is the assumption that the provision or withdrawal of certain types of remuneration can be used to reinforce the behaviour of employees concurrent with the objectives of the organization. In addition to the provision of remuneration in the form of a basic wage or salary and associated remunerative benefits, it is becoming increasingly common for organizations to provide an additional aspect of remuneration related to the performance of the individual, work group or organization – performance related remuneration (PRR). The author, on examining the use of systems of performance related remuneration within UK organizations (Hume, 1993), found that 78.5 per cent of the organizations surveyed operated at least one system of PRR, although the majority operated more than one system. These findings would seem to support the viewpoint that systems of PRR have become an increasingly common feature of the remuneration policy of many organizations and have consequently become regarded as part of the normal remuneration package. The author also found that within the organizations surveyed, systems of PRR were more commonly used for white collar and managerial employees rather than for blue collar or manual employees. Within the survey, the most commonly used systems of PRR were merit pay, either in the form of a bonus or salary increase, and profit related pay. Where organizations operated a system of PRR, the most common method of assessing the work performance of employees was performance appraisal. The trends in the use of PRR are examined fully in chapter 5.

When organizations make a decision to incorporate a performance related element into their remuneration strategy, the hope is that PRR will motivate the employees to behave in a manner which will contribute to the achievement of organizational objectives. Whilst PRR can be used to assist in the achievement of many organizational objectives, the single most important reason for using a system of PRR is to improve organizational performance through motivating the effective performance of individual employees (Lawler, 1983).

Improving Performance

In the modern commercial world, with high levels of competition and technological advances, it is clear that if organizations are to survive, they must ensure a high level of organizational performance. Whilst organizational performance can mean many things, it is most commonly interpreted as meaning financial performance which can be measured in terms of profitability, turnover, return on capital and capital growth. If we consider the public sector and the National Health Service, however, organizational performance cannot be measured in terms of financial returns but instead can be measured in terms of service and quality. Organizational performance can therefore mean many things including:

• financial performance (profits/liquidity/capital);
• customer service;
• quality of product/service;
• efficiency/productivity.

Throughout the 1980s, systems of performance related remuneration have become extremely popular as a method of improving and maintaining organizational performance through the improved performance of employees. Since the 1940s, a number of studies have been performed to investigate the effect of financial incentives on organizational performance.

Argyle (1989) refers to a survey carried out in the United States which examined 514 incentive schemes initiated in the late 1940s. This survey discovered increases in output of 39 per cent, increases in earnings of 17.5 per cent and decreases in labour costs of 11.5 per cent. Davidson *et al.* (1958) report on a 1958 study of six British companies which found that the use of financial incentives increased output by 60 per cent with a corresponding increase in earnings of 20 per cent.

More recently, in a United Kingdom survey carried out between 1977 and 1980, Bowey *et al.* (1982) found that of 52 firms operating incentive schemes, 71 per cent had increased effort, 68 per cent had increased productivity and 85 per cent had increased the earnings of the workforce. In addition to the above findings, Bowey *et al.* report that 55 per cent of the firms had improved quality whilst obtaining these quantitative improvements.

A survey carried out in 1991 by the Institute of Personnel Management (IPM, 1992) found that 74 per cent of organizations surveyed reported the use of a system of PRR. Of those organizations who operated a system of PRR but no formal performance management system (PMS), 62 per cent reported that the use of PRR had led to an improvement in organizational performance. In contrast, of those organizations which reported the use of a system of PRR *and* a formal performance management system, 94 per cent stated that the introduction of such systems had led to improved organizational performance. These results therefore support the suggestion that the most successful schemes are set within a wider framework of enlightened employee relations policies and management practice (McBay, 1989).

Overall, systems of PRR attempt to improve organizational performance by:

(1) Rewarding those employees whose performance is assessed to be of a high standard. Such an approach communicates to the individual (or group) that their contribution to the work of the organization is highly valued. The overall message is simple – improved performance results in improved remuneration. An important issue which must be addressed when establishing a correlation between the remuneration of individuals or groups to their performance is the notion of equity. Essentially, workers should feel, or perceive, that their remuneration in relation to their effort, performance and contribution is fair when compared with the remuneration

and work performance of colleagues. As Smith (1989) suggests, equity can be said to exist when people compare their reward and contribution with those of other workers and feel that any differences or similarities in reward are justified and acceptable. Armstrong and Murlis (1991) suggest, however, that whilst absolute equity is an unattainable ideal, the objective of organizations should be to achieve as high a degree of equity as possible. This may be achieved by organizations adopting a policy based on establishing the value of employee effort, performance and contribution in relation to the internal context of the organization and external market pressure. The importance of equity in relation to the payment of salaries and the provision of performance related remunerative rewards must not be underestimated and as Smith 1989 states:

> Although equity, justice and fairness are somewhat difficult to measure, and perceptions of equity differ among different people, the issue is real in the minds of employees and can influence the degree of success achieved by the application of an incentive scheme. Management should, therefore, be careful to implement incentive schemes in a manner which structures the reward/effort relationship.

(2)   Motivating all employees to perform well. Whilst the principle of rewarding high performers may well reinforce their behaviour, it is important to motivate those employees who are not performing so well. Good PRR systems must not therefore concentrate only on those employees who are already performing well, but must also consider the motivation of other employees – all employees must be encouraged to improve their performance, and the attraction of increased remuneration may assist and support a change in behaviour.

(3)   Supporting a performance orientated approach to work. PRR systems are based on the output from work rather than the effort put in by individuals, as, for example, in a reward system based on the amount of time employees spend at work. Employees are encouraged to concentrate on the standard of the end product rather than the input or effort. PRR systems are based on output rather than input.

(4)   Encouraging the use of work systems appropriate to the organization. By establishing a correlation between remuneration

and the performance of individuals or groups, different work systems can be emphasized. For example, work systems based on individual performance (personal initiative and contribution) or work systems based on collective performance (teamwork and co-operation).

(5) Promoting forward planning and objective setting. The central feature of many systems of PRR is the assessment of performance based on the achievement of previously established plans and objectives. This management technique therefore encourages individuals and groups to plan their work activity and achieve predetermined objectives.

Further aims of PRR which are related to the underlying objective of improving organizational performance include:

* *Increasing the earnings of employees.* The introduction of an equitable system of PRR gives the employee who attains the appropriate performance level the opportunity to increase their earnings.
* *Improving quality/reducing wastage.* By focusing on the output of employees and linking such output to their remuneration, employees should be motivated to provide a high quality product or service.
* *Improving labour flexibility.* By establishing a link between the acquisition of new skills and remuneration, employees will be motivated to become multi-skilled, which will result in a more flexible workforce.
* *Improving control over wage costs.* By replacing traditional annual salary reviews and automatic incremental salary increases with salary increases related to the performance level of the individual employee or group of employees, the organization can be confident that any salary increases given to employees are given in return for an appropriate contribution to the overall performance of the organization. This situation eliminates the provision of salary increases to employees who do not maintain satisfactory levels of performance that are concurrent with the objectives and strategy of the organization.
* *Reducing industrial stoppages.* One of the most common reasons behind industrial stoppages is employee remuneration. If employees are given the opportunity to 'control' their remuneration through their performance level, such industrial stoppages are likely to become less common.
* *Reducing absenteeism.* Employees are less likely to have high absence levels when being absent affects remuneration levels – an employee who has frequent absences is less likely to reach performance targets.

- *Reducing overtime.* If it is possible to improve the performance of employees through a system of PRR, higher productivity levels should result. This should enable organizations to reach production targets without relying on overtime.
- *Reducing manpower.* By improving the performance level of employees, it may be possible for some organizations to maintain a high production level with a reduced workforce. Whilst the prospect of redundancies is not welcomed by employees, a reduced workforce may help to guarantee the future survival of the organization.

Whilst the primary objective of performance related remuneration is to improve organizational performance through the improved performance of employees, systems of PRR can be used to assist in the achievement of additional objectives. Such objectives include:

- organization change;
- attracting, recruiting and retaining employees;
- encouraging employee involvement;
- flexibility of pay bargaining;
- maintaining or establishing employee differentials.

Organization Change

PRR is one management technique that is often used to help facilitate changes within organizations. Although changes are normally introduced to improve the performance and effectiveness of organizations, most changes, be they minor or major, are usually regarded with suspicion by the workforce. Such suspicion can often result in operational problems and therefore make the implementation of change very difficult. PRR is often considered to be a 'sweetener' for the 'bad taste' of organizational change. As Lawler (1983) states: 'When the reward system is considered and made part of the change strategy, it can make a positive contribution to a change effort.'

PRR can generally assist in the acceptance and implementation of the following types of change:

Change in organizational culture

Throughout the 1980s and into the 1990s there has been a continuing trend towards a performance culture within organizations. Employees are being encouraged to monitor their own performance and maintain or improve this performance in line with the overall objectives of the organization. Employees are now being given responsibility for their own or their group's work performance and subsequent remuneration through individual or group PRR. This culture is in sharp contrast to the position earlier in the century when the performance of employees was a management problem.

From the management standpoint, one major change in organizational culture has been the move towards treating employees as assets rather than costs or liabilities. As a result of this culture change, managers are increasingly being held accountable for the performance and effectiveness of their human resources, or human assets, and are being given delegated control over the remuneration of their human resources – employees.

In both of the situations mentioned above, it is essential that the reward management procedures of the organization take into consideration the changing culture within organizations. In many cases, PRR has been introduced in an attempt to assist such a transformation in organizational culture and encourage both management and employees to accept and participate in the performance orientated culture of the organization.

Change in technology

One of the most significant developments in organizations throughout the past 20 years is the increased use of technology within most workplaces. Traditionally, workers have been sceptical about the introduction of new or improved technology; technology is often considered to be a threat to jobs, with machines doing jobs once done by workers. In an attempt to overcome such scepticism, management often involve the employees in decision making about new technology and generally provide a full training programme. In addition to such tactics, PRR is often used to illustrate clearly the benefits to be gained by the employee from the new technology – new technology can result in improved individual (and organizational) performance which will result in improved remuneration. As Smith (1989) states: 'Incentive schemes may do more than improve employee performance, for example, by clearing the obstacle to technical or organizational change.'

Changes in work design

In order to maintain organizational efficiency and competitiveness, organizations must adopt suitable working methods. Occasionally, it is necessary to introduce new work designs which could include job enlargement, job rotation, group working, flexibility schemes and job enrichment. To facilitate the introduction of new work designs, organizations often introduce PRR. Again, this is to develop an association between the performance of individuals, groups or the organization, and their remuneration. This association should encourage the employees to accept changes in work design which will improve their work performance.

Overall, where organizations seek to improve their performance through some form of organizational change, the introduction of a system of PRR may not only improve performance in its own right, but may be a contributing factor leading to the acceptance of the change on the part of employee and management. Lawler (1983) does, however, provide a cautionary note regarding the use of PRR for the management of change: 'Pay systems can either facilitate or inhibit organizational change, although they should not automatically be assumed or counted on to do either.'

Attracting, Recruiting and Retaining Employees

During the past ten years, some employers have experienced difficulty in attracting, recruiting and retaining appropriately qualified and skilled employees. Such circumstances have arisen even though unemployment levels within the United Kingdom have remained significantly high. When organizations are faced with such a skills shortage it is essential that attractive and competitive compensation packages are available to attract and retain appropriately qualified and skilled employees. Such compensation packages normally include some element of PRR. The skills shortage can be explained in three ways:

1   some occupations appear unattractive to potential employees;
2   some skills and qualifications are in extremely high demand;
3   the demographic trend suggests that there is/will be a shortage in the supply of school leavers.

Unattractive occupations

Within the modern industrial and commercial world, there remain some occupations which appear unattractive to the majority of job seekers. Such unattractiveness could be the result of poor working conditions, long and unsociable hours of work, or perhaps the general unpleasantness of the type of work. Faced with the problem of finding employees to perform unattractive types of work, employers are required to lure employees with tactics such as appealing remuneration packages which could be wholly or partly based on a system of performance related pay.

Skills and qualifications in high demand

In any industrialized country, there are likely to be a range of skills and qualifications which are in high demand. Such high demand is linked closely with the trends within the manufacturing and service industries. Currently, one trend is towards the use of computerized technology, which means that there is significant demand for computer operators and programmers. Another trend is the forecasted shortage in graduates and higher qualified people in the 1990s. Essentially, job seekers who possess skills and qualifications which are in high demand can command attractive remuneration packages from potential employers. As Nash and Carroll (1975) state: 'Jobs that require greater preparation, are more hazardous, and require skills that are in scarce supply are usually thought to deserve more pay than less demanding jobs.'

Whilst an attractive basic pay is essential in the competition for scare human resources, Curnow (1989) suggests that many employers are also including an element of PRR as part of the total remuneration package.

Demographic trends

The current demographic trends suggest that there is/will be a shortage in the supply of school leavers entering the labour market. The demographic trends for the 15–19 and 20–24 age groups are illustrated in table 4.1.

Although unemployment levels within the United Kingdom remain high, most employers tend to recruit a certain number of school leavers to fill junior positions or commence training pro-

Table 4.1   *Age distribution of United Kingdom population (in thousands)*

Age groups	1981	1986	1989	1991[a]	1996[a]	2001[a]
15–19	4735	4479	4079	3707	3499	3681
20–24	4284	4784	4651	4496	3724	3517

[a] Indicates projection
Source: *Annual Abstract of Statistics*, 1991

grammes and apprenticeships. If the supply of school leavers falls below the demand level from industry, the school leavers will need to be attracted to organizations through such tactics as appealing remuneration packages which could involve some system of performance related pay. In its report in 1988 entitled 'Young people and the labour market' the National Economic Development Council stated that, 'over the next five years, the number of 16–24 year olds in the labour force will fall by 1.2 million, a decline of one-fifth – with a decline of 23 per cent in the 16–19 year old age group. Employers are going to find it much more difficult to recruit young people in sufficient numbers in the future' (Curnow, 1989).

Faced with such a position, employers will need to examine very closely their recruitment and retention policies. This will inevitably involve an examination of their remuneration policies and the role of PRR.

Overall, if employers are to attract, recruit and retain an effective workforce, it is important that satisfactory working conditions are provided. An important element of good working conditions is an attractive remuneration package. The trend over the past ten years has been to make remuneration packages attractive by developing a correlation between the performance of employees and their remuneration – performance related remuneration.

Encouraging Employee Involvement

An increasingly popular trend in organization management is to encourage employee involvement in the fulfilment of organizational objectives. Occasionally, employees become involved in organizational decision making and forward planning through consultation or employee representation on executive committees. Alternatively, employees can become involved by feeling that they are an integral part of the organization and that their work effort and commitment are an essential part of the organizational performance, efficiency and future survival. This integration of employee performance and organizational objectives can be achieved through PRR. This way, the employee infers an association between their own perform-ance, the performance of the organization and the provision of remunerative rewards.

In a study in 1989 by Kinnie and Lowe (1990) which looked at the use of performance related pay on the shop floor, they found a strong correlation between the use of PRR and increased employee involvement and commitment. More specifically, Kinnie and Lowe found that 100 per cent of the organizations surveyed stated that PRR improves employee commitment and capability. In addition, 75 per cent of those organizations surveyed said that PRR was beneficial in that it led to better two-way communications. Perform-ance related remuneration therefore encourages employee involve-ment and commitment by making employees feel that they are an integral part of the organization and that their own performance has an influence on the performance of the organization as a whole.

Flexibility of Pay Bargaining

Within many large organizations with several sites geographically widespread throughout the United Kingdom, pay negotiations have tended to take place on a centralized basis, usually at head office. Such a position left individual workplace managers with little or no control over remuneration budgets. Wage and salary systems within such organizations were generally rigid and left very little room for managerial flexibility. Since the cutthroat competitive markets of the modern commercial world call for optimum levels of organizational performance and efficiency, it is essential that managers are given control over remuneration budgets and are allowed some degree of flexibility in their operation. As Armstrong and Murlis (1991) state:

> Some central control over the implementation of salary policies and salary costs is necessary, but the aim should be to delegate as much authority as possible to the managers. The reward management pro-cedures of the company must, therefore, be designed to achieve a delicate balance between the extremes of rigidity or anarchy.

Within the United Kingdom, the 1980s witnessed a sharp decline in the power and influence of trade unions. Factors contributing to this decline were:

- the failure of trade union campaigns in the late 1970s;
- the dramatic reduction in trade union membership since 1979;
- the anti-union legislation introduced by the 1979 Conservative Government led by Margaret Thatcher.

The reduction in trade union power and influence has allowed employers to decentralize pay bargaining to a local level and introduce flexible payment systems. PRR is one of the most popular systems of remuneration to be introduced into organizations since the mid 1980s in an attempt to bring about or increase managerial flexibility concerning remuneration. PRR allows managers to remunerate employees according to their performance and also lets managers modify, if not replace, the traditional concept of an annual inflationary salary or wage increase. Once again, the emphasis is on a performance orientated culture. As Vicky Wright, writing in Neale (1991), states: 'In the current business environment performance related pay, whether in the form of incentives or rewards is frequently used to support a performance orientated "culture".'

Overall, PRR allows managers to control the remuneration of employees concurrent with the objectives of the organization.

Maintaining or Establishing Employee Differentials

Whilst many employers have sought to harmonize the terms and conditions of employment for all employees including management, white and blue collar workers, they have tended to retain, or establish, wage and salary differentials. Such differentials mean that employees of the same grade can be awarded different remuneration packages according to their performance or contribution to the organization. The message to employees is clear – an improved performance will result in improved remuneration. One of the most popular methods of creating remunerative differentials is through the use of a system of PRR. Performance related remuneration establishes a direct correlation between the performance of employees and their subsequent remuneration, and, by rewarding employees of the same grade differently, creates employee differentials.

To summarize, the primary objective of performance related remuneration is to improve the overall performance and effectiveness of organizations. This should be achieved through the improved performance of individuals or work groups within the organization. In addition, PRR can assist in the achievement of organizational objectives by:

- helping with various types of organization change;
- helping the organization to attract, recruit and retain the correct quantity and quality of employees;
- encouraging employee involvement and commitment;
- improving managerial control and flexibility over the remuneration of employees;
- maintaining or establishing employee differentials.

Dysfunctional Effects of PRR

Under the correct conditions, there is proof to show that the use of performance related remuneration *can* assist in the achievement of a variety of organizational objectives. As Smith (1989) states:

> A survey in the United States of 514 incentive schemes applied in the late 1940s discovered increases in output of 39 per cent, labour costs lower by 11.5 per cent, while earnings increased by 17.5 per cent. A 1958 study of six British companies found that the use of financial incentives increased output by 60 per cent, while earnings increased by 20 per cent. More recently, in 1985, an American survey of 330 programmes to improve worker performance found that financial incentives had by far the greatest influence on productivity.

Although PRR can have a positive effect on the achievement of organizational objectives, there are many occasions where the use of a system of PRR can have negative implications. These negative implications can be explained by examining some of the dysfunctional aspects of PRR. Such dysfunctional aspects include:

- the belief that one system of PRR will suit all organizations;
- subjectivity of performance assessment;
- PRR being used for the wrong reasons;

- excessive amounts of bureaucracy;
- lack of communication;
- negative impact on employee morale.

One system for all organizations?

One factor which leads to the downfall of PRR is the belief that one system of PRR is appropriate for all organizations. This belief rejects the suggestion that all performance management strategies, including reward systems, have to be designed in line with such factors as:

- the objective(s) of a performance related reward strategy;
- the philosophy and objectives of the organization;
- the characteristics of the product or service;
- the production process;
- the expectations and demands of the workforce.

If a system of PRR is designed and introduced without careful consideration of the environment within which the organization operates, the success and subsequent life span of the system of PRR is likely to be extremely limited. As Armstrong and Murlis (1991) suggest: 'Badly conceived performance related pay schemes . . . can encourage people to focus narrowly on a task to do it too quickly and to take few risks. This is short termism, a major contributor to poor performance and hardly the behaviour we want in the innovative, flexible and responsive organizations of the 1990s.'

In addition to considering the unique demands of the organization and its employees when selecting or designing a system of PRR, it is important to consider the position of PRR in relation to the wider performance management strategy of the organization. Where an organization depends entirely on performance related rewards to improve or maintain the level of employee performance, the effect is likely to be minimal. The effect of a system of PRR on employee performance is likely to be more dramatic where PRR is set within a comprehensive performance management strategy. As Smith (1989) states: 'Effort or performance is more likely to remain at higher levels if money is mixed with such elements as job satisfaction, cohesive groups and self actualization in a synergistic effect which brings forward the types of contribution which management require and pay for.'

Subjectivity of performance assessment

One of the most common grievances regarding the operation of PRR relates to the lack of standardization in the assessment of employee performance. Whilst some systems of PRR, including payment by results, can be based wholly or entirely on quantifiable and objective measurements, many of the other systems of PRR rely on the subjective judgement of a line manager. Since all individuals are unique, and different personal relationships and personalities inevitable, any subjective assessments of performance are likely to be influenced by many factors not directly related to the performance of the individual. Where employees do not perceive equity in the operation of PRR, the success of PRR in contributing towards the achievement of organizational objectives may be limited. In addition, explicit inequality in performance assessment can be divisive and demoralize employees. A successful performance based reward strategy therefore not only requires a well-designed and carefully implemented system of PRR but requires committed and well-trained managers who are capable of operating the system and who can be as objective as possible when making assessments of performance.

The purpose of using PRR

The earlier part of this chapter focused on the objectives of using a system of PRR. Whilst it can be seen that the objectives can be many and varied, they all essentially relate to improving the work performance or output of employees. In certain circumstances, however, systems of PRR are often used for ulterior motives. Managers often use PRR not to reward employees according to their performance, but as a means of retaining key staff. In addition, where an employee is not eligible for promotion within an organization, the system of PRR is often used to enable the individual to progress to the maximum of their pay scale in the shortest possible time. Whilst PRR may be a useful method of achieving these ends, they tend not to be the purpose for which systems of PRR are designed.

Excessive bureaucracy

Whilst successful systems of PRR appear to be characterized by operational procedures which are straightforward to manage and monitor, many organizations design systems of PRR which are not only bureaucratic but are also difficult to understand. The complexities of such systems are not only difficult for the managers to comprehend, but are often outwith the understanding of the employee. In response to the criticism relating to the subjectivity of performance assessments, many organizations introduce complex performance appraisal systems which attempt to remove or at least minimize subjective judgements. In addition to these complicated methods of assessing performance, many systems of PRR incorporate intricate mechanisms which translate the performance assessment into an actual reward. Altogether, this increasing complexity and bureaucracy results in systems which are difficult to understand and which in turn prove costly in terms of time and money.

Lack of communication

Unless the objectives and operational details of the system of PRR are effectively communicated to both management and all other employees, there are likely to be problems regarding the use of PRR. Firstly, it essential that everyone within the system of PRR is aware of their responsibilities. Without a comprehensive understanding of the operational aspects of the system, it is almost certain to fail. With regards to effective communication to employees, it is essential that the employees are made aware of how the system operates and how it may affect them. This in turn will help to ensure that the perceived expectations of the employees are realistic and capable of being achieved. Should the expectations of employees be unrealistic as a result of misinformation or poor communication, the effects of PRR are likely to be negative.

Negative impact on employee morale

Whilst systems of performance related remuneration can have a positive impact on the morale and work performance of employees, there are occasions when the introduction of PRR can have the opposite effect. It is not unusual for some employees to oppose the use of PRR for a variety of reasons. For example, some employees feel insulted by the use of PRR on the grounds that they would give their best performance for the employer irrespective of whether or not this resulted in a remunerative reward. On the other hand, there are other employees who view the introduction of PRR as manipulation of the workforce by the employers and therefore object strongly to any management policy which can be conceived as manipulative. In addition, whilst those employees who actually receive a performance related payment are likely to be happy, those who do not receive such a payment are very likely to be discontented. This is likely to be particularly true of those employees whose performance levels are judged to be just below the level required for a performance related payment. As a result of the possible negative impact of PRR on employee morale, and performance, it is essential that employers ensure open communication regarding the introduction and implementation of systems of PRR, and ensure that as far as possible the expectations of employees are realistic. In addition, the negative impacts of PRR are likely to be minimized if employees are consulted very early in the design stage and their views and opinions given careful consideration before PRR is implemented within the organization.

Conclusion

Whilst there are several dysfunctional aspects relating to the operation of systems of PRR which may limit the success of PRR in helping to achieve organizational objectives, a well-designed system of PRR which is set within a carefully thought out performance management strategy can have a significant impact upon the performance of individual employees and the ultimate achievement of organizational objectives. As Income Data Services (1989b) state:

> Performance related pay is not a simple panacea for all the problems of an organization. However, when carefully designed to meet particular circumstances and when set within a much wider context of performance management, it can act as a powerful agent for reinforcing organizational change and helping to improve efficiency and effectiveness. Whatever the pitfalls, the use of performance pay is likely to continue to increase.

5
Developments in Payment Systems

Introduction

The practice of paying, or remunerating, individuals for their labour is not new, it dates back at least to the time of Christ. Reference to payment for labour is made in the Holy Bible, the Gospel according to Matthew 20: 1–2: 'For the Kingdom of heaven is like a landowner who went out in early morning to hire men to work in his vineyard. He agreed to pay them a denarius for the day and sent them into his vineyard.'

Whilst this chapter will consider the general developments in remuneration systems over the past century, the main aim of the chapter is to examine recent developments in one approach to employee remuneration – the practice of establishing a direct correlation between the remuneration of employees and their work performance (performance related remuneration – PRR). Whilst PRR has been present in various forms for several hundreds of years, the main developments in PRR have occurred since 1900.

Around 1900, employers tended to remunerate employees in one of two ways – on a time basis or an incentive basis. If the employer used a time based system, the employee would be paid according to the amount of time worked – typically, an hourly rate for the job which could be used to calculate a daily, weekly or monthly wage. The main problem with the time based system was that two employees could be paid identical amounts even though their work effort and performance differed significantly. This problem tended to result in an overall low level of production and employee performance.

In order to try and improve employee performance, some employers adopted a system of PRR – an incentive based approach to the remuneration of employees. As Smith (1989) states, incentives motivate, at least to a point, and organizations are increasingly eager to capture this motivational effect by paying for, and thus recognizing, achievement and contribution. Currie (1963) also emphasizes the need for a relationship between performance and remuneration by suggesting that the success or failure of management will depend in large part on their ability to provide adequate incentives of the right type for all in industry. Under a system of PRR, the level of employee remuneration is directly related to the level of work accomplished (performance) – the emphasis being on the results of work rather than the time spent at work.

Following the First World War, there was a spurt of activity regarding the use of incentive schemes as the base for remuneration systems. Such developments were, however, cut short by the depression of the early 1920s with high levels of unemployment, the development of organized labour unions and organizations fighting for survival. Further use of incentive based remuneration systems occurred around the late 1920s but this again was affected by a depression in the 1930s. During the 1930s, organizations were so embroiled in conflict, which arose when their employees were organized into labour unions, that attention to personnel issues, including compensation programs, waned substantially.

Large-scale use of incentives as a base for remuneration systems started to occur following the Second World War. It should be noted that the trend towards the use of incentive based remuneration systems was closely associated with the development, power and influence of personnel departments within organizations. As personnel management became recognized as an important and necessary branch of good general management, the influence of personnel managers on organization policy increased. Such increased influence affected the development, introduction, utilization and overall effectiveness of incentive based remuneration systems. A feature of the 'new' remuneration system was the increasing use of job evaluation.

Before it is possible to relate the remuneration of employees directly to their work performance, it is essential that each organization ensures that the philosophy and technicalities of their basic remuneration system are sound. Job evaluation is a management technique often used to enable organizations to rationalize and validate their remuneration system by removing anomalies and creating an easily understandable pay structure. The topic of job evaluation will be discussed fully in chapter 7.

Overall, however, the use of job evaluation has been increasing for many years and has been proven to assist with reviewing/implementing grading structures, technological/organizational change, avoiding discrimination and ameliorating anomalies in payment systems. As a note of caution, however, it should be remembered that job evaluation systems must be designed/chosen, implemented, maintained and evaluated properly if they are to be successful.

Since the late 1930s the number of employees receiving incentive payments has increased gradually. This trend is illustrated in the list below, which shows the percentage of male employees in all industries in Britain receiving incentive payments during the period 1938–83. (Statistics from the *Ministry of Labour Gazette*, 1987.)

Year	Percentage of employees
1938	18
1947	24
1951	28
1961	30
1974	41
1983	47

Although the use of incentive based remuneration systems has continually increased since the period around the Second World War, the presence of incomes policies in the 1970s had a major effect on the introduction and use of such systems.

In February 1974, a Labour Government came into power under the leadership of Harold Wilson, although Wilson was to be succeeded by James Callaghan in October 1974. On defeating Edward Heath's Conservative Government, the newly formed Labour Government had to deal with the serious problem of increasing inflation.

One approach adopted by the Government in an attempt to control inflation was the introduction of various stages of incomes policy. The Stage 1 incomes policy was introduced in 1975 and set a limit of £6.00 per head per week increase in pay, but only for those employees earning up to £8,500 per annum. Employees who had annual earnings in excess of £8,500 were to be given no increase. The Stage 2 incomes policy was introduced the following year and set a 5 per cent pay limit with a £2.50 minimum and a £4.00 maximum increase per week per head.

At the same time as the introduction of incomes policies, the trend in management philosophy was moving away from the use of incentive schemes as the best method of controlling and motivating employees to work better. The trend at that time was towards the use of job enrichment, group working and participation as methods of encouraging better performance from employees. The effect of the Stage 1 and Stage 2 incomes policies together with the fashionable management philosophies was a reduction in the proportion of employees who received incentive payments between 1974 and 1977. This reduction is illustrated in table 5.1.

The table shows that the proportion of male manual workers in all industries who received incentive payments dropped from 41.4 per cent in 1974 to 36.8 per cent in 1977. This trend, however, was to be reversed by the final stage of the Labour Government incomes policies.

The Stage 3 incomes policy was introduced in August 1977 and was to be labelled the 'social contract'. This policy set a maximum increase of 10 per cent of a company's wage bill. However, extra payments above this 10 per cent limit were allowed providing they arose as a result of a self-financing productivity scheme. In addition to the introduction of the Stage 3 incomes policy, management philosophy appeared to change between 1977 and 1979 to one which considered incentive payment systems to be the only way of improving productivity. As a result of the Stage 3 incomes policy and the changing management philosophy, the period between August 1977 and May 1979, when the incomes policies ended, saw a considerable growth in the coverage of performance related incentive schemes.

Table 5.1 *Percentage of male employees receiving incentive payments 1974–1979*

	1974	1975	1976	1977	1978	1979
Manual employees						
All services and industries	41.4	41.2	37.9	36.8	42.3	44.0
Manufacturing	43.4	40.9	39.9	39.5	45.0	47.0
Non-manufacturing	39.2	41.5	36.1	34.3	39.8	41.1
Non-manual employees						
All services and industries	7.9	7.3	7.6	7.2	10.6	12.9
Manufacturing	8.2	8.5	8.6	7.9	15.3	18.0
Non-manufacturing	7.7	6.8	7.3	6.9	8.8	11.0

Source: Department of Employment, New Earnings Surveys

Whilst the developments of the mid/late 1970s catalysed a growth in the use of performance related remuneration systems, the conditions behind such renewed interest were not common across all industries.

Several years prior to the mid 1970s, many parts of the public sector had been making preparations for the introduction of work-measured payment-by-results schemes on a large scale for manual workers. In the health service, coal mining, water authorities and local authorities, for example, decisions had been made (in some cases as far back as the late 1960s) to introduce several forms of performance related remuneration. There were two identifiable problems in certain public sector industries – low pay and poor productivity – and it was hoped that such problems could be remedied by the introduction of incentive based remuneration systems.

In general, therefore, most of the public sector schemes had a long gestation and preparation period and were generally introduced by managers who believed that this was the best way to proceed. Only a few of the public sector groups had hastily drawn up incentive schemes in an attempt to combat the problems associated with the incomes policies of the 1970s.

The picture in the private sector was radically different, especially in the manufacturing industries where the recent trend had been a steady decline in the use of incentives. Following the introduction of the Stage 3 incomes policy in 1977, many private sector industries adopted incentive schemes as a method of financing increased remuneration via increased productivity.

Within the first few months of the introduction of Stage 3, many incentive based remuneration systems were hastily designed and quickly implemented with little thought for the suitability of the scheme. The nature of incentive schemes in the late 1970s also changed from systems which were complicated and difficult to implement to systems which were simple in nature and easy to implement. The simplistic nature of the 'new' incentive schemes resulted directly from the immediate need for a way round the restrictions imposed by the Stage 3 incomes policy.

Another feature of the 'new' incentive schemes which assisted speedy implementation was the base for measuring performance. Whereas many previous incentive schemes were based on individual performance, the 'new' incentive schemes tended to be based on group or organizational performance since this did not require complex procedures for measuring performance and could be applied to all levels of staff.

Overall, the incomes policies of the 1974 Labour Government were instrumental in reversing the increasing trend in favour of the use of incentive based remuneration systems which was present in the early 1970s. Since the late 1970s, and the introduction of the Stage 3 incomes policy, the trend towards performance related remuneration is again increasing on an annual basis.

Up until the late 1970s, the main type of incentive based remuneration system was payment by results (PBR), in which employees were paid according to the number of tasks performed/units produced. Since the early 1980s, however, there has been a move away from 'traditional' PBR schemes to remuneration systems such as merit pay, profit sharing and employee share ownership. There have been several studies throughout the 1980s which have attempted to determine the level of usage of performance related remuneration schemes and the different schemes in operation.

Two studies which examined the use of performance related remuneration were carried out by ACAS – *Labour Flexibility in Britain: The 1987 ACAS Survey* and *Developments in Payment Systems: The 1988 ACAS Survey*.

Labour Flexibility in Britain: The 1987 ACAS Survey

The aim of the 1987 survey was to examine the extent to which employers had introduced labour flexibility into their organizations, and the different forms such flexibility could take. Among the forms of flexibility examined were:

• flexibility in numbers;
• flexibility in crafts and skills;
• flexibility in hours of work;
• flexibility in labour costs and rewards.

In addition to examining the forms of flexibility which had been introduced, the survey sought to establish the reasons for introducing flexibility. The findings could be illustrated as in figure 5.1. Among the reasons given for introducing various forms of flexibility, the most commonly cited reasons amongst the 584 organizations

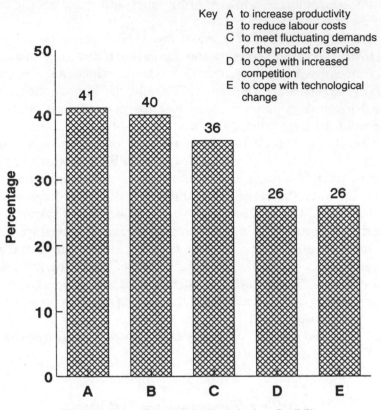

Figure 5.1   *Reasons for introducing flexibility*

surveyed were: to increase productivity (41 per cent); to reduce labour costs (40 per cent); to meet fluctuating demands for the product or service (36 per cent); to cope with increased competition (26 per cent); and to cope with technological change (26 per cent).

The survey highlighted some important developments in payment systems, in particular, the trend towards performance related remuneration. The results of the 1987 survey, which relate to performance related remuneration, could be summarized as in figure 5.2.

Clearly, the statistics show that of the 584 organizations participating in the survey, around a quarter had introduced some form of merit pay (24 per cent) or profit sharing (26 per cent) between 1984 and 1987. In addition, around one-fifth of respondents had plans to either introduce or increase merit pay (19 per cent) or profit sharing (18 per cent). Whilst the survey concentrated on private manufac-

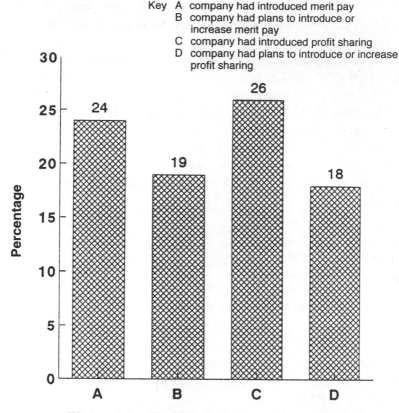

Figure 5.2 *Flexibility in remuneration systems*

turing companies and is not fully representative of UK organizations, it is clear that even within this category of organization the
interest and use of performance remuneration systems has grown
substantially since the early 1980s.

The 1987 survey also identified a trend towards the harmonization of the terms and conditions of employment. Harmonization is
defined within the survey as: 'a narrowing or elimination of the
differences in the basis of the treatment of manual and non-manual
workers regarding pay, fringe benefits and other conditions of
employment.'

The survey indicated that in the period 1984–7, around 40 per
cent of those organizations surveyed had harmonized terms and
conditions such as holiday arrangements, car parking, restaurants,
pension schemes, sick pay schemes, and working hours. In addition,
a further 13 per cent of respondents indicated that they had plans to
harmonize terms and conditions.

Developments in Payment Systems:
The 1988 ACAS Survey

In the 1980s, much of the conciliation and advisory work of ACAS was related to the difficulties faced by employers and employees in the design and operation of payment systems. As a result, ACAS felt that they should know about the trends and developments of payment systems within UK organizations and therefore conducted the 1988 ACAS survey, *Developments in Payment Systems*. In particular, ACAS wanted to know what payment systems employers used and developed to deal with the major organizational problems present at that time, such as:

* recruiting employees;
* retaining employees;
* motivating employees;
* maintaining high productivity/profit levels;
* coping with managerial accountability.

Whilst this ACAS survey again overrepresented private manufacturing establishments, the findings of the survey are useful for drawing broad conclusions about the development of payment systems in the UK around 1988.

The first aspect to be examined in relation to the development of payment systems was the use of time–rate payment systems where employees are paid a flat rate for each hour, day, week or longer period which they work. From the 664 respondents to the survey, around two-thirds confirmed that they used some form of time based payment system for at least some of their employees. The second area to be examined was the use of payment systems based on incremental increases, where employees move through a pay or salary scale according to their length of service. Around three-fifths of respondents used this payment system for at least some of their employees although the use of such systems was most common in public administration, education, health, banking and financial services. The first two areas of the survey therefore indicate that time based and incremental increase based payment systems are very common within organizations in the UK. The majority of the survey was concerned with how employers formed an association between the performance of employees and their remuneration.

The overall results of the survey indicated that payment systems based on performance related remuneration were very widely used. Indeed, some three-quarters of respondents confirmed the use of some form of payment system which linked the performance of employees to their remuneration. The payment systems used varied widely in their design and included individual incentives (piecework, commission payments, merit pay) and collective incentives (work-group based, enterprise-wide based, and profit related incentives). From the respondents who used some form of PRR, 54 per cent reported that they used individual incentives for at least some of their staff, whilst 53 per cent reported using some form of collective incentive. The use of different systems could be illustrated as in figure 5.3 and figure 5.4.

From figure 5.3, it is clear that the most preferred method of relating performance to remuneration on an individual basis was

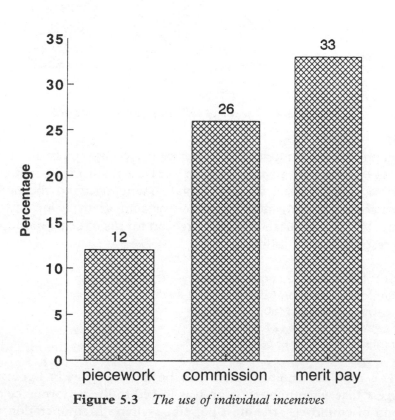

Figure 5.3 *The use of individual incentives*

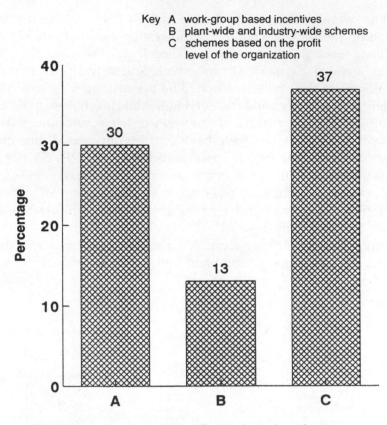

Key A work-group based incentives
     B plant-wide and industry-wide schemes
     C schemes based on the profit
        level of the organization

Figure 5.4   *The use of collective incentive schemes*

through the use of merit pay (33 per cent). Whilst commission also seems to have been popular (26 per cent), it is surprising that even from a survey biased towards private manufacturing, the use of piecework as an individual incentive was comparatively low (12 per cent). Where organizations cited a reason for introducing merit pay, the responses were as follows:

• unable to measure output of employees (29 per cent);
• improve motivation (45 per cent);
• reward individuals (80 per cent);
• reward extra skills (24 per cent);
• other reasons (7 per cent).

The research findings which can be illustrated as in figure 5.4 suggest that when remuneration was linked to the performance of a group of employees, the most popular system of remuneration was via the use of schemes based on the profit level of the organization (37 per cent). The next most popular method of remunerating performance on a collective basis was through the use of work-group based incentives (30 per cent). In comparison to the use of pay schemes linked to profits and work-group incentives, the use of plant-wide and industry-wide schemes was significantly lower (13 per cent).

One part of the survey also examined which categories of staff were covered by differently based systems of performance related remuneration. The survey used two simple staff categories, manual and non-manual, and identified which of three systems of PRR were related to each category. The three systems of PRR used were merit pay, work-group schemes and plant-wide schemes. The results could be summarized as in figure 5.5.

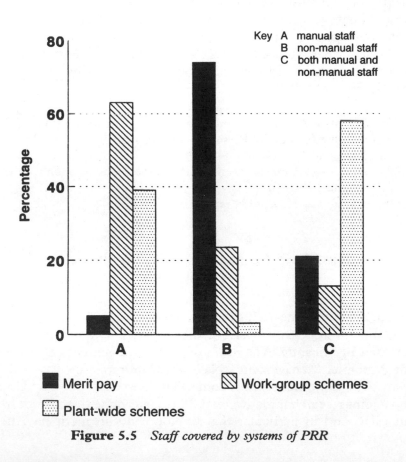

Figure 5.5 *Staff covered by systems of PRR*

From the figure, it is clear that those organizations which used merit pay generally used it for non-manual staff whilst those organizations which used work-group and plant-wide schemes concentrated on applying them to manual staff.

The main finding of the 1988 ACAS survey was that, whilst the types of performance related remuneration systems used in UK organizations varied greatly, the overall trend was towards an increasing interest in all types of incentive payment with the use of such schemes being directed at the fulfilment of a series of organizational objectives.

The two ACAS surveys together show that during the second half of the 1980s, the use and popularity of performance related remuneration systems within modern organizations was highly significant. Although the surveys were biased towards private manufacturing organizations, the introduction of merit pay, profit sharing and other forms of incentive payments between 1984 and 1987 was obviously substantial, and in 1988 three-quarters of the respondents to the survey used some form of performance related remuneration system.

Four further studies concerned with the use of performance related remuneration systems have been carried out by Income Data Services:

1985: *The Merit Factor – Rewarding Individual Performance* (in association with the Institute of Personnel Management)
1988: *Paying for Performance*
1989: *Paying for Performance in the Public Sector* (in association with Coopers and Lybrand)
1990: *Putting Pay Philosophies into Practice*

The Merit Factor – Rewarding Individual Performance

Since the end of the 1970s incomes policies in 1979, the popularity and use of systems of performance related remuneration has increased significantly. As a result of such developments, the Institute of Personnel Management's National Committee on Pay and Employment Conditions and Income Data Services' Top Pay Unit set up a joint research initiative in 1985 to determine the current trends in PRR, and in particular the developments in merit pay. In the introduction of the research publication, the objective is stated as being to 'provide personnel professionals and others interested in this area with a briefing on current practice and developments to help them analyse, devise or refine merit policies for all categories of employee to whom they are appropriate.'

The research was based on interviews carried out by the IDS Top Pay Unit with 125 organizations across a wide range of organizations and industries. One finding of the research was the identification of six reasons for introducing or amending merit payment systems:

- *the board of directors* – to establish greater control over pay;
- *line managers* – to be able to exercise more control over their employees' pay and to reward on the basis of performance;
- *the personnel department* – to gain greater flexibility over remuneration budgets;
- *employees* – to gain appropriate rewards for high levels of performance and effort;
- *market pressures* – to enable organizations to address the increasing problem of recruitment, retention and motivation;
- *the Government* – being a major employer, the Government sought to use merit payments as an aid to greater managerial control.

The research also identified the main areas of change in relation to merit pay and performance related remuneration in general:

- *changing to 'all-merit' increases* A trend was identified where organizations had replaced the traditional 'across the board' annual wage/salary review with a system where an increase in wage/salary was dependent on an individual merit review. Whilst such systems were most common in non-negotiated management layers, some companies had achieved such change in collectively bargained staff areas. None of the companies interviewed had been successful in introducing 'all-merit' reviews to shop floor staff.
- *changing from increments to merit* It was found that some organizations had replaced incremental pay systems based on automatic wage/salary increases with systems where wage/salary progression was dependent on a merit review.
- *increased use of performance appraisal* Together with, and as a result of, the move towards merit pay, many employers had introduced formal and systematic methods of appraising employee performance. Such methods normally involved some system of objective-setting.
- *increased use of job evaluation* Several organizations were found to have introduced or expanded the use of job evaluation to assist with salary structures and merit progression.

Overall, the 1985 survey by the IPM and IDS highlights the increased use of, and reliance on, PRR as a management tool to assist with ensuring the most effective use of human resources within organizations.

Paying for Performance

This research file was undertaken by the IDS in 1988 and was considered to be a follow-up to the 1985 survey rather than a replacement for it. The aim of the research was firstly to identify any developments in the use of performance related remuneration in the private sector since the publication of *The Merit Factor* in 1985, and secondly to examine any developments in the public sector. With regards to the private sector, the research highlighted two main developments:

• an increasing trend towards the replacement of incremental pay systems with wage/salary systems based on merit progression;
• the extension of performance related remuneration – in addition to senior/middle management, many other categories of employees were now covered by systems of performance related remuneration.

On examining the public sector, the main development which was identified was the marked increase in the use of performance related remuneration systems in public sector organizations such as the National Health Service, the Civil Service, British Rail, the Audit Commission and the Civil Aviation Authority. The research file proposed that the increased use of PRR in the public sector was a direct response to:

1   the recruitment and retention problems being experienced due to the competition for staff from the private sector, and
2   the requirement for increased managerial accountability for human resources.

An additional finding of the research was the changing role of trade unions in pay negotiations related to payment systems based on employee performance. Whilst one of the primary functions of trade unions is to negotiate wage and salary agreements on behalf of their members, the trade union negotiating role within PRR is generally much less significant and often reduced to a consultative role. Inevitably, as PRR gives managers more control over remuneration budgets, the control of trade unions over the pay of their members is reduced, if not taken away.

The research also focused on the use of performance appraisal, since some form of performance assessment was considered to be a prerequisite for performance related remuneration. Whilst most of the organizations interviewed used a formal and systematic method of performance appraisal, there appeared to be great diversity in the type of systems used.

Paying for Performance in the Public Sector

As has been highlighted by the four surveys previously mentioned, the period from 1979 to the late 1980s was characterized by an increasing use of performance related remuneration, particularly in the private sector. The introduction of such systems was essentially aimed at motivating staff by rewarding performance in the hope that such improved individual performance would be reflected in organizational performance and would help organizations cope with the problems of competition and economic recession. After the mid 1980s the enthusiasm for performance management and PRR began to spread into the public sector. Up until 1989, there had been no specific research on the use of PRR within the public sector so the research project *Paying for Performance in the Public Sector* was an attempt by the IDS, with part funding by Coopers and Lybrand, to redress the balance. The objective of the project was to examine the use of PRR within the public sector, and highlight any identifiable trends.

Whilst the underlying reason for introducing PRR into the public sector was the move towards a performance culture, several additional influences were identified:

- recruitment and retention difficulties;
- devolving decision making to a local level;
- the recruitment of managers with private sector experience;
- the belief of the 1979 Conservative Government that higher rewards should be given to the best performers;
- the move from traditional incremental pay structures to systems which allowed managerial flexibility over pay.

Overall, the survey identified five main trends in the use of performance related remuneration within the public sector.

1 PRR was introduced to the public sector as part of the process of organizational change with an emphasis on devolved management control and a performance culture.
2 PRR was largely confined to managerial staff but plans were being made in some areas of the public sector to extend the coverage of PRR to other staff levels.
3 Most organizations operated a system of performance appraisal where the emphasis was on target based appraisals.
4 Two strategies for introducing PRR were identified – evolution and revolution. The evolution approach involved the adaptation of existing salary structures whilst the revolution approach involved replacing existing salary structures with completely new salary arrangements.
5 Three systems of PRR were identified – incremental based schemes, salary range schemes and schemes based on 'spot salaries' with one-off lump sums.

Putting Pay Philosophies into Practice

This research file published by the IDS in July 1990 described PRR as the 1980s 'flavour of the decade'. The research concentrated on nine major organizations and by means of case studies sought to identify the likely trend in pay philosophies and resulting remuneration systems for the 1990s. Throughout the case studies, several recurring themes become apparent:

• salary policy and PRR was considered to be an effective tool for bringing about cultural change within organizations;
• flexibility in remuneration systems was required to enable employers to recruit and retain key staff;
• for some levels of staff (particularly managers and professionals) a link between performance and remuneration was taken for granted;
• careful monitoring was required when using a system of PRR to ensure fairness and consistency between individuals and/or groups;
• computerization had enabled performance and remuneration to be correlated in increasingly sophisticated ways.

Together, the four IDS studies reveal five major trends in the development of performance related remuneration between 1985 and 1990:

1   the move away from performance assessment based on merit ratings to performance assessment based on work objectives;
2   the increasing use of performance related remuneration systems in the public sector;
3   the increased coverage of performance related remuneration systems to include different categories of staff in addition to senior management;
4   the move towards substituting annual increases for all staff with individual remuneration levels dependent on the performance of each employee/group of employees;
5   the increasing complexity in forming a correlation between the performance of an individual and their subsequent remuneration package.

Merit ratings versus work objectives

Central to the PRR systems developed in the early to mid 1980s was the assessment of performance based on merit ratings – the rating of an individual's personal qualities such as commitment, dependability and initiative. Such assessments were not directly related to the ability to do a particular job or actual work performance but were based on the input to work by scoring the personal qualities of an individual. One of the main criticisms of merit ratings was that it was the personality of an individual which determined their remuneration reward rather than their actual work performance. The recent trend, however, has moved away from the assessment of performance based on merit ratings to the assessment of performance based on work performance and the achievement of working objectives. Such an approach centres on the setting of individual objectives (related to the organizational goals) and the assessment of performance against the achievement of such objectives. PRR systems using such an approach are therefore rewarding output rather than input. The trend therefore is towards PRR systems where the assessment of performance is based on work objectives.

PRR in the public sector

Traditionally, the managerial approach within the public sector, and in particular the British Civil Service, was one of impersonal uniformity where consistency of service depended on all employees doing the same job being treated equally. The concept of PRR, identifying some employees as being better than others and rewarding them accordingly, is inconsistent with such an approach and it is only since 1985 that PRR systems have been developed to a larger extent within the public sector. There are two main reasons for this increased interest in PRR:

1 PRR systems have been used in an attempt to achieve a more commercial or managerial attitude within the public sector, and
2 some services within the public sector have experienced the beneficial effects of PRR systems within the private sector, such as improved organization performance and efficiency.

Overall, the presence of PRR systems within the public sector has increased dramatically since 1985, particularly in the British Civil Service, the National Audit Office, the Audit Commission and the National Health Service.

The coverage of PRR systems

Whilst the early PRR systems were on the whole restricted to senior management, the recent trend has been to extend the coverage of PRR systems to lower level jobs such as professional, technical, clerical and secretarial staff. Some organizations, such as Nissan UK Ltd, even have PRR systems which extend to shop floor workers. Four main reasons for extending the coverage of PRR can be identified.

1 Some organizations see PRR as one method of assisting a change of organizational culture. It is therefore important that the staff are treated as a whole and are encouraged to act as a team. In such circumstances, if PRR is restricted to senior management and does not apply to all or at least most levels of staff, the change in organizational culture is unlikely to succeed. Organizations using a system of PRR and seeking a change in organizational culture therefore find it necessary to extend the coverage of their PRR system.
2 Where an organization seeks to be a single status organization, PRR is a method of rewarding different individuals according to their performance level although all employees enjoy a single status situation.
3 The reduction in real trade union power throughout the 1980s has meant that management control over payment systems has increased whereas the power and influence of trade unions in the areas of pay negotiation and collective bargaining has weakened. Such a situation has made it easier for management to introduce PRR into staff levels which the previously strong trade unions would have effectively protected. Whilst the trade unions may still be opposed to the principle of

PRR in some areas, their ability and power to oppose and reject the implementation of such systems is substantially weaker than it was in the 1970s.

4 In order to attract, recruit and retain suitable staff, some organizations use PRR systems as a method of making salary levels attractive. Such an approach is especially necessary in industries with skill shortages and in geographical areas with low unemployment levels.

Replacement of annual increases

As mentioned previously, the power of trade unions within the field of pay negotiation was reduced greatly throughout the 1980s. This situation has allowed employers to replace the traditional annual pay award with some system of PRR or with a minimal annual award alongside some system of PRR. The first situation means that any improvement in an individual's remuneration package is entirely dependent on their work performance. The second situation is less severe and consists of an annual pay award for all staff and the possibility of an additional improvement in the remuneration package dependent on the performance of the individual. Overall, there is a trend away from the traditional annual pay award towards a system where all improvements in the remuneration package are dependent on the performance of the individual.

Increasing complexity

Whilst the notion of paying individuals according to their performance is relatively simple, the administrative procedures involved in any PRR system are becoming increasingly complicated. Firstly, there has to be some formal method of assessing performance – and there are a whole range of possible alternatives, none of which can be described as simple. The second requirement is a method of translating an assessment of performance into a suitable remuneration system. Again the possibilities are many and tend to be at least administratively complicated. Overall, whilst the idea may be simple, the administrative requirements behind any system of PRR are becoming increasingly complicated.

New Earnings Surveys

A further source of data regarding the use of performance related remuneration can be obtained from the New Earnings Surveys

(NES) published by the Department of Employment. These surveys date from 1968 and attempt to identify trends in the remuneration of employees within the United Kingdom. One part of the annual survey relates to the percentage of full-time employees in all industries who as part of their total remuneration have an element which is performance related. The data from the surveys carried out between 1982 and 1993 is illustrated in the following list.

Year	Percentage of employees
1982	54.7
1983	58.6
1984	59.1
1985	54.4
1986	53.5
1987	51.9
1988	50.0
1989	51.7
1990	49.2
1991	46.3
1992	44.5
1993	43.1

The data in the list suggest that during the period 1982–93, the percentage of full time employees receiving an element of performance related remuneration has varied between 59.1 per cent and 43.1 per cent. In addition, the data suggest that since 1989, there has been a steady decline in the use of PRR amongst full time employees, from 51.7 per cent in 1989 to 43.1 per cent in 1993.

On examining the findings of the New Earnings Surveys, two points require to be clarified. Firstly, on comparing the data with the findings of the 1988 ACAS survey, *Developments in Payment Systems*, which suggested that the use of systems of PRR is likely to cover around 75 per cent of all employees, there appears to be a substantial difference. It should be noted, however, that the New Earnings Surveys only provide data on full time employees whilst the ACAS survey, and most other surveys, provide data on *all* employees. It is suggested therefore that if the New Earnings Surveys included data on both full and part time employees, the coverage of PRR would be similar.

Secondly, from the NES data, it appears that the popularity of PRR as a performance management technique has steadily declined since 1989. This would also appear to conflict with the findings of other studies performed by ACAS and IDS. On examining the number of employees in full and part time employment between 1989 and 1992, however, an explanation can be provided. Since 1988, the number of employees in full time employment has steadily declined whilst the number of employees in part time employment has continued to rise. The decline in the popularity of PRR, as suggested by the finding of the New Earnings Surveys, may not be a consequence of a decline in the use of systems of PRR but the result of a steadily decreasing number of employees in full time employment.

Overall, the annual publication of *The New Earnings Survey* demonstrates that although the total number of full time employees within the workforce is declining, the use of systems of PRR remains high.

To recap, the main developments in performance related remuneration have taken place since around 1900, although significant progress in the development and utilization of PRR systems was hindered during the early part of the century firstly by the First World War, and secondly by the economic depressions in the 1920s and 1930s. Since the late 1930s, however, the popularity of PRR systems has continually increased to a point where most organizations, in both the private and public sectors, operate some system of PRR.

The 1980s saw PRR systems being adopted as a fundamental management technique in the struggle to improve organizational performance and efficiency. Whilst the traditional systems of PRR were based on incentive payments, the most popular systems in the 1980s were merit pay (on an individual basis) and profit related pay (on a collective basis).

Summary

At the beginning of this century, the payment of employees primarily took place on a time based system where each worker would be paid according to the amount of time worked. Such a system, however, took no account of different levels of employee performance, and could have resulted in two employees being paid identical amounts even though their levels of work performance were significantly different. In an attempt to try and resolve this problem, some employers introduced an incentive element into their remuneration policies whereby part, or the whole, of an employee's pay would be determined by their level of performance. The use of incentive schemes increased around the time of the First World War, although such developments were cut short by the depression in the 1920s. The popularity of incentive schemes among employers tended to fluctuate during the late 1920s and 1930s, depending on the economic climate of the time, with large-scale use of incentive based systems of remuneration not taking place until the end of the Second World War. From the early 1940s, the use of incentive schemes steadily increased until in 1974, 41 per cent of all male employees in Britain were receiving an incentive payment as part of their total remuneration package.

In 1974, the Labour Party became the governing party in the House of Commons and had to deal with the increasing problem of soaring inflation. In an attempt to combat the problem, the Government introduced a series of incomes policies. This move resulted in a decline in the popularity of incentive schemes between 1975 and 1977. It was only with the introduction of the Stage 3 incomes policy in 1977 that the use of incentive schemes once again increased – this time in an attempt to get around the restrictions of the incomes policy.

Several studies have been undertaken since the early 1980s in an attempt to identify the reasons for using various systems of performance related remuneration and also to determine their level of use. These studies have shown that in the United Kingdom around three-quarters of all employees have some aspect of their wage/salary determined by a system of performance related remuneration. The systems of PRR in operation have varied over the past ten years although the main trend has been away from the traditional systems of payment by results to systems of merit pay, profit sharing and employee share ownership. From the studies, it would appear that non-manual/white collar staff are more likely to be covered by a system of individual merit pay whereas manual employees/blue collar staff are more likely to be covered by a bonus system based on collective/group performance.

The various studies have also identified the main reasons for introducing systems of PRR into the remuneration policies of organizations. Among the main reasons cited were:

- to establish greater management control over pay;
- to reward employees on the basis of performance;

- to enable organizations to address the increasing problems of recruitment, retention and motivation;
- to assist in the achievement of organizational objectives such as efficiency, profitability and quality.

In addition to identifying the main reasons for introducing systems of PRR into organizations, the studies also identified a number of trends regarding the use of PRR within organizations. These trends included:

- the replacement of annual salary/wage reviews with a system in which an increase in wage/salary is dependent on the level of employee performance;
- the replacement of automatic wage/salary incremental increases with systems in which wage/salary progression is dependent on the level of employee performance;
- the increased use of formal and systematic methods of assessing employee performance, such as performance appraisal based on work objectives;
- the increased use of job evaluation to assist with salary structures and merit progression;
- the extension of PRR to most categories of employee within organizations;
- the increased use of PRR to assist with cultural change within organizations;
- the increased use of PRR within the public sector as well as the private sector.

Overall, therefore, the current trend towards increased application of PRR systems in all sectors of employment suggests that the high level of interest in PRR will continue at least throughout the 1990s. Whilst the birth of PRR has been slow, and significant developments have been hindered in many ways, the popularity of PRR as a management technique to assist with the achievement of various organizational objectives has increased substantially during the twentieth century, and in particular since the early 1980s.

6

Establishing Remuneration Systems

Introduction

A key factor affecting the recruitment, retention and motivation of an effective workforce is a carefully researched and appropriately designed remuneration system. To be successful in assisting with the recruitment and retention of the correct quality and quantity of employees for the organization, the remuneration system should take account of market pressures and be designed in line with organizational and business objectives. Such considerations should ensure that the organization is in a position to recruit the best to do the best. A poorly designed remuneration system, on the other hand, is likely to manifest itself in the recruitment of poor quality staff, undesirable levels of employee performance and motivation, and high levels of staff turnover. All remuneration systems should encompass the following aims:

- to enable the organization to recruit and retain employees of the desired standard to facilitate the achievement of objectives;
- to ensure fairness and equity regarding payment for service to the organization;
- to reward performance, responsibility, skills, achievement and loyalty;
- to establish a clear link between effort and reward;
- to motivate employees to work towards the achievement of objectives.

In order to design a potentially effective remuneration system, there a number of factors that should be considered when making decisions regarding payment levels and payment structures. This chapter will examine some of the issues to be addressed, including the characteristics of the organization, internal and external factors influencing payment levels, sources of information on remuneration trends, and the various payment structures which could be utilized.

Characteristics of the Organization

Within organizations there are a number of factors which have a direct influence on the formation of management policies, including the remuneration policy. The main consideration is that any policy should be appropriate to the needs of the organization and should take into account the characteristics of the organization, the industry and the workforce.

Size of the organization

The size of an organization, in terms of the number of employees, tends to have a major impact on the design of the remuneration system. For smaller organizations, there is likely to be little need for complicated and bureaucratic remuneration systems since the employer will know each employee well and be able to base the payment level of each individual on their contribution to the organization. This position, however, does not mean that small employers can ignore market forces. All employers, be they large or small, must be able to recruit and retain an effective workforce, and this normally requires employers to offer remuneration packages which are at least comparable to that of competing employers. As organizations increase in size, there is likely to be a need for different payment structures for various categories of staff which take into account the impact of market forces. In such a situation, there is a need for a formalized and established remuneration system. As the number of employees within an organization increases, it is important for the employer to have a remuneration system which can cope with complex payment issues and potentially high levels of bureaucracy. In addition, employers must demonstrate to a large workforce that the overall remuneration policy is carefully planned and based on equity.

Organization structure

An important factor affecting the formation of any remuneration policy is the structure of the organization. Organizations which function in one location, or have multi-site operations which are centrally managed, are likely to have a remuneration policy with unified payment levels and payment structures which apply to all employees. Organizations with multi-site operations, each with devolved management responsibilities, however, may have a very complex remuneration system comprising of a series of payment levels and structures which cater for the particular needs of each site. Occasionally, as organizations grow and acquire other businesses, they will perhaps inherit various remuneration systems and end up with a remuneration policy comprising a series of remuneration systems with a multitude of payment levels and payment structures. In such a situation, the employer may decide to harmonize the various remuneration systems into one system which applies to all locations.

Nature of employment

Historically, different areas of employment have developed remuneration systems with particular characteristics. For example, the payment system for employees within an engineering company is likely to be radically different to the payment system for employees within a service organization such as a hotel or restaurant. The characteristics of such payment systems may have developed as a result of influencing factors such as industry-wide agreements and the former Wages Councils. The payment system adopted by an organization therefore has to take account of the characteristics of the area of employment and reflect the needs of the particular business, industry, occupation or profession.

Composition of the workforce

Where an organization has a workforce composed of groups of homogeneous employees, there are likely to be payment systems for each group. In such a situation, it is relatively straightforward to analyse the job content of each employee, establish areas of similarity and create a number of groupings to which various payment systems can be applied. Where it is difficult to establish similarities in job content, the result is likely to be a very fragmented and complex remuneration system with a significant number of payment structures. The most common difference in the composition of the workforce is between manual and non-manual employees. Whilst the remuneration system for manual employees is likely to be characterized by an hourly rate and weekly wage, the remuneration system for non-manual employees is more likely to consist of an annual salary paid monthly.

Factors Influencing Payment Levels

Establishing the correct payment levels for employees is important for several reasons. For example, in order to recruit and retain a workforce of the correct calibre, it is essential that the organization establishes and maintains payment levels which are at least comparable to that of competing employers. It is therefore imperative that any remuneration system takes account of current market forces and potential trends in payment levels. In addition, since the payment of salaries and wages is a considerable cost to any organization, it is important for employers to get a satisfactory return on such expenditure in terms of employee performance, commitment and loyalty. In order to motivate employees to behave in such a manner, it is essential that the remuneration package offered is considered to be of significant value by the employee, and an appropriate reward for their efforts.

When attempting to establish payment levels for employees, employers must take account of the following factors:

- the external labour market;
- internal differentials;
- individual skills and performance;
- collective bargaining;
- company performance;
- government intervention.

The external labour market

The main purpose of examining the external labour market is to establish what competing employers are paying to recruit and retain employees with similar skills, abilities, qualifications and experience. It is important not only to establish particular payment levels but also to find out about the provision of any other remunerative benefits and associated terms and conditions of employment. Once an employer is aware of the payment trends in their geographical location, industry, business area or in particular occupations or professions, they will be in a position to establish or modify payment levels and remuneration packages to assist with attracting and retaining a workforce of the correct calibre.

Once the payment levels of competing employers are established, most employers aim to be within the upper quartile of the relevant salary market. By being in the upper quartile, the employer will be among the top 25 per cent of their comparators in terms of payment levels. An unfortunate consequence of many employers seeking to be in the upper quartile is high levels of salary inflation. As each employer is tries to meet or exceed the payment levels of other competing employers, the result tends to be an ever increasing pay bill. An important factor affecting the payment levels of particular categories of employee is the principle of supply and demand. When particular skills and abilities are high in demand but short in supply, as with computer programming in the 1980s, the payment levels are likely to be very high. On the other hand, when skills and abilities are low in demand and yet high in supply, as with general office staff perhaps, the converse is likely to be found – low levels of pay.

Since the composition and characteristics of the labour market are constantly changing, it is essential that employers remain aware of any developments which may affect their remuneration system and, in particular, their payment levels. There are numerous sources of information on payment trends within the labour market and these are examined later in this chapter.

Internal differentials

Within most organizations, the workforce tends to be arranged into a number of categories or grades of employee. Once established, these grades are normally ranked and reflected in a hierarchy of pay levels using a series of payment structures. Employees quickly become aware not only of their own grade and its corresponding salary level, but also of their relative position within the organization in relation to employees in other grades. It is therefore important that when establishing and reviewing salary levels, careful consideration is given to both the grading structure and the influence that pay levels for particular jobs can have on other jobs within the organization. An increasingly common method used to grade employees within organizations is the use of job evaluation systems.

The main purpose of job evaluation exercises is to grade jobs and then use the gradings as the base for a remuneration system. The key feature of job evaluation is an assessment of the job content of each job, not an assessment of the job holder. Once each job has been assessed using criteria such as skill, responsibility and physical effort, jobs with a similar score are banded together into a series of job grades to which payment levels are subsequently attached. The topic of job evaluation is discussed fully in chapter 7.

Individual skills and performance

Although an organization may have a carefully planned remuneration system with established payment levels and payment structures based on market comparisons, there are occasions when the organization may have to deviate from the established guidelines. One such occasion is when the organization desperately requires particular skills or abilities. In these circumstances, whilst there may be established market rates for such skills and abilities, the organization may be willing to pay above the market rates in order to ensure the speedy appointment of an appropriately skilled individual.

The organization may also deviate from market rates when the remuneration system incorporates a performance based element of pay. In such circumstances, should the performance of an individual employee reach or go beyond a predetermined standard, they become eligible for a remunerative reward, be it a bonus, salary increase or a non-cash benefit. Under such a system, the inclusion of a performance related payment may take the payment level for the individual beyond established market rates for the job. The recent trend towards the increasing use of performance related pay, however, has resulted in performance related rewards becoming incorporated into many remuneration systems and therefore subject to market pressures.

Collective bargaining

An important influence on remuneration policy, including payment levels, are the demands made upon employers by employee representatives such as trade unions. Within most organizations, it is very rare for employees to negotiate their individual terms and conditions of employment; this procedure normally takes place on a united basis via collective bargaining. Collective bargaining is a process of joint negotiation between the employer and the trade unions, or other employee representative, regarding all aspects of the employment relationship. Perhaps the most common item on the collective bargaining agenda is the issue of pay and the terms and conditions of employment. Although the British system of collective bargaining is based on a voluntary process, around half of all firms still have their payment levels determined by a process of collective bargaining. In order for a system of collective bargaining to operate effectively, the following two conditions must exist:

- the employees must be willing to act collectively with a representative body, and must recognize their common interests;
- the employer must recognize the representative body as the legitimate bargaining agent for the workforce.

Irrespective of whether collective bargaining takes place on a formal or informal basis, any pressure applied by a united workforce is likely to have an impact on the remuneration policy and must be considered when establishing payment levels if frustration of the employment relationship is to be avoided.

Company performance

Perhaps the most crucial factor influencing the review of payment levels is the simple economic fact that in order to provide payment increases, the organization must have adequate resources to cover the additional expenditure. If the organization does not have sufficient funds to pay for increased remuneration levels, then to agree to such changes is likely to result in the demise of the business. Within the highly competitive business world of today, both private and public sector organizations are becoming increasingly aware of the need to fully justify any expenditure. When negotiating payment levels, therefore, a trend has emerged whereby organizations aim to establish a correlation between pay increases and identifiable productivity levels. In such circumstances, if the workforce seeks a particular pay increase, they must be able to justify this increase with a corresponding increase in productivity levels.

Government intervention

Occasionally, payment levels within organizations can be affected by government intervention, either in an attempt to control salary inflation or to guarantee minimum wages. During the 1970s, the British Government introduced a series of income policies which placed restrictions on the amount by which wages and salaries could be increased. In some cases, payment increases were limited to 5 per cent whilst in other cases no increase was permitted. In contrast to controlling the level of payment increase, the British Government has also intervened to establish minimum payment levels for particular categories of workers.

In 1948, the Agricultural Wages Board and the Agricultural Wages Committee were set up under the Agricultural Wages Act. The Agricultural Wages Board fixes minimum rates of pay and holidays and other terms and conditions of employment for those employed in agriculture. These statutory bodies remain in existence within Britain. Other minimum rates of pay were established in Britain by the 1986 Wages Act which set up a series of Wages Councils. These Wages Councils were empowered to set minimum rates of pay in certain industries where it was considered that no adequate form of collective bargaining existed. The Wages Councils were, however, rather short-lived since they were abolished by the Trade Union Reform and Employment Rights Act of 1993. Whilst the councils have been abolished, employers formerly governed by Wages Council Orders cannot automatically disregard the terms of the Wages Orders. Examples of industries once governed by Wages Councils include the hairdressing industry, retail trades (non-food) and clothing manufacture.

With each of the above factors having a potential influence on the payment levels within organizations, it is very clear that careful consideration must be given to such factors when establishing or reviewing the overall remuneration system. The success or failure of any remuneration system in contributing to organizational and business objectives is largely dependent on adequate account being given to the significance of internal and external influences.

Data on Remuneration Trends

When attempting to gather information on remuneration trends, there are various types of data which can be obtained from a variety of sources. This section of the chapter will highlight the type of data which organizations may require and examine the potential sources of such data, including a discussion of some of the factors which may affect their validity.

Type of data

Whilst there may be an abundance of information available on remuneration trends, organizations are likely to require data of a particular nature relating to specific aspects of their remuneration policy. Among the types of data likely to be sought are the following:

Basic payment levels   Perhaps one of the most important facts to establish when designing or reviewing a remuneration policy is the issue of basic payment levels, as discussed above. It is essential that an organization is able to compare their current payment levels with those of competing employers to ensure that they provide a competitive basic pay to assist with the recruitment, retention and motivation of a quality workforce.

Performance related pay   In addition to basic pay, many organizations are now including a performance based monetary reward as part of the total remuneration package (see chapter 5). As mentioned above, such rewards can be paid in a variety of ways including cash bonuses and salary increases. The payment of such rewards is usually dependent on the attainment of a predetermined performance target. As a result of the increasing use of performance related pay, it is essential that organizations are able to determine the use of such remuneration strategies within their geographical area, industry or profession, and where appropriate incorporate the payment of such rewards into their remuneration policy.

Remunerative benefits   A common component within most remuneration packages is a range of remunerative benefits. Such benefits may include the provision of items such as a personal pension scheme, private health care, company car, luncheon vouchers and child care. In order to be competitive within the employment market, employers must be aware of the types and level of benefits offered for the different categories of employees within their business. Whilst the exact content of the benefits package does not need to be identical to that of a competing employer, it is important that the package as a whole is perceived to be of a similar value in the eyes of the employee.

Total earnings   As has been illustrated above, the total remuneration package can include a number of components such as basic pay, performance related pay and remunerative benefits. When comparing a remuneration package to those of competing employers, it is important to consider not only the individual components of the package but also the package as a whole. Whilst one employer may offer a high basic pay with no performance pay and few remunerative benefits, another employer may offer a low basic pay with high levels of performance related pay and remunerative benefits. In such circumstances, the important issue is the value of the total package and not necessarily the characteristics of the component parts. The overall content of the remuneration package is therefore a crucial decision for any organization, but the key consideration must be the needs of both the organization and its constituent workforce.

Salary structure Whilst the issue of salary structures is discussed fully later in this chapter, it is important to realize that employers should not only be aware of the types of salary structures which may be used but also the types of structures which are actually used within their industry or type of business. Once again, whichever salary structure(s) an organization utilizes, it must be appropriate to the needs of the organization and be competitive within the employment market.

Sources of data

Whilst there are many sources of information available on remuneration trends, the organization must establish what type of data it requires and which source is most appropriate to its needs. The following are examples of sources of data, each of which may be appropriate for gathering different types of data:

* general salary surveys;
* consultants/bespoke surveys;
* recruitment agencies;
* recruitment advertisements;
* professional institutions;
* pay clubs;
* periodicals/journals;
* government surveys;
* informal sources.

General salary surveys Within the United Kingdom, there are many organizations which conduct research into salary trends and publish their findings in various formats. Such organizations include Income Data Services (IDS), the Industrial Relations Service, PE International plc, Charterhouse Group Ltd, The Wyatt Company (UK) Ltd, Hay Management Consultants, Remuneration Economics Ltd, Reward Group, the Institute of Personnel and Development, the British Institute of Management and Monks Publications. Such organizations generally produce information on trends relating to base salaries, total remuneration, remunerative benefits and annual salary movements. Within published surveys, the information tends to be grouped according to such factors as job titles/function, company size, type of employment, industrial sector, number of employees, turnover and geographical location.

Consultants/bespoke surveys Occasionally, organizations employ consultants to conduct surveys to meet their specific requirements. Such surveys are generally referred to as bespoke surveys since they are conducted to the customer's specifications and are likely to provide information on a specifically targeted selection of jobs and issues. Whilst consultants can be used to conduct remuneration surveys on the customer's behalf, they can also be used for a wide range of human resource management issues such as recruitment and selection, training and development, industrial relations and health, safety and welfare. Consultants tend to be used for the following reasons:

- to provide specialist expertise and knowledge not available within the organization;
- to act as a catalyst for ideas and developments;
- to provide an independent view;
- to help develop a consensus when there are divided opinions within the organization.

Whilst the use of a consultant can have many advantages for the organization, the cost of employing a consultant can be very significant, perhaps ranging from £200 to £300 per day upwards. Therefore, organizations must always take great care when employing a consultant and should perhaps consider a checklist similar to the one outlined below:

1 use consultants with whom you are familiar;
2 obtain recommendations from other users;
3 establish which consultants have specialist expertise within your industry/occupation;
4 check the advertisements of consultants for professionalism and the names of previous clients;
5 meet with the actual consultant you will be employing, not simply a representative of the company;
6 discuss the consultancy agreement including aspects such as the consultancy specifications, consultancy programme and timing, reporting

details to the employing organization and the basis for costs and expenses;

7   obtain written confirmation regarding all aspects of the consultancy agreement;

8   trust the consultant!

Recruitment agencies   Since recruitment agencies are employed by organizations to advertise and perhaps shortlist and select appropriate candidates for particular positions, they have a large source of information regarding the pay and terms and conditions of employment relating to a large number of jobs. Many recruitment agencies regularly publish information from their data banks on remuneration trends either for general release or to their client base. Whilst such information may be of considerable use to employers, it is important to realize that there may be a significant difference between the remuneration packages advertised and the actual pay and terms and conditions of employment offered to successful candidates.

Recruitment advertisements   Information on remuneration trends, similar to that obtained through recruitment agencies, can be obtained by analysing information on pay and terms and conditions of employment found in recruitment advertisements. Whilst this may be a laborious process, organizations can concentrate on particular jobs and competing employers, and it is a very cheap source of data. As with recruitment agencies, however, organizations must not assume that the payment levels advertised necessarily reflect the actual terms offered to successful applicants.

Professional institutions   Should an organization require information on the payment trends of a particular profession or occupation, they may be able to obtain such data from the representative professional institution. Whilst some professional bodies may only release information on payment trends to its membership, others make such information generally available, perhaps with a corresponding charge.

Pay clubs   Occasionally, groups of companies within the same industry or of a similar size may join together to carry out surveys on remuneration trends. Such surveys can either be run by one of the participating companies or alternatively can be placed with a consultant. Usually, the results of the surveys are only made available to members of the pay club. The pay clubs can be organized either formally or informally and can be on a local, national or industry-wide basis. Within the UK, examples of pay clubs organized on an industry-wide basis include the pharmaceuticals, electronics, oil and food and drink industries.

Periodicals/journals   Within the personnel management profession, there are a number of journals which constitute a valuable source of general information regarding trends in human resource management. Such journals often provide useful up-to-date information on payment trends. Examples of this type of journal include *People Management*, *Personnel Today*, *Personnel Review* and the *British Journal of Industrial Relations*. In addition to these general personnel management journals there are several specialized journals which concentrate on developments in remuneration issues. Examples of this type of journal include *Benefits and Compensation International*, the *Employment Gazette*, *IDS Reports*, *IDS Studies* and *Industrial Relations Europe*.

Government surveys   The British Government produces two main surveys which are valuable sources of information on payment trends. The Department of Employment produces *The New Earnings Survey*, an annual publication produced in six volumes. The survey includes data on gross weekly earnings with and without overtime, payment by results and shift premiums. Whilst the data presented are analysed according to a number of factors such as industry, occupation, age, sex and geographical region, the survey tends to have a small sample size at management level and is therefore probably a more valuable source of information on the pay of manual employees than non-manual and managerial employees. The other survey is produced by the Office of Manpower Economics and focuses on top pay levels in the private sector. Whilst the main purpose of the survey is to assist the Top Salaries Review Body in making recommendations to the Government on the remuneration levels of top government officials, it does provide a good and readily accessible source of information on the payment trends for managers. The survey provides information on basic salary and total remuneration, and analyses such data according to finance and non-finance sectors, company size, and job level.

Informal sources   Within the personnel profession, it is common for groups of personnel managers to meet either formally or informally to discuss issues of common interest. In addition to such meetings, valuable information is often made available via the personnel grapevine. Whilst information obtained through informal sources may often be inaccurate, due to secrecy as a result of business pressures, it can be a potential source of information on current trends within the area of pay and benefits.

Factors to be considered

Whilst there are many potential sources of data on remuneration trends, employers must be highly confident that the information provided is valid and appropriate to the needs of the organization. In order to assist with making a decision regarding the validity of such data, organizations should perhaps use a checklist similar to the one outlined below.

1 *Scope of the data* Do the data provide information on companies of a similar size, geographical location, business type, employee type, organizational structure or status? Whatever the source of the data, it is essential that the organization is able to use the information to make an accurate comparison of general remuneration trends with their own remuneration system.

2 *Up-to-dateness of the data* Were the data collected and analysed recently, and therefore indicative of current trends, or are they based on information gathered some time ago? It is very important that the organization is aware of the date for which the data were valid. This will enable the organization to make any necessary adjustments to the data to make it possible to make an accurate comparison.

3 *Method of collecting data* Was the information collected through personal visits or questionnaire surveys and was the information based on the responses of employers or employees? Whilst the best method of collecting data is through personal visits to either employer or employees, since this allows full discussion of important points, this is also the most expensive method.

4 *Size of sample* If the information is based on a survey, was the sample size sufficient to allow valid analysis? In addition to the scope, up-to-dateness and method of collecting data, organizations must be confident that any survey had an adequate number of participating organizations within the sample. Where a survey has been based on a minimal number of participants, the user organization should be made aware of such limitations.

5 *Basis for comparison* Is the nature of the information such that it allows a comparison of like with like? To be most useful, any data

used should be detailed enough to allow the user organization to make valid comparisons of similar aspects of the remuneration system. For example, the organization must be clear that they are comparing their basic payment levels to the basic payment levels of other organizations, and not their total earnings levels. The types of comparison likely to be made normally relate to aspects such as basic pay, cash bonuses, total earnings, remunerative benefits and salary structures.

6 *Inclusion of other data* In addition to remuneration trends, does the data source provide information on other terms and conditions of employment? It may be useful when making comparisons regarding different aspects of the remuneration system to refer to the wider terms and conditions of employment.

7 *Presentation of data* Is the information presented in such a way that it is easily interpreted and understood. Whilst a data source may provide copious amounts of information, it is essential that the user organization can access this information and use it for the purposes for which it was intended.

Overall, employers must carefully assess the value of any data and be confident that any information used is both valid and appropriate to the business objectives of the organization.

Payment Structures

Once an organization has established appropriate levels of payment for each category of employee, it must then select a payment structure, or series of payment structures, congruous with the characteristics of the organization and its strategic objectives. In addition, whatever payment structure(s) the organization adopts, it must also:

- be flexible;
- allow for the inclusion of some system of performance related pay;
- allow payment for skills and/or qualifications low in supply;
- encourage employee retention;
- be consistent and fair.

There are a number of types of payment structure which an organization can utilize, each one being appropriate to particular circumstances and needs of the organization. Among the most commonly used payment structures are:

- graded salary structures;
- individual job ranges;
- progression pay curves;
- job family systems;
- spot rate structures;
- pay spines;
- rate for age scales.

Graded salary structures

The basic aim of a graded salary structure is to group together jobs of a similar value to the organization with a view to attaching a particular salary range. The starting point of such a payment structure is therefore the establishment of a number of job grades. Such grades can be determined either as a result of a formal or informal job evaluation exercise, job ranking or according to existing remuneration levels. Where the organization uses a job classification evaluation system, a grading structure can be established using the same point scores. For example, where a job evaluation exercise has scored jobs between 1 and 200, it might be possible to create eight grades as follows:

Score	Grade
1–25	1
26–50	2
51–75	3
76–100	4
101–125	5
126–150	6
151–175	7
176–200	8

Once a grading structure has been established, and a hierarchy of jobs formalized, the organization must allocate a salary range to each grade. Before deciding on the salary ranges, however, there are a number of important points to be considered:

- Each salary range should have a minimum and a maximum salary level with the mid-point representing the market level for effective performers of jobs in that grade.
- The width of each range (the difference between minimum and maximum) should be sufficient to allow some flexibility in the payment of employees in the same grade. Such flexibility should allow employees to

progress through the salary structure as a result of performance, length of service, or both, enable additional payments in relation to employee performance and enable the organization to react to external market pressures. Whilst the width of the salary grade may be low for junior grades, perhaps 20 per cent of the minima, the width for senior grades may increase to as much as 60 per cent of the minima.

• If different salary structures are to overlap, the level of overlap requires careful consideration. Grade overlap can be expressed as the proportion of the salary range of one grade covered by the salary range of the next lower grade. Whilst grade overlap is very common within graded salary structures and demonstrates that employees at the higher points of the salary range may be more valuable to the organization than a new employee at the bottom of the salary range of a higher grade, it is important that the degree of overlap is not excessive. An overlap of 40–50 per cent, however, is not uncommon.

Table 6.1 is an example of the skeleton of a graded salary structure for three grades of employee. The example given provides details of salary ranges with three different widths although each has a salary differential of 20 per cent between each grade.

Whilst there are several formats which graded salary structures can take, such as narrow banded and finely graded structures, the most commonly used graded salary structure is the broad banded, overlapping structure. Such structures normally involve a differential

Table 6.1 *Example graded salary structure*

	Range width (£)		
Grade	*20%*	*30%*	*40%*
1	10000 ⇓ 12000	10000 ⇓ 13000	10000 ⇓ 14000
2	12000 ⇓ 14400	12000 ⇓ 15600	12000 ⇓ 16800
3	14400 ⇓ 17280	14400 ⇓ 18720	14400 ⇓ 20160
Grade overlap	0	27.7%	41.6%

Salary

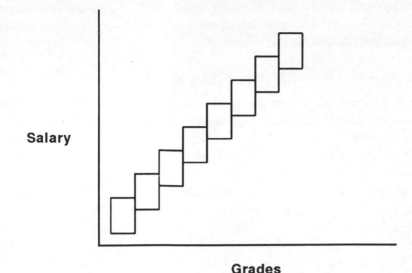

Grades

Figure 6.1   *Broad banded, overlapping salary structure*

of around 15-20 per cent between the minimum levels in each grade and may incorporate a grade overlap of up to 50 per cent. Whilst such systems enable a number of progression steps within each grade and allow employees to be promoted to the next grade without coarse salary changes, they have sufficient differentials to make different grades identifiable. A broad banded, overlapping graded salary structure is illustrated in figure 6.1.

Individual job ranges

Individual job ranges form a simple payment structure in which a salary range is defined for each individual job. Whilst in principle this is similar to the approach taken with graded salary structures, the main difference is that instead of assigning salary ranges to various grades of employee, the salary range is assigned to each particular job. The mid-point of each salary range is related to external comparisons and the upper and lower limits defined as plus or minus a percentage of the mid-point. This system of salary structure is particularly useful where the context of various jobs within the organization is significantly different or where market pressures demand high levels of flexibility from the remuneration system. Such payment systems do, however, tend to result in high levels of administration and bureaucracy and hence the use of individual job ranges tends to be limited; they are most likely to be applied to senior positions within organizations.

Progression pay curves

For any particular job, or group of jobs, progression pay curves seek to reward individuals according to the competence level which they have attained. The assumption is that an individual will not progress along a pay curve unless they have attained the correct level of competence. Refinements can also be made to the pay curve to allow for different levels of performance. In addition to the competence level of the individual, progression pay curves relate to the market rates for each type of job. Progression pay curves can therefore take into account: (a) the competence level of the individual in relation to the content and context of their job, (b) the extent to which individuals contribute to meeting objectives, (c) individual performance levels, and (d) market rates. A progression pay curve is illustrated in figure 6.2.

Job family systems

This approach is based on the assumption that within each organization there are various identifiable groups of employees, each group, or family, being subject to different market pressures. As a result of the different market pressures faced by such groups, it is occasionally necessary for some groups to be treated differently from other groups of employees within the same organization. In its most extreme form, the job family system of payment structures can result in a separate salary structure for each group of employees, perhaps with different salary limits and rates of progression. Consequently, organizations with a multitude of job family systems have a corresponding administrative burden.

Spot rate structures

Spot rate structures are very widely used amongst manual or blue collar employees and are based on specific rates of pay for particular jobs – there are no upper or lower limits. The rates of pay are normally fixed by reference to market rates and often through negotiation with employee representatives such as trade unions. Occasionally, spot rate structures are modified by the addition of

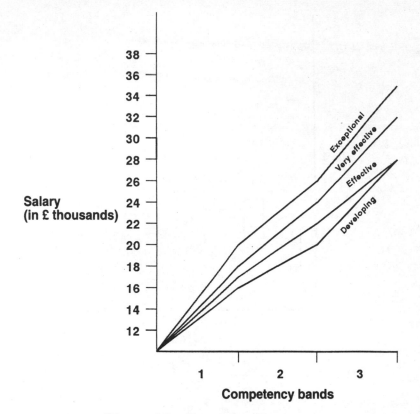

Figure 6.2 *Progression pay curves*

performance related bonuses, shift payments or payments for additional skills or responsibilities.

Pay spines

Pay spines are very common in the public sector and consist of a series of incremental salary points which extend from the lowest salary level to the highest salary level for jobs covered by the system. The differential between each salary point on the pay spine normally represents a salary increase of 2 or 3 per cent. Once the pay spine is constructed, with a continuous number of salary points, pay scales or ranges are superimposed on the pay spine. Occasionally, the pay range for particular employees is extended beyond the set limit to allow for performance related payments. A pay spine is illustrated in figure 6.3.

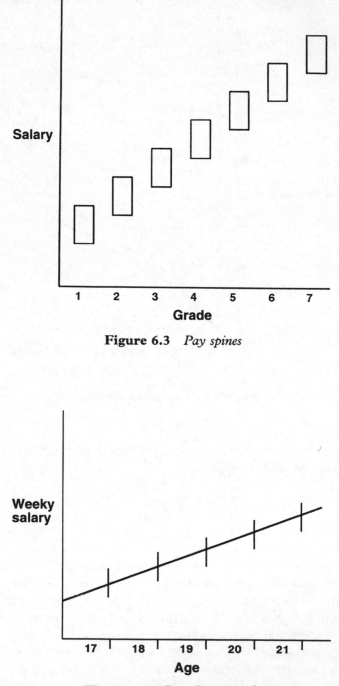

Figure 6.3   *Pay spines*

Figure 6.4   *Rate for age scale*

Rate for age scales

Rate for age scales are normally associated with young employees and consist of an incremental pay scale in which an association is drawn between the age of the employee and the pay range for particular jobs. A rate for age scale is illustrated in figure 6.4.

Conclusion

Whatever payment levels and payment structures are adopted by an organization, they must be appropriate to the needs of the organization and be flexible enough to respond to internal and external pressures. In addition, the payment levels and structures should facilitate rewards for performance and achievement ensuring that there is equity and consistency in both salary levels and salary administration.

7

Job Evaluation

Introduction

Job evaluation is a management technique often used to enable organizations to rationalize and validate their remuneration system by removing anomalies and creating an easily understandable pay structure. Whilst possibly the best method of determining payment levels for particular jobs would be to establish the worth or contribution that job makes to the organization, the level of worth of each job is usually impossible to identify. As a result, the basis for many payment structures involves the comparison of what each job involves and establishing the internal relativities of the jobs within organizations – the key function of job evaluation. Job evaluation schemes, however, do not determine payment levels but instead provide a foundation upon which payment structures and levels of payment can be based. As chapter 6 explains, actual payment levels and payment structures can only be determined once a series of factors have been considered, such as market pressures, trade union negotiations, skill and performance levels and internal differentials. Whilst the main objective behind the use of job evaluation is to provide a structure for a remuneration system, this comprises the following aims:

1 to ensure that the pay for each job reflects fair market rates;
2 to eradicate any horizontal or vertical internal pay differentials;
3 to enable a comparison of the pay rates for different jobs, functions and departments within the organization;
4 to identify the tasks, skills and responsibilities associated with each job;
5 to provide a method of establishing pay rates for new jobs and skills and redesigned jobs within the organization;

6 to identify strengths and weaknesses of the organizational structure;
7 to provide a base for salary negotiations and performance related aspects of remuneration.

The underlying approach of job evaluation is to create a job hierarchy where the relative position of each job within an organization can be easily identified. One very important issue regarding job evaluation is raised by Armstrong and Murlis (1980) who emphasize the fact that job evaluation schemes should set out to measure the relative value of the job not the job holder. Whilst the performance of the individual should not be evaluated, this may be extremely difficult where the individual is or has been in a position to personally influence what he/she does. Job evaluation schemes, on the whole, do not determine rates of pay but instead create a job hierarchy by evaluating different jobs using the same yardstick so that the relative importance of one job to another is clear. Job evaluation is therefore essentially concerned with relationships – comparing jobs with other jobs and comparing jobs against a predefined standard in order to create a hierarchical framework of jobs which reflects the relative importance of any job to another. Writing in 1990, Richard Greenhill attempted to explain job evaluation by using the following analogy:

> Jobs of the same type and specification can be likened to a particular variety of apple which can be judged, one apple against others, by prescribed criteria of, say, weight, volume and sugar content. When more than one variety of apple has to be judged, and certainly when other types of fruit enter into the comparison exercise, more subjective standards of assessment have to be employed. A company with many different types of job – accountants, machine operators, fitters, sales representatives, designers, laboratory technicians, personnel administrators, etc. – can be likened in this respect to a 'basket of mixed fruit with different varieties of any one fruit'. The evaluation of such a mix of jobs must be undertaken objectively in a consistent and relevant manner, but the final judgement on each job, by one or more people carrying out the evaluation, is subjective.

Since the early 1980s, it would appear that there has been an increasing use of job evaluation systems within many types of organizations and for a variety of purposes. Research by Millward *et al.* (1992) has shown that the use of job evaluation systems is particularly common in manufacturing and nationalized industries and tends to increase with organization size. In particular, Millward *et al.* found that between 1984 and 1990 the proportion of workplaces with 25 or more employees using a system of job evaluation rose from 21 per cent to 26 per cent.

Types of Job Evaluation

There are generally considered to be four main types of job evaluation which can be classified into two groups:

Non-analytical	Analytical
Ranking	Points rating
Job classification	Factor comparison

The non-analytical types of job evaluation are concerned with making comparisons between 'whole jobs' – the jobs are not broken down into constituent parts or factors. On the other hand, the analytical types of job evaluation are concerned with comparing jobs by reference to the different aspects or factors of each job. Millward *et al.* (1992) found that the most frequently used system of job evaluation was points rating with 45 per cent of organizations in their study using such a system. The other analytical type of job evaluation, factor comparison, accounted for 15 per cent of organizations in the study. In contrast, 36 per cent of organizations in the study used non-analytical systems of job evaluation.

Ranking

Ranking is considered to be the simplest method of job evaluation. It aims to judge each job as a whole and place it in a hierarchy of jobs by comparing one job with another, using job titles and job descriptions, and arranging them in order of importance. Whilst this technique is simple and does not attempt to break down the job in any way, it is normally only effective when used for small units. When used for larger units, the judgements become multi-dimensional and are open to inconsistencies. A further drawback of ranking is that it does not measure the difference between jobs – whilst it can show that one job is more important than another, it does not show how much more important. One variant of ranking is the use of paired comparisons where each job within the organization is compared with all the other jobs and given a score depending on the demands of the position in contrast to the other jobs. If a job is considered to be more demanding than the job it is being compared with, it scores two points. If the job is equally demanding, it scores one point and if it is less demanding, it scores no points. Once all the comparisons have taken place, the score for each job is totalled up and all the positions in the organization ranked. Table 7.1 illustrates how this process would work in an organization with six employees.

Whilst the use of paired comparisons for six different jobs appears to be relatively straightforward, involving 15 different comparisons, it becomes increasingly difficult as the number of jobs and subsequent comparisons increases. For example, an organization with 100 different jobs would be required to undertake 4,950 comparisons.

Job classification

Job classification is concerned with placing jobs in predetermined grades. The grades are defined using recognizable characteristics such as the levels of skill, responsibility, knowledge, equipment, education and training required to do the work. Once the grades are determined, each job can be allocated a grade by comparing the job description with the definition of the grade. Whilst job classification is also a simple method of job evaluation, it is not suitable for complex jobs which do not fit neatly into one grade.

Points rating

The points rating method of job evaluation was devised by M. R. Lott in 1924 and analyses jobs in terms of separately defined characteristics or factors. The starting point for points rating is to select a

Table 7.1 *Paired comparisons*

Job	A	B	C	D	E	F	Score	Rank
A	–	2	0	0	0	1	3	5
B	0	–	1	2	2	1	6	2
C	2	1	–	2	2	2	9	1
D	2	0	0	–	1	0	3	5
E	2	0	0	1	–	2	5	3
F	1	1	0	2	0	–	4	4

series of main factors which are common to all or nearly all of the jobs within an organization. Such main factors could include skill, responsibility, effort and decision making. These factors are analysed for each particular job and allocated points which reflect the relative importance of each factor in the job. Within each main factor, sub-factors can be identified, defined and allocated points which relate to the weighting of the main factors. It is also possible for sub-factors to be further broken down and analysed into degrees with points being allocated for each degree up to a maximum of the points allocated to the sub-factor. For example, if one of the main factors is responsibility and is allocated 100 points, the sub-factors could be:

Responsibility: Staff (20 points)
(100 points)   Equipment (20 points)
              Raw materials (30 points)
              Finance (30 points)

In addition, if we take the sub-factor, responsibility for staff, this may be broken down into degrees as follows:

Responsibility: Staff: Supervisors (4 points)
              (20 points) Manual workers (10 points)
                           Clerical staff (6 points)

When all jobs have been analysed using the points rating system, a system of ranking by points allows a number of grades (normally around eight) to be fixed in a hierarchical fashion. Points rating job evaluation is commonly used in organizations within the United Kingdom and has the advantage that it provides a rationale for explaining why jobs are ranked differently and therefore appears to be objective, even if it is not. The main disadvantage of a points rating system is that it is complex and potentially expensive to develop, install and maintain.

Factor comparison

Factor comparison is a method of job evaluation which attempts to ascribe monetary values to key job factors. The factor comparison method of job evaluation is based on the examination of a series of benchmark jobs in terms of selected factors of which the jobs are thought to be composed (the benchmark jobs should be jobs which are considered to be properly paid). Normally, five factors are con-

Table 7.2 *Evaluating the total rate for any job*

Benchmark jobs	Basic rate (£ pw)	Skill		Mental requirements		Physical requirements		Responsibility		Working conditions	
		%	£	%	£	%	£	%	£	%	£
Shift leader	200	20	40	30	60	10	20	30	60	10	20
Technician	180	30	54	30	54	10	18	20	36	10	18
Production operator	160	25	40	25	40	15	24	15	24	20	32
Production trainee	120	20	24	20	24	25	30	10	12	25	30
Cleaner	100	15	15	15	15	30	30	15	15	25	25

sidered: skill, mental requirements, physical requirements, responsibility and working conditions. Each benchmark job is analysed factor by factor to determine what proportion of the job is accounted for by each factor. Once this is known, a monetary value is attached to each factor using the basic rate of pay as a base for the calculation. Table 7.2 illustrates an example of factor comparison.

Once the benchmark jobs have been analysed, and monetary values attached to each factor, any other job can be allocated a rate of pay by considering each factor in turn, comparing it with the key jobs and allocating an appropriate monetary value. The main criticism of the factor comparison method of job evaluation is that it links together the processes of remuneration and job evaluation which are best kept separate although they may be indirectly related.

Non-analytical versus analytical

When examining the two main types of job evaluation, non-analytical and analytical, it is clear that both approaches have a number of advantages and disadvantages. With non-analytical systems of job evaluation, one of the main advantages is that these systems tend to be simple to operate and as a result tend not to be costly in terms of time and money. In addition, non-analytical systems of job evaluation tend to provide data in a short time period. On the negative side, however, the disadvantages of using non-analytical systems of job evaluation include:

• it is difficult to justify ranks or grades created as a result of non-analytical job evaluation;

- where non-analytical job evaluation is used in large organizations with many different jobs, the judgements used become multi-dimensional;
- non-analytical job evaluation is not suitable for analysing complex jobs;
- within non-analytical job evaluation, there is little or no method of identifying the difference between ranks or grades;
- non-analytical systems of job evaluation cannot be used for equal pay claims;
- although it is relatively simple to identify jobs at both ends of the spectrum, it is difficult to identify differences in jobs within the 'middle area'.

Considering the above advantages and disadvantages of non-analytical systems of job evaluation, such systems are likely to be most effective when used within smaller organizations. Analytical systems of job evaluation are perhaps the most commonly used systems since they enable the consideration of a large number and wide range of jobs. In addition, analytical job evaluation avoids simplistic assumptions and can be used in equal pay claims. The main disadvantage of using analytical systems of job evaluation centres around the fact that they tend to be complex to develop, implement, maintain and evaluate. Whilst analytical systems of job evaluation appear to be scientific and rely on objective judgements, the reality involves people making a number of subjective judgements based on certain information available to them.

Whilst the aforementioned are the four most popular systems of job evaluation, there are in addition many proprietary brands of job evaluation which have been developed in recent years. Some of these proprietary brands are based on the same foundations as those previously described whilst others are based on new theories of work content and subsequent remuneration. The most well known and most widely used proprietary brand of job evaluation throughout the world is the Hay guide chart-profile method marketed by Hay/MSL, a leading firm of international management consultants. The foundation of this system of job evaluation is an assessment of jobs based on three standards factors – know-how, problem solving and accountability. For any given job, each factor is evaluated on two dimensions. The know-how factor is evaluated depending upon the amount of planning, organizing and controlling (breadth of management know-how) and depth and range of technical know-how. With regards to problem solving, each job is evaluated according to the thinking challenge and the thinking environment (freedom to think). The final factor, accountability, is assessed according to the area and type of impact, and the level of freedom to act. Armstrong and Murlis (1991) conclude that the complete evaluation process characterizes jobs not only by the levels or size of each factor, but also by the balance between the factors – the profile – which reflects the 'shape' of the job. Other important proprietary brands of job evaluation include:

• Inbucon – direct consensus method
• Urwick Orr – job profile method
• Professor Paterson – decision band theory
• Professor Jaques – time-span of discretion theory

When deciding which system of job evaluation should be utilized within an organization, it is essential that the system which is chosen is appropriate for the requirements of the organization and takes account of the characteristics of the organization. As Armstrong (1990) states: the 'choice will depend on the size and complexity of the organization, the types of job to be evaluated, the time and resources available and the extent to which the scheme has to be "sold" to staff.'

Introducing Job Evaluation

Once an organization has decided to introduce a system of job evaluation, there are a number of implementation stages for the management of the organization to consider. Figure 7.1 provides an outline of the implementation process, and each stage is discussed below.

Formation of Job Evaluation Committee

The overall purpose of the Job Evaluation Committee should be to manage the introduction, administration and subsequent reviews and evaluation of the job evaluation system. Membership of the Job Evaluation Committee is likely to be led by a senior executive of the organization (perhaps the Director of Human Resource Management), and include two or three senior managers and a similar

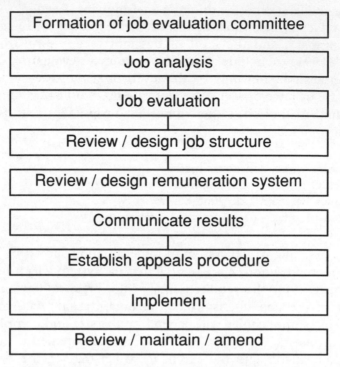

| Formation of job evaluation committee |
| Job analysis |
| Job evaluation |
| Review / design job structure |
| Review / design remuneration system |
| Communicate results |
| Establish appeals procedure |
| Implement |
| Review / maintain / amend |

Figure 7.1   *Job evaluation: implementation process*

number of staff representatives. Essentially, the committee will be concerned with project management which is likely to involve a number of responsibilities including:

- establishing the organizational strategy regarding job evaluation – the purpose of job evaluation in relation to the needs of the organization;
- selecting the approach to be used – whether the system of job evaluation should be devised 'in-house' or alternatively with the assistance of a consultant;
- establishing a programme for the introduction and implementation of job evaluation;
- selecting the most appropriate system of job evaluation – whether it should be a new system developed for the organization, a customized version of an existing system or a proprietary system of job evaluation;
- identifying the jobs to be evaluated as 'benchmarks' – the jobs against which all other jobs will be compared;
- selecting personnel to be involved in the job evaluation process – the Job Evaluation Team;

- developing a communications strategy in order that all employees are aware of why job evaluation is being introduced, the process of job evaluation and the effect which this may have on individuals and groups of employees;
- encouraging employee involvement in the job evaluation programme (employee involvement is generally considered to be a prerequisite for the operation of a successful job evaluation system);
- consultation with employee representatives regarding all issues of concern relating to job evaluation.

Job analysis

Before it is possible to carry out a job evaluation of the benchmark jobs, it is essential that comprehensive information about each job is available for those involved in making decisions. Such information is readily gathered through job analysis which can be defined as a process of collecting information about the tasks, responsibilities and context of jobs. This information includes details of the job title, the organizational context (location, department, supervisory and reporting relationships), the tasks/duties of the position, working conditions, performance requirements and individual physical, educational, experience and psychological requirements. It is only once this information is available that an accurate evaluation can be made. Such information can be gathered by various means including the use of interviews, group discussions, observation, work diaries, questionnaires and the examination of existing records. The result of job analysis should be a comprehensive job description which can then be used for job evaluation. In addition, job analysis is a useful method of providing valuable information to assist with recruitment, training, performance management and work design.

Job evaluation

Using the system of job evaluation selected by the Job Evaluation Committee, the Job Evaluation Team can proceed with the evaluation of the benchmark jobs. The benchmark jobs should be selected to provide the Job Evaluation Team with an indication of any potentially contentious issues, and in addition should highlight any problem areas with the system of job evaluation being used. Once the Job Evaluation Team is satisfied with both the evaluation of the benchmark jobs and with the operation of the job evaluation system, making any necessary modifications, it can proceed with evaluating the remaining jobs within the organization.

Review/design job structure

Using the results of the job evaluation exercise, the next step for the Job Evaluation Team is to either review and amend the existing job structure or alternatively to introduce a new job structure. The purpose of this exercise is to create a hierarchy of jobs which can then be used to establish the internal relativities of each job within the organization. Once the job structure is established, it can then be used by management for a number of purposes including the formulation of a remuneration system.

Review/design remuneration system

Once a job structure has been established, the organization is in a position to consider which system of remuneration is most appropriate to the needs and characteristics of the organization. Whilst the actual levels of payment will be determined by a multitude of factors including external pay comparisons, skill and performance levels and the relativities determined by the job evaluation exercise, the organization must decide whether to utilize its existing system of remuneration, with or without amendment, or alternatively introduce a new system of remuneration (see chapter 6).

Communicate results

Once the process of job evaluation has been completed, and the job structure and remuneration system established, it is essential that detailed feedback is given to the employees. The employees must be made aware of what changes, if any, are to be introduced into the organization and how they are likely to affect them as individuals or groups of employees. Such feedback is necessary in order to appease the concerns or fears which employees may have regarding their position within the organization. At this stage, it is also important that the employee representatives are consulted on an official basis to protect harmonious industrial relations.

Establish appeals procedure

Following the communication of results to employees, there are likely to be some employees who are not completely satisfied with the effect of the job evaluation exercise on their position within the organization. This may be the result of a fault in the job evaluation system, an error on the part of the Job Evaluation Team, or internal politics within the organization. No system of job evaluation is perfect and a few grievances on a range of related issues can be expected. Therefore, it is important that the Job Evaluation Committee formulates an appeals procedure which allows individuals within the organization to intimate their objections. The Job Evaluation Committee may decide to devise an appeals procedure exclusively for job evaluation appeals or alternatively may incorporate this within the normal company grievance procedure.

Implement

After completion of the job evaluation and the subsequent development of job structures and payment systems, and when communication on the results of the exercise is ongoing, the organization should be in a position to implement the most appropriate course of action. Throughout the process of implementation, it is vital that communication is maintained between the Job Evaluation Committee, the Job Evaluation Team and the employees. In addition, in order to maximize the commitment of the employees towards any changes resulting from the job evaluation exercise, it is beneficial to involve the employees at all stages of the implementation process.

Review/maintain/amend

If it is to be successful, job evaluation must be viewed as a system which should be reviewed, maintained and amended as necessary. It should not be considered as a one-off system which can be installed and left to function without any consideration about its role within the overall strategy of the organization. It is essential, therefore, that when utilizing a system of job evaluation within an organization, careful consideration is given to a systematic reviewing procedure which takes significant account of the ongoing and developing strategy of the organization.

Job Evaluation and Equal Pay

Under the Equal Pay Act 1970, a woman or a man can claim equal pay if they can show that in relation to pay, they are or have been treated less favourably than someone of the opposite sex who is employed on work which has been rated as equivalent under an analytical job evaluation study such as points rating or factor comparison. Once a person's work has been rated as equivalent under such a study, they are entitled to enforce the results through the Industrial Tribunal procedure to gain equal pay.

The Equal Pay Act states that a woman/man is to be regarded as being employed on work rated as equivalent with that of a man/woman if:

- their jobs have been given an equal value under an analytical job evaluation study which has considered the demands made on all or any of the employees in an undertaking, or a group of undertakings, under headings such as effort, skill and decision making, or
- their jobs would have been so rated but for the fact that different values have been given to the jobs done by men and women even though they had the same level of skill, effort, etc. – that is, where the system of job evaluation itself is discriminatory.

An important issue relating to the use of job evaluation to assist equal pay claims is the validity of the job evaluation system. To be eligible as evidence in a case of 'work rated as equivalent', the job evaluation system must be shown to be valid. This essentially focuses on three main factors:

- It is essential that the system of job evaluation to be used in the equal pay claim is analytical. This requires that the system of job evaluation is undertaken with a view to evaluating jobs done by all or any employees in terms of the demands made upon an employee under various headings such as effort, skill, decision making, etc. The system of job evaluation will not be considered valid if it simply compares the jobs of the applicant and any comparator on a 'whole job' basis. This requirement means that whilst points rating and factor comparison systems of job evaluation are likely to be considered as valid, ranking, paired comparison and job classification are not.
- It is also a requirement that the system of job evaluation to be used can be shown to be objective. This means that the actual job evaluation process must not overtly discriminate by attaching different values to the jobs done by men and women when it can be shown that the demands on both sexes are equivalent. The job evaluation system must therefore focus on the job and not the job holder.

- Perhaps the most important requirement for a valid system of job evaluation is that it should be acceptable to both the employer and the employee (or employee representative).

Whilst job evaluation studies can be used in certain circumstances to support a claim of equal pay, it should be noted that there are occasions when the employer can block the use of job evaluation studies, or use the results of job evaluation studies as evidence against a claim of equal pay.

On certain occasions, it is possible for an employer to defeat a claim of equal pay by using the results of a job evaluation study. Such an occasion would arise where the results of the job evaluation study show that, on examining the various aspects of the positions in question, there are significant differences in the value levels attached to each position, that is, the work of the applicant and the comparator are rated as being unequal. In such circumstances, providing the job evaluation study was valid, the claim by the applicant would be defeated. A further method by which the employer may be able to defeat a claim of equal pay is by establishing a defence based on the existence of a 'genuine material factor'. In such circumstances, the employer is attempting to prove that any inequality, in terms of pay, is due to a genuine material factor which is not the difference of sex. The foundation for any defence based on a genuine material factor is the proof that a difference in pay is necessary for a 'business need'. The main issue for an Industrial Tribunal to consider when deciding whether the argument of a genuine material factor should be allowed is whether or not the material factor can be objectively justified. Examples of potential genuine material factors are:

- *market forces* An argument under this heading would be based on the fact that the employer had to set a higher rate of pay for a particular job in order to recruit and retain employees with particular skills and abilities.
- *red circling* Where an employee is moved from a higher paid position to a lower paid position as a result of an organizational regrading exercise or perhaps personal incapacity, it is common for that individual to retain their higher pay level, either on a temporary or permanent basis.
- *geographical differences* Where an organization has employees employed in different parts of the country, it is perhaps necessary to pay employees in particular areas higher levels of pay to take account of the cost of living in that particular location.

- *hours of work*   Where employees have different hours of work, or different holiday levels, it is obvious that their annual payment level is likely to be different. Such differences are permissible so long as there is no significant difference when the annual amounts are translated into a notional hourly rate.
- *time of work*   The time at which work is carried out may constitute a material factor and permit the payment of a shift premium or a payment for working unsociable hours.

In equal pay cases where the results of job evaluation studies are presented as evidence on behalf of the applicant, it is sometimes possible for the respondent (employer) to block the use of job evaluation results. If the employer succeeds in blocking the use of the job evaluation results, the applicant cannot use the results as evidence and would have to rely on alternative forms of evidence. The employer would be able to block the use of job evaluation results in the following circumstances:

- should the system of job evaluation used to provide values on the work of the applicant and comparator not be valid (as described above), then the respondent is at liberty to block the use of job evaluation results;
- it is essential that the job evaluation studies apply to the positions in question, that of the applicant and the comparator; should this not be the case, the respondent may block the use of the job evaluation results.

It is clear that the issue of equal pay and the use of job evaluation studies as evidence is very complicated and normally requires the advice and services of legal experts and job evaluation professionals. It is therefore an area of human resource management which managers should at least be aware of when considering the introduction of job evaluation studies, because of its potential impact on the remuneration systems and policies of the organization.

Conclusion

Throughout the past decade, the use of systems of job evaluation within organizations of various sizes and industrial backgrounds has been steadily increasing. The use of such systems has been proven to assist in a positive manner with reviewing and implementing grading structures, technological and organizational change, avoiding discrimination in the area of remuneration and ameliorating anomalies in payment systems. If the use of job evaluation is to be successful, however, it is essential that those responsible for establishing, implementing, managing and reviewing the job evaluation policy of the organization take account of the following important issues.

1 *Reasons for using job evaluation* Should an organization decide to introduce or develop a system of job evaluation, it is essential that this is done for the correct reasons. Although the use of job evaluation is increasing within many organizations, it is important that systems of job evaluation are not utilized simply because it is 'trendy' within the modern business world. The organization must be confident that the reasons for introducing or developing job evaluation support the overall objectives and strategy of the organization and will assist, in some manner, the management of human resources.

2 *Type of system to be used* Since there are various options regarding the type of job evaluation system to be utilized within organizations, it is important that the system chosen is appropriate to the needs and objectives of the organization. The decision of which system of job evaluation to select will depend on various factors such as the size and nature of the organization, the reasons for introducing job evaluation, the existing human resource policies within the organization and the outcome of consultation with employee representatives. Whichever system of job evaluation system is chosen by the organization, the decision must be based on a number of factors which together take significant account of the mission or direction of the organization.

3 *Implementation* As with any other management policy, it is vital that the job evaluation policy of an organization is implemented in a manner which will help to ensure that it functions in a way which will contribute to the objectives and strategy of the organization. Figure 7.1 provides a suggested implementation procedure which should ensure that the job evaluation policy, and subsequent job evaluation system, is designed, introduced, managed and reviewed in an effective manner.

4 *Job evaluation and equal pay* When devising or developing payment systems within organizations, current legislation requires that careful consideration is given to the equality of remuneration packages awarded to employees doing the same or similar work. In addition, as outlined above, it is a requirement that employees

rated as equivalent under a job evaluation system are also treated equally regarding their remuneration. As a consequence, employers must be fully aware of the potential impact which the results of job evaluation may have on the payment structure and associated payment levels within their organization.

In summary, therefore, it should be remembered that an organization's job evaluation policy should be designed or chosen, implemented, maintained and evaluated in an appropriate manner if it is to successfully contribute to the business objectives and strategy of the organization.

8

Equal Pay

Introduction

History has shown that for many years there has been substantial inequality regarding the rewards given to female employees. This discrimination has not only applied to conventional salaries and wages but has also extended to more wide-ranging issues such as the terms and conditions of employment, recruitment, training, promotion, transfer and even redundancy and dismissal. As a result of such inequality, it has now become recognized that the state has the responsibility to protect women, and men, from discrimination. Whilst there have been several statutes, covering all aspects of employment, introduced to protect employees from discriminating employers, this chapter is specifically concerned with the 1970 Equal Pay Act. This Act was designed specifically to protect employees from inequality in relation to pay and the terms and conditions of employment. Whilst the Act protects both men and women from discrimination regarding their terms and conditions of employment, this chapter, like the wording of the Act itself, will assume that we are considering the status of the female employee.

It is important to appreciate that whilst the Equal Pay Act is a statute of the British Government, there are also aspects of European law which have to be adhered to. For example, Article 119 of the Treaty of Rome also requires all member states to ensure equal pay between the sexes, as does the Equal Pay Directive (No.75/117/EEC). It should be noted, however, that whilst British and European laws are similar in that they protect men and women against sexual discrimination, in all forms, the European courts have tended to overrule judgements made in British courts by imposing harsher penalties on employers by ordering compensation payments to claimants which have been much larger than the maximum compensation levels awarded by the British legal system.

Although the Equal Pay Act was passed on 29 May 1970, it did not come into effect until 29 December 1975. This time delay was a conscious strategy aimed at giving employers the opportunity to rectify any discriminatory practices which may have existed regarding pay and the terms and conditions of employment. Since the Act came into force, the average gross hourly earnings of women in full time employment compared to that of men has improved significantly, as shown by Income Data Services statistics on the average gross hourly earnings of women as a percentage of men's earnings.

Year	Percentage of male earnings
1970	60.1
1977	75.5
1987	73.6
1992	78.9

There remains, however, substantial inequality regarding male and female remuneration.

The 1970 Equal Pay Act provides that all employees have an equality clause implied into their contracts of employment. This clause gives them the legal right to complain if they are being given unequal terms and conditions of employment on the grounds of their sex. As originally drafted, the Act specifies that a female employee can complain of discrimination regarding the terms and conditions of employment if:

(a) she is employed on *like work* with a man in the same employment, or
(b) she is employed on *work rated as equivalent* with that of a man in the same employment.

In 1983, however, following a European Court of Justice decision (*Commission of the European Communities* v. *United Kingdom* (1982)) it was found that the Equal Pay Act did not comply with European law (see above). The Act was subsequently amended by the Equal Pay (Amendment) Regulations 1983 to include an additional right. In addition to (a) and (b) above, a female employee also has the right to complain of discrimination regarding pay and the terms and conditions of employment if:

(c)   she is employed on work which, not being work in relation to which (a) and (b) above applies, is, in terms of the demands made on her, of *equal value* to that of a man in the same employment.

The equality clause, however, shall not operate if the employer can prove that a variation between a woman's contract and a man's contract is genuinely due to a material difference (other than the difference of sex) between her case and his. Each of the above provisions will be discussed fully later in this chapter.

Scope of the Equal Pay Act

Within Great Britain, there are two Acts of Parliament which relate to discrimination on the grounds of sex – the Equal Pay Act 1970 and the Sex Discrimination Act 1975 (subsequently amended by the Sex Discrimination Act 1986). Whilst these two Acts have a common objective – to eliminate sex discrimination within employment – the provisions of the two Acts are mutually exclusive. The Equal Pay Act covers discriminatory contractual terms, and although it does cover all contractual terms, the main feature of the Act is the issue of pay and the terms and conditions of employment. The Sex Discrimination Act, on the other hand, covers discrimination in the formation, operation, variation and termination of the contract of employment and includes issues such as recruitment and selection, training, promotion, transfer, redundancy and dismissal. Although the two Acts are complementary to each other, it is essential when proceeding with a claim of discrimination that it is known whether the claim falls within the scope of the Equal Pay Act or the Sex Discrimination Act.

Employees Protected

The provisions of the Equal Pay Act apply to anyone, male or female, who is employed at an establishment in Great Britain. The Act specifies the meaning of 'employed' to include:

1   those employed under a contract of service;
2   those employed under a contract of apprenticeship;

3   those employed under a contract personally to execute any work or labour.

The Act does not apply, however, to those Crown employees holding a statutory office, or to those employed in any office listed in Schedule 2 (Ministerial offices) to the House of Commons Disqualification Act 1975. Since the Act only applies to individuals employed at establishments in Great Britain, it excludes employees in Northern Ireland, the Channel Islands and the Isle of Man. It does, however, include British territorial waters. Although the Act does specify an 'establishment in Great Britain', the Act will apply to an employee wherever they work, so long as it can be said that they are *based* at an establishment in Great Britain, unless they work 'wholly or mainly' overseas. Unlike some other employment laws such as the Employment Protection (Consolidation) Act 1978, there is no service qualification required by employees before they become protected by the legislation. In addition, the provisions apply equally to part time and full time employees.

Definition of Pay

As mentioned above, the Equal Pay Act covers all contractual terms, the focus being on pay and the terms and conditions of employment. The Act does not, however, specify what is meant by the locution 'pay'. Relating back to European law, however, cases which have arisen under Article 119 of the Treaty of Rome have been concerned with the interpretation and meaning of 'pay'. Article 119 states that 'pay is the ordinary basic or minimum wage or salary and any other consideration, whether in cash or in kind, which the worker receives, directly or indirectly, in respect of his employment from his employer.' Whilst this is a very broad statement, it can be considered to include the following elements:

* *Money*   Whilst a woman may be eligible for the same financial remuneration as a man, be it an hourly rate or salary, this does not necessarily mean that she will get the same amount. It may be that whilst the man and woman are put on the same remunerative rate or scale, there may be other material differences which determine the individual's place on the rate or scale. For example, length of service, special skills/aptitudes and shift allowances.

- *Fringe benefits* If fringe benefits are associated with the employment relationship, they will fall within the definition of pay as determined by Article 119. Employees are therefore entitled to equality regarding benefits such as travelling expenses, clothing allowances, company cars and discounts, so long as they can satisfy the criteria of the equality clause.
- *Leave payments* If an employer provides employees with a certain amount of paid leave, this constitutes pay for the purposes of Article 119. The basis for the calculation of the amount of paid leave should be applied equally to both sexes.
- *Sick pay* Whilst there has been some debate surrounding the issue of whether sick pay does fall within the scope of Article 119, previous cases have established that sick pay does fall within the meaning of pay and should therefore be applied equally.
- *Redundancy payments* Both statutory and contractual redundancy payments constitute pay under Article 119 since they are referable to the employment relationship. The criteria for calculation of redundancy payments and actual payment should therefore be applied equally to both sexes.
- *Pensions* This is one of the most problematic areas regarding the definition of pay for the purposes of equal pay. The arguments surrounding this area are therefore discussed fully in chapter 10: Pension Schemes.

Selecting a Comparator

When a woman submits a claim under the Equal Pay Act, she must demonstrate to the Industrial Tribunal that there is a male comparator whose work they can compare against hers. This comparison is the base for the ultimate decision regarding equal pay and therefore the comparator should be selected only after careful consideration. The choice of the comparator rests with the applicant and whilst she is free to select more than one comparator, this is not an invitation to have a wide range of comparators in order to increase the chances of success. Instead of selecting one or more comparators, the applicant may select a particular group of workers to be compared against. The danger with this option is that the Industrial Tribunal has the freedom to select a representative sample of the group in order to alleviate the administrative and logistical burden.

The Equal Pay Act places one restriction on the selection of the comparator – he must be 'in the same employment'. This restriction is explained in Section 6 of the Act as follows: 'Men shall be treated

as in the same employment with a woman if they are men employed
by her employer or by any associated employer at the same establishment or at establishments in Great Britain which include that one
and at which common terms and conditions of employment are
observed either generally or for employees of the relevant classes.'
This restriction has two main issues: (a) common terms and conditions of employment and (b) associated employers.

Should the male comparator be from the same establishment,
there is no need for the applicant to prove common terms and
conditions of employment. If, however, the comparator is from
another establishment, then whilst the applicant need not prove that
the terms and conditions of employment are identical, she must
prove that they are generally common across all employees or relevant groups of employees at the other establishment(s). In relation
to associated employers, it is necessary for the applicant to prove that
the comparator is from the same employer or an associated employer
– an associated employer is defined within the Act as being 'a
company of which the other (directly or indirectly) has control or if
both are companies of which a third person (directly or indirectly)
has control'.

Like Work

When a woman lodges a claim of equal pay on the grounds of 'like
work', she is essentially claiming that, in relation to a male comparator, she is being paid less for doing the same job. Section 1(4) of
the Equal Pay Act defines like work as follows:

> A woman is to be regarded as employed on like work with men if, but
> only if, her work and theirs is of the same or a broadly similar nature,
> and the differences (if any) between the things that she does and the
> things they do are not of practical importance in relation to terms and
> conditions of employment; and accordingly in comparing her work
> with theirs, regard shall be had to the frequency or otherwise with
> which any such differences occur in practice as well as the nature and
> extent of the differences.

When hearing a claim of equal pay (like work), Industrial Tribunals have two issues to consider: (a) is the work the same or of a

broadly similar nature? and (b) is there a difference between the work of the applicant and the work of the comparator, and if so, is it of practical importance?

The onus of proof regarding *the same or similar work* rests with the applicant. Whilst attempting to prove like work, it is not necessary for the applicant to prove that their work is identical to that of the comparator, only that it is broadly similar. Essentially, a tribunal will consider the nature of the work actually done by both the applicant and the comparator together with the skills required to do them. It is important for the tribunal when making a comparison to take account of the whole job and not to focus on minute details and insubstantial differences.

The onus of proof regarding *differences of practical importance* rests with the employer. If it is shown that the work of the applicant and the comparator are broadly similar, the tribunal must then consider whether there are any differences of practical importance between the work of the man and the work of the woman. The Equal Pay Act itself gives guidance, and suggests that regard should be given to:

- the frequency or otherwise with which such differences occur in practice
- the nature of the differences
- the extent of the differences

Examples of differences of practical importance may include: differing and/or additional duties, flexibility, responsibility, experience, skills, supervision and physical effort.

An example of an equal pay claim based on 'like work' can be found in the case of *NCB* v. *Sherwin and Spruce* (1978). In this case, the two female applicants worked in a canteen and were claiming equal pay with a man who also worked in the canteen, but worked permanent night shift. As the applicants did not work nights, but worked the day and afternoon shift, they were only claiming the same basic hourly rate – they were not claiming basic pay plus the shift premium for working nights. The Industrial Tribunal found that the employees were engaged on like work, and the Employment Appeals Tribunal agreed. Another claim of equal pay based on 'like work' can be found the case of *Eaton Ltd* v. *Nuttall* (1977). In this example, the female claimant was a production scheduler and was claiming equal pay with another production scheduler, a man, who was paid more. The employer argued, however, that based on the value of the items dealt with, the man had more responsibility and therefore was entitled to a higher rate of pay. Whilst the Industrial Tribunal agreed with the applicant, the employer appealed to the Employment Appeals Tribunal who rejected the decision of the tribunal, stating that responsibility was a factor which could be taken into consideration when paying different amounts.

Work Rated as Equivalent

In contrast to a claim for equal pay based on the similarity of jobs, as above, this aspect of the Equal Pay Act allows a woman to claim equal pay with a male comparator even though their jobs may be entirely different. Such a claim, however, is dependent on the applicant being able to prove that she is employed on work rated as equivalent with that of a man in the same employment. The proof of such a claim rests on the outcome of a job evaluation study.

Whilst the whole issue of job evaluation is discussed fully in chapter 7, it is useful to summarize the main features of a job evaluation scheme in relation to this aspect of equal pay. The underlying approach of job evaluation is to create a job hierarchy where the relative position of each job within an organization can be easily identified. Job evaluation schemes, on the whole, do not determine rates of pay but instead create a hierarchy by evaluating different jobs using the same yardstick so that the relative importance of one job to another is clear. It should be noted that, whilst job evaluation is concerned with measuring the relative importance of the job and not the performance of the job holder, this may be difficult when the individual has been in a position to personally influence what he or she does. Job evaluation is therefore essentially concerned with relationships – comparing jobs against other jobs using predefined standards with the aim of creating a hierarchical framework of jobs which reflects the relative importance of any job to another.

Basically there are two main categories of job evaluation, non-analytical schemes and analytical schemes. The non-analytical schemes are concerned with making comparisons between 'whole jobs' – the jobs are not broken down into constituent parts or factors. On the other hand, the analytical job evaluation schemes are concerned with comparing jobs by reference to the different aspects or factors of each job. For the purposes of equal pay claims, only analytical job evaluation schemes may be used when trying to prove work rated as equivalent. The two main analytical job evaluation schemes most commonly used are points rating and factor comparison. Points rating is a system whereby each job is assessed under a number of different headings such as skill, responsibility, effort and decision making. Different scores, or points, are allocated under each heading giving each job a total score. The various jobs can then be graded accordingly. Factor comparison job evaluation is similar to points rating but is based on the examination of a number of key jobs. Each key job is analysed using five factors: skill, mental requirements, physical requirements, responsibility and working conditions. Once the ranking order for each factor is determined, the amount to be paid for each factor is established. Once the key jobs have been analysed, and rankings and rates of pay established for each factor, any other job can be allocated a rate of pay by considering each factor in turn, comparing it with the key jobs and allocating an appropriate monetary value.

For a claim of equal pay based on work rated as equivalent to succeed, the job of the applicant and the comparator must either be equally rated or fall within the same range of the hierarchy established using the job evaluation scheme. The onus of proof regarding work rated as equivalent falls upon the applicant. Should an applicant prove that her work is rated as equivalent to that of a comparator, there is no further requirement to establish that she is employed on like work.

An example of a claim of equal pay based on 'work rated as equivalent', can be found in the case of *Ratcliffe & others* v. *North Yorkshire County Council* (1992). In this case, the female applicants were employed as school dinner ladies by the County Council – a group of employees which was exclusively female. They were claiming equal pay with higher paid male employees of the equivalent grade working at other institutions within the Council. Such employees included road sweepers, refuse collectors and gardeners – these categories of worker being exclusively male. In 1987, a job evaluation study was undertaken within the County Council which concluded that the jobs of the applicants and the comparators were rated as equivalent and that the school dinner ladies were indeed underpaid against the male comparators. As a result, new rates of pay were applied to the applicants with effect from January 1988 to bring about equality in terms of pay.

Work of Equal Value

Prior to 1984, the only grounds on which a woman could claim equal pay was if she could prove 'like work' or 'work rated as equivalent'. As a result of a ruling in 1983 by the European Court of Justice that the Government of Great Britain failed to fulfil its obligations under European law regarding equal pay for work of equal value, the Government introduced the Equal Pay (Amendment) Regulation 1983. From 1 January 1984, this regulation gave women the right to claim equal pay on the grounds of work of equal value. In addition to claims of equal pay on the grounds of like work or work rated as equivalent, women now have the right to claim equal pay to that of a man even though their jobs may be entirely different and/or there is no job evaluation scheme to prove that the work is rated as equivalent.

Equal pay for work of equal value entitles a woman to equal pay where she can prove that in terms of the demands made upon her, such as effort, skill and decision making, for example, she is employed on work of equal value to that of a man in the same employment. The basic argument of such a claim is that the work of the woman is of the same worth to her employer as that of a man and she should therefore be paid the same rate for the job.

Should an Industrial Tribunal find that the initial application by a woman for equal pay has reasonable grounds for a full hearing, they will appoint an independent expert to prepare a written report on whether the jobs can be said to be of equal value. There remains a certain amount of uncertainty, however, regarding what constitutes work of equal value – does it imply 100 per cent parity or 95 per cent, 90 per cent . . . ? On receipt of the written report from the expert, the tribunal will hold a full hearing to consider the evidence of the expert, the applicant and the employer. The independent expert is a person drawn from a panel of suitably qualified people designated by the Advisory, Conciliation and Arbitration Service (ACAS).

An example of a claim of equal pay based on 'work of equal value', can be found in the case of *McAuley & others* v. *Eastern Health and Social Services Board* (1991). In this case, the female applicants were employed as domestic assistants and were claiming equal pay with that of a male domestic porter and a man employed as a groundsman. After a hearing lasting 14 days, the Industrial Tribunal found in favour of the applicants and therefore found that the work of the female applicants and the male comparators were of equal value.

Employer's Defence

Should an applicant be able to prove that she is employed on like work, work rated as equivalent or work of equal value, an Industrial Tribunal is likely to enforce an equality clause and order the employer to pay 'equal pay'. In order to stop the enforcement of such an equality clause, the employer must be able to demonstrate that any variation in pay or the terms and conditions of employment is due to a material factor and not due to a difference in sex. As the Equal Pay Act states: 'an equality clause shall not operate in relation to a variation between the woman's contract and the man's contract if the employer proves that the variation is genuinely due to a material factor which is not the difference of sex.' The onus of proof regarding a 'material factor' other than sex rests with the employer. Essentially, the employer's defence is based upon an admission that the woman and the male comparator *are* employed on like work, work rated as equivalent, or work of equal value but that any variation in pay is genuinely due to a material factor and not the difference of sex.

It should be noted that since the employer is essentially admitting that the work of the woman and the male comparator are of equal value in terms of skill, responsibility, decision making, etc., it is not possible for the employer to use as a 'material factor' any issue which falls within the scope of the comparison regarding like work, work rated as equivalent or work of equal value. The employer cannot therefore use, for example, any issue relating to such factors as skill, mental requirements, physical requirements, responsibility and working conditions.

An important issue for an employer to consider when preparing a defence against an equal pay claim is whether the variation in pay and/or terms and conditions of employment constitutes discrimination, and whether or not such a variation can be justified by a material factor. As a result of previous cases, it has become clear that the criteria to be applied regarding a 'material factor' is very complicated and tends to vary with each decision of the Court of Appeal. However, the following are examples of factors which have been considered as acceptable 'material factors' in particular cases:

- *market forces* It has become established that the varying state of the employment market can result in particular skills and abilities becoming scarce. In such a situation, market forces make it necessary for employers to increase the pay of particular categories of employees in order to attract, recruit and retain an appropriately skilled workforce. Under such circumstances, it is acceptable for employers to have a variation in pay and the terms and conditions of employment for economic reasons.
- *red circling* Occasionally, it is necessary for employers to protect the salary, either temporarily or permanently, of an employee who, for reasons such as incapability or redundancy, has been transferred from a higher to a lower paid job. So long as the red circling exercise is not discriminatory, the resulting variation in pay and the terms and conditions of employment may be acceptable as a material factor.
- *geographical/location differences* Where the applicant and the comparator are employed at different locations, there may be customary reasons which can be used to defend a variation. A common example is the payment of a London weighting to compensate for the higher cost of living in the London area.
- *time of work* It is generally accepted that the particular time at which work is carried out may justify an additional shift allowance to compensate for working unsociable hours. In such circumstances, so long as the payment of shift premiums is itself not discriminatory, this would constitute an acceptable material factor.

Additional examples of potentially acceptable material factors include qualifications, age, experience and length of service.

Industrial Tribunal Procedure

The initial procedures for initiating and progressing a claim of equal pay are very similar to that for other types of tribunal applications. There are, however, specific differences in the latter stages of an equal pay claim if it is a claim of 'work of equal value'. The provisions of the Equal Pay Act allow any individual, male or female, who is employed at an establishment in Great Britain to initiate a claim of equal pay. In order to initiate such a claim, the individual should present to the appropriate Central Office of the Industrial Tribunals an originating application form (IT1) within the prescribed time limit which is either:

1 For those no longer employed by the respondent (employer) – within six months of termination.

2 For those still employed by the respondent – at any time so long as the applicant has been in the relevant employment during the six months preceding the date of the reference.

Whilst it is not necessary for the originating application to contain comprehensive details regarding the case, it should contain basic information such as:

- the applicant's name and address, and job description
- the employer's name and address
- full details of pay and contractual benefits
- the name of the comparator, and job description
- details of the claim

On receipt of the originating application, the Secretary to the Industrial Tribunal will forward to the employer a copy of the application together with a Notice of Appearance Form (IT3) which should be returned to the tribunal within 14 days. If the claim is to be defended by the employer, the IT3 should contain information regarding the grounds on which the claim is to be defended, for example, a genuine material factor defence. At the same time, the Secretary to the Industrial Tribunal will forward a copy of the IT1 to ACAS. ACAS will then appoint a Conciliation Officer, who has a duty to try and promote the settlement of the dispute. Attempts at settlement can be initiated either by the applicant or the respondent contacting ACAS or by the Conciliation Officer if he/she considers that there is a prospect of settlement.

Prior to the hearing, there are a number of stages which can occur depending on the particular case. The following is a brief explanation of each stage:

- *further particulars* Occasionally, the information contained in either the IT1 or IT3 may be insufficient. In such circumstances, either party may apply to the Industrial Tribunal for further particulars regarding the grounds of the case or facts.
- *discovery of documents* Central to most claims of equal pay are the personnel records of the employer. To enable the applicant to prepare their case as fully as possible, they can ask the tribunal to request copies of documents relevant to the proceedings. The tribunal reserves the right to refuse such a request if it would be oppressive or if the nature of the documents is confidential.
- *consolidation of claims* An Industrial Tribunal reserves the right to allow the consolidation of a number of claims if: (a) a common question of law

or fact arises, (b) the relief claimed arises out of the same set of facts or (c) for some other reason it is desirable to do so.

- *preliminary hearing over jurisdiction* The tribunal may allow a preliminary hearing over jurisdiction if the tribunal, or either party, feels that the matter of the complaint is outwith the jurisdiction of the tribunal.
- *hearing for direction* Particularly in complex cases, either party can request a hearing for direction with the tribunal to discuss such matters as further particulars and discovery of documents.
- *pre-hearing review* The tribunal, or either party, may request a pre-hearing review at which both parties will give brief details of their case. Should the tribunal consider that one party has no reasonable prospect of success, they can request a deposit of an amount not exceeding £150 as a condition of the case being able to continue.
- *striking out* Should the tribunal consider an equal pay claim to be scandalous, frivolous or vexatious, they reserve the right to strike it out.
- *adjournment* Prior to the actual hearing, the tribunal may allow an adjournment if requested by either party, particularly if a settlement seems possible.

Once an equal pay claim reaches the hearing stage, cases based on like work or work rated as equivalent go down one route whilst cases based on work of equal value go down another, more complicated, route. Cases based on like work and work rated as equivalent follow the sequence of events common to other types of tribunal cases: written evidence, oral evidence and cross-examination. The tribunal hearing of cases based on work of equal value has a series of stages.

1 *An initial hearing* At such a hearing, the tribunal may dismiss any claim which it considers to have no possible chance of success. In addition, at such a hearing, the respondent has the opportunity to prevent the claim progressing by demonstrating that any variation in pay and/or the terms and conditions of employment can be explained by a genuine material factor.

2 *Referral to an independent expert* Should the tribunal decide not to dismiss a work of equal value claim at the initial hearing stage, they will refer the case to an independent expert. On considering all the facts of the claim, the independent expert will prepare a written report on whether or not the jobs can be said to be of equal value.

3 *The hearing* On receipt of the written report of the independent expert, the tribunal will hold a full hearing. At this hearing, the tribunal will consider the claim for equal pay for work of equal

value, taking into consideration the report and any further evidence given by the applicant and/or respondent.

4 *The decision* Following the hearing, the tribunal must inform both parties, in writing, of the decision, giving full reasons. Should either party wish to challenge the decision, they have two options: to seek a review of the decision or lodge an appeal to the Employment Appeals Tribunal. A review of the decision is only available in limited circumstances and a request for such a review should be made in writing, stating the full grounds for the review, to the tribunal within 14 days of the decision being sent to both parties. An appeal against the decision should be made in the normal fashion by forwarding a notice of appeal to the Employment Appeals Tribunal within 42 days of receiving the decision of the tribunal.

Remedies

Should an applicant be successful in her claim for equal pay, her contract of employment will be deemed to include an equality clause. The inclusion of such an equality clause may have several consequences:

1 The pay and/or terms and conditions of employment of the woman should be modified to ensure that they are now comparable to that of the male comparator.
2 The tribunal may make an award of arrears in relation to remuneration (including compensation for non-pay benefits) and/or damages for breach of an equal pay clause. Arrears awards are limited to payments in respect of the two-year period prior to the date on which tribunal proceedings were initiated. It should be noted that whilst the validity of this limitation has been challenged with reference to Article 6 of the Equal Treatment Directive, the British Government, at this stage, has made no attempt to remove the limitation.

Conclusion

Whilst the Equal Pay Act of 1970 should give employees protection against unequal pay and terms and conditions of employment, the complexity of the Act and necessary Industrial Tribunal proceedings may make it difficult for an individual employee to prepare and present a valid claim. The Industrial Tribunal proceedings within the United Kingdom are aimed at providing employees with a rapid and informal method of resolving disputes in the employment relationship. In reality, however, the intricacies of the Equal Pay Act, and most other employment acts, together with the demands of presenting a case at an Industrial Tribunal, make it very difficult for an individual to pursue a claim for equal pay without legal representation. Such legal representation can be very expensive and, since there is little likelihood of legal costs being awarded, this is yet another barrier for the potential applicant.

It is a fact, however, that the inequality regarding the remuneration of male and female employees has reduced in recent years, although a considerable amount of inequality still remains. At the moment, there is no real penalty for an employer who is found to be in breach of an equality clause; they only have to pay to the employee what is rightfully theirs – equal pay and terms and conditions of employment. Such a situation may encourage some employers to continue to pay male and female employees different amounts until an Industrial Tribunal instructs otherwise. If employers were faced with a substantial penalty for breaching an equality clause, in addition to paying an award of arrears, it may encourage them to provide equal pay before they are faced with Industrial Tribunal proceedings. In the near future, however, it may be the case that further European rulings will impose very high penalties on employers and, as a result, employers may take more notice of equal pay legislation and consequently ensure equity with regards to pay and other associated terms and conditions of employment.

9
Remunerative Benefits

Introduction

In addition to the provision of pay in the form of a salary or wage in return for service given, employees are increasingly expecting a range of other remunerative benefits to be provided. Such benefits are many and varied and may include such items as pensions, company cars, holidays, relocation packages, child care and medical services. Together, the provision of pay and remunerative benefits form the total remuneration package. This chapter considers the policy of providing remunerative benefits and discusses many of the types of benefit which can be included within the total remuneration package.

Benefits Policy

When considering the inclusion of benefits within the remuneration package, there are several issues which organizations must consider regarding their benefits policy. Perhaps most important, in addition to examining the reasons behind the introduction of benefits which are examined below, organizations must consciously consider the relationship between the total remuneration package (including the provision of benefits) and the overall business strategy. Whatever the reasons are for providing remunerative benefits, their introduction into an organization must be part of a strategic approach to remuneration and should assist in the achievement of organizational objectives. Each benefits package therefore requires to be tailored to meet the needs of each organization – there is no 'set' benefits package which will be appropriate to all organizations. The following

are issues which must be addressed when formulating an organizational benefits policy.

1   *Which benefits should be provided?*   For any benefit to be effective,
it must hold a value for the employee, either immediately or in
the long term. It is therefore essential that when deciding upon
the content of the benefits package, the actual or perceived needs
of the employees together with their expectations are taken into
account. From the organization's point of view, the provision of
a package of benefits will prove very costly. As a result, the
organization must be sure that the provision of any benefit is
cost-effective in that it should, in some manner, assist in the
achievement of organizational objectives and therefore justify
expenditure. In addition to considering the effect of each individual benefit, it will be important for the organization to consider the package as a whole. Overall, each benefit and the
package of benefits as a whole should be a strategic element of
the total remuneration package and should be in harmony with
the organization's business objectives and strategy.

2   *On what scale should the benefits be provided?*   As mentioned
above, the provision of remunerative benefits will necessitate a
considerable amount of expenditure on the part of the employer,
the level of such expenditure being dependent on both the type
of benefits provided and the scale to which they are provided. It
is therefore important that when designing the benefits package,
thought is taken regarding the cost of the package in relation to
the cash element of remuneration in the form of salary or wage.
The employer must decide what proportion of the total remuneration package he or she is willing to devote to benefits. For
some employers, the proportion of benefits in relation to total
remuneration may be 10 per cent whilst for others it may be as
much as 40 per cent. Once again, whatever scale of benefits the
organization decides upon, it must support the objectives, or
mission statement, of the business.

3   *Should employees be given an element of choice regarding their benefits
package?*   When devising a benefits policy, it is important to
consider the question of choice within the benefits package. This
concept of allowing employees a choice regarding the content of
their benefits package is commonly referred to as 'cafeteria benefits' and is discussed fully later in this chapter. Since every
individual has a unique set of physiological, cognitive and social

needs, it is inevitable that each employee's opinion regarding the ideal benefits package will be different. In an attempt to overcome this problem, it may be desirable to allow employees a certain amount of choice regarding the content of their benefits package. Whilst this may well be desirable, the logistical problems of operating a cafeteria system of benefits are substantial and are referred to later in this chapter.

4 *How should the benefits be allocated?* Within many organizations, there is a trend towards the harmonization of the terms and conditions of employment. Such harmonization would be typically found within a single status organization. Within such an environment, the content of the benefits package would be identical for all employees, any differentiation regarding such aspects as responsibility and contribution being reflected only in pay. In contrast to this situation, organizations may decide to construct a hierarchy of benefits, the type and range of benefits being dependent primarily on grades of employee and seniority within the organization. Some organizations may decide to have partial harmonization of the terms and conditions of employment, that is, a core range of benefits for all employees with an additional range of benefits dependent on the individual's position within the organizational hierarchy.

5 *What, if any, relationship should there be between the benefits package and the financial position of the organization?* An important factor to consider when devising a benefits policy is the past and present financial position of the organization. In addition, it is necessary to identify the potential effect a growth or decline in business would have on the total remuneration package, including the provision of remunerative benefits. Whilst it may be beneficial and socially acceptable to provide employees with a comprehensive and competitive benefits package, the current and future financial position of the organization must be able to support such an initiative. As Smith (1989) suggests: 'with this kind of approach, benefits are more likely to relate cost to the performance of the company . . . and relate the total benefits package to the particular circumstances faced by the company.'

6 *What are the likely taxation implications of the benefits package?* When devising or reviewing a benefits policy, it is essential that considerable attention is given to taxation regulations. Historically, the provision of some benefits have carried with them certain taxation benefits, making the provision of some benefits

more attractive than the provision of additional cash. Within the United Kingdom in recent years, however, taxation cuts have resulted in the provision of such benefits becoming less attractive. Each year, as the Chancellor of the Exchequer announces the Government's Budget Statement, remuneration and benefit managers throughout the country are consciously aware that any change to corporate and/or personal taxation may have a dramatic effect on the financial implications of benefits packages. Whilst there may be particular taxation benefits to be gained through the provision of certain remunerative benefits, taxation levels and regulations tend to be very unstable. The taxation implications for the benefits package therefore require careful monitoring.

7   *Should employee representatives be consulted regarding the benefits policy?*   Irrespective of whether the employees within an organization are represented by a staff association, consultative committee, trade union or similar body, it is probably sensible to involve them in negotiations regarding the formulation of a benefits policy. Like most decision making processes, if the individuals likely to be affected by the benefits package are involved at the design stage, they are far more likely to be committed to the end product. One key role of employee representatives is to protect the interests of their group membership. If representatives are involved in policy formulation, and see that the benefits policy is in the general interests of the employees, the level of resistance when the benefits package is implemented will be minimal.

8   *What should be the approach to devising a reward package for key employees?*   Within the employment market, there are always likely to be skills, qualifications, etc. which are short in supply. In order to attract and retain employees who possess such characteristics, it is often necessary to offer a total remuneration package which not only equals that of competing employers but is considered to be more attractive. In relation to the benefits package, it may be appropriate to offer to key employees a competitive selection of benefits even although this may go against the principle of equity (see chapter 8: Equal Pay). Such a package may include an executive company car, enhanced health care provision or improved pension arrangements.

In summary, the formulation or review of a benefits package should take adequate account of a series of influencing factors.

Overall, the benefits package should be a strategic aspect of the total remuneration package and should be consistent with business objectives. Once formulated, it is essential that the benefits package of the organization is systematically evaluated and reviewed to ensure that it continues to contribute to organizational success.

Reasons for Providing Remunerative Benefits

When establishing a reward strategy and remuneration packages for employees in return for their service to the organization, it is generally accepted that such packages should include a range of employee benefits. Whilst this situation may be the result of historical developments in the remuneration of employees, it must always be remembered that the main purpose in providing remunerative benefits for employees should be to assist in the achievement of organizational goals. If you were to ask the executives of an organization to state the reasons why they provide benefits, however, there are likely to be a multiplicity of reasons given. Among the main reasons likely to be cited are the following:

- Many employers will claim that a range of employee benefits are provided because this is an effective method of rewarding employees without incurring the taxation implications applied to cash payments. Historically, there were recognized tax benefits in rewarding employees using non-cash benefits rather than monetary payments. Recent changes in taxation regulations, however, have resulted in such taxation advantages being greatly restrained.
- Occasionally, some jobs necessitate the provision of certain remunerative benefits – the benefit is considered to be a requirement for the job. In such circumstances, the job itself requires that the employees are provided with particular benefits which will allow them to fulfil the duties of the post. Such benefits may include items such as a company car, mobile telephone, special equipment, specific clothing or a staff uniform.
- A common reason given for the provision of benefits is that a competitive benefits package is a useful method of attracting and retaining employees. Even though the employment market may be characterized by high unemployment levels, there are always likely to be particular skills and qualifications which are high in demand yet short in supply. In such circumstances, the provision of an attractive benefits package may help to ensure that the organization is able to recruit employees of the desired specification. In addition, after employees have joined an

organization, it is essential that if high levels of staff turnover are to be avoided, the total remuneration package, including employee benefits, is at least comparable to that of competing employers.

- Many employers believe that one method of motivating employees is to increase their commitment to the organization through the provision of particular remunerative benefits. The belief is that if employees have a stake in the organization through such benefits as share ownership, pension schemes or service rewards, they will become increasingly committed to the organization and will be motivated to behave in a manner which will assist in the achievement of organizational goals.

- The provision of some benefits can have the effect of encouraging specific forms of behaviour. If, for example, the organization wishes to encourage employees to develop their careers either through part time study or affiliation to a professional association, they may provide, as an employee benefit, payment of course fees or the subscription fees for a professional body.

- The employment practices of many employers within Britain are historically based on a welfare or Quaker tradition which promotes a paternalistic and caring attitude towards the conditions of employment for employees. Whilst most employers are now primarily concerned with business issues and organizational performance, there are certain employee benefits which demonstrate that the employers still have a caring attitude. Such benefits include sick pay schemes, pensions, child care and life and health insurance.

- Whilst some employers are moving towards the harmonization of the terms and conditions of employment, as mentioned above, there are still employers who use particular benefits to recognize the status of certain categories of employees. For example, it is common for employees in senior management positions to have such benefits as executive company cars, enhanced pension schemes and wide-ranging expense accounts.

- In response to recent legislation regarding equal opportunities within employment practices, most employers are keen to demonstrate that they are 'equal opportunity employers'. As part of this employee relations exercise, employers may include in their benefits package a number of benefits which would reflect such an equal opportunities attitude. Such benefits may include child care, flexible working patterns, career breaks, job sharing and paternity leave.

- Perhaps wisely, a primary concern for employers when introducing a range of employee benefits is the actual needs or desires of the employees. As mentioned above, if employee benefits are to be effective as part of the remuneration strategy, any benefits provided must hold a value for the employee. It is therefore essential that employers do not concentrate on what they consider to be the perceived needs of the workforce, but actually determine through various means their actual needs.

Types of Benefits

The principal remunerative benefits provided for employees can be divided into three categories: financial security, financial assistance and personal needs.

Financial security

There are many benefits which are designed to give employees an element of security regarding their future financial position. Benefits of this nature include the following:

Pensions   As a result of the complex nature of pension provision, this type of benefit will be discussed separately in the following chapter, chapter 10.

Life assurance   This type of benefit can be covered either as part of a comprehensive pension scheme or as an independent life assurance provision. The basic purpose of life assurance is to guarantee a lump sum payment to the dependants of an employee should he or she die before the normal company retirement age. The amount paid to dependants is normally based on a multiple of the employee's pensionable earnings and can vary from one to four times such an amount. The link between some life assurance benefits and pension schemes is also discussed in chapter 10.

Personal accident insurance   Personal accident insurance is a benefit designed to provide compensation to employees who are involved in an accident which causes serious injury or death. It should be noted that any compensation paid to dependants on the death of an employee through accident will be in addition to any payment made under life assurance provision. Whilst most organizations make some provision regarding personal accident insurance, it is rare for such a benefit to be applied equally to all employees. The level of cover provided is normally dependent on the employee's relative position within the organizational hierarchy. For example, whilst senior management may be covered permanently irrespective of whether they are at their place of work, on business travel, at home or on holiday, other categories of employee may only be covered for accidents at their place of work or whilst on company business.

Business travel insurance This benefit is normally provided as a matter of routine to all employees involved in travelling on company business. Travel insurance generally provides cover in two main areas. Firstly, compensation for serious injury or death and, secondly, insurance cover for loss of personal effects, medical treatment and public liability.

Additional sick pay Whilst all employees paying the appropriate National Insurance contributions are covered by the provisions of statutory sick pay (SSP), many employers take the initiative to supplement statutory sick pay by increasing the amounts payable to employees and/or extending the statutory sick pay period. It is common for employers to provide a period of sick leave at full pay and an additional period at a reduced rate, perhaps two-thirds or half pay, although this still tends to be greater than the SSP minimum level. In addition to providing enhanced sick leave payments, employers occasionally extend the sick pay period beyond the customary six month limit. Should an employer decide to offer this benefit, careful checks are required regarding the levels of absence to ensure that the enhanced provisions are not being abused.

Permanent health insurance Should an employee be in the unfortunate situation of facing long-term absence from work as a result of injury, or chronic or terminal illness, this benefit goes some way towards providing financial security. Once payments under sick pay schemes are exhausted, normally after six months, permanent health insurance provides regular payments to employees during absence related to incapacity to work. Such payments, which represent a proportion of normal earnings, generally continue until death or retirement, at which stage the employee or their dependants become eligible to receive pension payments. Such provisions are generally incorporated into the company's pension scheme, via ill-health retirement provisions, or alternatively can be covered by a separate insurance scheme.

Private health insurance Whilst the provision of private health insurance can be a considerable cost to the employer, the main advantage of having employees who can receive private health care is that they can generally be treated quickly and at a time which is convenient to both the employee and the organization. Should the organization decide to provide private health insurance at no cost to the employee, the cost of doing so tends to be very restrictive. As a result, this type of benefit tends to be reserved for particular categories of employee such as company directors and senior management. One method of encouraging all employees to take out private health insurance, with little or no cost to the employer, is to arrange a group discount with an appropriate company whereby the employees can purchase private health insurance at a reduced rate. Among the main providers of private health insurance within the United Kingdom are BUPA and PPP.

Additional redundancy pay Whilst there are statutory redundancy payments available in the United Kingdom, the maximum amount of compensation available under this provision is very limited. For any employee, the maximum statutory redundancy payment is limited to 30 times the weekly pay of the individual, with an additional statutory limit on the amount of weekly pay used for the calculation. Under such circumstances, a statutory redundancy payment, even if it is the maximum, could be considered particularly insignificant when given to an employee who has given considerable service to the organization or who has commanded a high salary level. In an attempt to overcome the shortfall in statutory provision, some employers provide additional redundancy payments based primarily on length of service and salary level. It would not be uncommon to find employers providing a redundancy payment of one month's salary for each year of service.

Financial assistance

In addition to providing security for employees regarding their future financial position, many employers provide a range of benefits aimed at giving employees financial assistance in particular areas. Benefits of this nature include:

Subsidized mortgages Mortgage assistance is considered to be one of the most significant benefits for employees. Instead of having to pay market interest rates on money borrowed for a house purchase, some organizations offer employees mortgages with subsidized interest payments. The subsidy given to employees can vary according to such factors as seniority and salary level but could range from a subsidy of a few per cent off the market interest rate to a mortgage with no interest. Whilst this type of benefit is most commonly found within the financial sector in such organizations as banks, building societies and insurance companies, there are companies within non-financial sectors which offer similar benefits. Within organizations offering subsidized mortgages, there are normally a few conditions which the employees must satisfy before they are eligible to take advantage of the benefit. Normally, employees are required to have a certain length of service and in addition may have to satisfy requirements relating to age, status and salary level. Once employees are given the benefit of subsidized mortgages, it is common to find low rates of staff turnover, since employees would find it difficult to start paying market interest rates if they were to leave the organization. In addition to subsidized mortgages for house purchase, some organizations offer a similar arrangement for home improvements and bridging loans.

Company loans   Occasionally, organizations offer employees loans for a variety of purposes. Like the provision of mortgage assistance, the basis of this type of benefit is normally a reduction in the interest rate, although the level of reduction can depend on the organization and the purpose of the loan. One example of a company loan is the provision of season ticket loans for travel purposes. Such loans are normally interest free and are given to enable employees to purchase annual season tickets for travel to and from their place of work on public transport. Employees normally repay the cost of the season ticket by monthly instalments throughout the year. Should an employee find themselves with a short-term financial crisis, some employers may offer an emergency loan as a method of overcoming a time of such personal hardship. These loans are normally considered to be an advance of salary to be repaid by weekly or monthly instalments and tend to be interest free. Employers may also offer employees larger loans at a reduced interest rate for a variety of purposes such as the purchase of a car, to pay for medical treatment or to pay school fees.

Relocation expenses   In order to recruit suitably qualified and skilled employees, it is often necessary for organizations to attract candidates from a wide geographical area. Alternatively, should the organization comprise multi-site locations, it may be necessary to transfer some employees from one location to another. In both of these scenarios, it would normally be expected that the employer would at least contribute to the costs of relocating. Greenhill (1990) suggests that employers may offer, as part of the relocation package, financial assistance which may include such things as:

- cost of removal and reasonable gratuities;
- insurance of furniture in transit;
- storage of furniture where necessary;
- legal fees, stamp duty, estate agent's fees;
- valuation and survey fees;
- alterations to electrical equipment, carpets, curtains, TV aerials, etc.;
- disconnection and reconnection of gas, electricity and telephone;
- assistance with bridging loans if appropriate;
- contribution towards changes of school uniform, and accommodation for children left behind in schools for temporary periods;
- travel and accommodation for employee and spouse whilst looking for new property;
- cost of temporary accommodation and weekend travel whilst in such accommodation;
- a grant towards the cost of essential replacements;
- disturbance allowance.

Company cars Ask a sample of employees within the United Kingdom to state three employee benefits and the majority are likely to mention the company car. Whilst the provision of company cars can be a divisive issue within organizations, between the 'haves and have-nots', the level of provision of company cars within the UK remains extremely high, and is generally considered to be amongst the highest in the world. The level of provision in some European countries and the USA is, however, on an upward trend.

The provision of company cars as a remunerative benefit can be a very delicate and complicated issue. Consequently, considerable skill is required when devising and managing a company car policy, and most large organizations tend to have a specialist with the key responsibility of car fleet management. When devising a company car policy, there are a number of issues for the organization to consider, these include:

(1) Which employees should be given a company car? A key factor to be considered when providing company cars as a benefit is an allocation policy. In order to minimize the potential divisive effect of company cars, every employee must have a clear understanding of the allocation policy regarding company cars. Company cars tend to

be allocated under three headings: job need (those employees with a specified need or high annual business mileage), status (employees above a particular position in the hierarchy) and market pressures (the provision of a company car being necessary to recruit particular employees).

(2)   Which make and model of car should be provided? The main issue to be addressed here is whether employees should be given a choice regarding the make and model of their company car. In general, company directors and senior managers are normally given a choice from a list of cars in a predetermined price range. Other employees. however, may have little or no choice, if the company cars are leased as a fleet. An additional issue regarding the choice of company cars is whether or not employees should be allowed to 'buy-up'. Such a policy would allow employees to pay any additional cost over a fixed amount to enable them to have either a different make and model or a higher specification vehicle. Whatever policy the organization decides to adopt, it should be adhered to rigorously if conflict is to be minimized.

(3)   How should the company cars be financed? Companies may decide to finance the provision of company cars in one of three ways. One method is to purchase the vehicles outright, selling them after a certain time period or predetermined mileage. Alternatively, the company may decide to purchase the vehicles through hire purchase, paying the cost of the vehicle and any interest charges. Finally, and perhaps most common, the company can lease the vehicles without any purchase commitment. Each method has a number of advantages and disadvantages, and it is important for the company to choose whatever method is most appropriate to the needs of the organization.

(4)   What costs should the company meet? Once again, the company has a choice regarding this policy decision. The company can either meet all the costs of the car including the purchase or lease, running costs, and fuel, or alternatively it can meet some of the costs. Normally, the company will pay all the major costs, and the main decision relates to whether the company should pay the costs of private mileage or whether a charge should be made to the employee for private use.

(5)   What should be the criteria for renewal? As mentioned above, the main criteria for the renewal of cars are the age of the vehicle and

the total mileage. The cars can be renewed after either a set time period (normally one to three years), a specified mileage (for example 55,000 miles), or a combination of time and mileage (after three years or 55,000 miles, whichever occurs first).

(6) Who should be allowed to drive the vehicle? The decision here is whether the spouse, family or other named drivers should be allowed to drive the car. One influencing factor over this decision is the insurance implications. There are also a few companies which provide second cars for the employee's spouse, although such a privilege is likely to be restricted to directors of the company.

(7) What are the taxation implications? When devising a company car policy, it is important that the company takes into consideration the taxation implications on the employees. The taxation treatment of company cars is very complicated and constantly changing (further details are available in Croner's *Reference Book for Employers*). A new regime for tax relating to company cars came into effect on 6 April 1994. The main feature of the regime is that an employee is liable for tax based on a percentage of the manufacturer's list price of the vehicle, including VAT and any other taxes and delivery charges. The liability for tax varies according to the amount of business miles as detailed in the following list.

Business miles	Tax liability
Up to 2500	35% of list price
2501–17999	23.33% of list price
18000 or over	11.67% of list price

In addition to being liable for tax on a percentage of the list price of the car, employees are also liable for tax in respect of fuel provided by the employer for private motoring on a scale illustrated in table 9.1.

Overall, whilst the provision of company cars within the United Kingdom remains commonplace, there are a number of important issues which require to be addressed by organizations when formulating a policy on company car provision.

In addition to the above benefits, other examples of financial assistance include company discounts, the payment of professional association subscriptions, company housing and travelling allowances.

Table 9.1   *Tax liability on fuel (1994–1995)*

Fuel	Cars with cylinder capacity (cc)	Tax liability (£)
Petrol	1400 or less	640
	1401–2000	810
	Over 2000	1200
Diesel	2000 or less	580
	Over 2000	750

Personal needs

Whilst the above two categories of benefits are primarily concerned with the financial welfare of the employee, there are a significant number of benefits which can be considered as personal welfare benefits aimed at fulfilling individual personal needs. Whilst some of these benefits may not incur significant costs for the employer, they tend to hold a high value for the employee. In addition, as more and more employers are providing a comprehensive range of personal benefits, such benefits are increasingly becoming expected as part of the total remuneration package. Although it is not possible to discuss all the personal benefits which may be offered to employees, it is useful to highlight a few of the most important ones.

Annual leave   Although the majority of employers provide their employees with a certain amount of paid annual leave, it should be recognized that this is a significant benefit for employers to provide. Although employers must allow their employees any statutory holidays, or days in lieu, there is no statutory duty to give employees any annual leave. As a result, whilst paid leave may have become a benefit expected by employees, it is an important benefit within the total remuneration package. The trend within the United Kingdom is for employers to provide employees with between 20 and 25 days leave per year, plus any statutory days. This leave entitlement may be increased, however, as a result of status or length of service. Because of the nature of their business, many employers feel that it is necessary to specify when employees may take their leave entitlement. Some employers have a shut-down for four weeks of the year to enable all employees to take their leave at the same time, normally two weeks in the summer and two separate weeks at other times in the year. Before becoming entitled to the full amount of annual leave, many employers insist on a qualifying period before which employees might be given a reduced amount.

Maternity leave and maternity pay Under current statutory provisions, a pregnant woman has the right to a period of maternity leave and the payment of statutory maternity pay, providing she satisfies certain requirements. The rules governing maternity leave and statutory maternity pay are extremely complicated and full details can be found in Croner's *Reference Book for Employers*. With regards to maternity leave, a pregnant woman, irrespective of length of service or number of hours worked, has the right to a minimum of 14 weeks maternity leave. This period of leave can be taken before and/or after the birth of the baby. In order to be eligible for this period of maternity leave, the woman must comply with a few procedural details. Should the woman satisfy a qualifying period of service, she may be eligible for extended maternity leave. Essentially, if a woman has two years continuous service working at least 16 hours per week, or five years continuous service working at least 8 hours per week, prior to the eleventh week before the expected week of childbirth, she may be eligible for a minimum period of 40 weeks maternity leave comprising 11 weeks before the expected week of childbirth and 29 weeks afterwards. Once again, to be eligible for this period of maternity leave, the woman must comply with a few procedural details. It should be noted that the above provisions are statutory minimum levels of leave and an employer is free to provide improved levels should he or she so desire.

With regards to statutory maternity pay, should a woman satisfy certain earning and length of service requirements, she may be eligible for the payment of statutory maternity pay. Statutory maternity pay is a payment for 18 weeks of the period of maternity leave. The minimum payment for an eligible woman is 18 weeks at £52.50 (April 1994) although the first 6 weeks of the payment period can be increased to nine-tenths of her salary should she satisfy an additional earnings requirement. Once again, these are statutory minimum provisions and an employer is free to increase the amount of payment and/or the period of payment.

Overall, whilst the rules and regulations governing maternity leave and statutory maternity pay are very complex, they remain a valuable benefit to pregnant employees, although, as always, any improvement to the statutory provisions are certain to be welcomed by both individual employees and their representative body.

In connection with maternity provision, a few employers are now considering the provision of paternity leave. Paternity leave is essentially a period of leave for the male partner to allow him to look after the newly born child and allow the mother to return to her employment. Whilst there are very few employers in the UK who provide extended paternity leave, the uptake in Europe is far more encouraging. Developments in the provision of paternity leave within the UK are sure to continue in future years and will be monitored closely by employers, employees and equal opportunity bodies.

Career breaks In response to the demand for equal opportunities within the employment field, many employers are consciously making an effort to retain employees with young dependent children. In addition to child care provision, some employers are now offering employees career breaks. The purpose of this benefit is to allow both male and female employees the opportunity to take a temporary break from employment (perhaps one to five years) to raise their children. Employees taking advantage of this benefit are normally encouraged to return to the organization for a short period each year as a familiarization exercise. At the end of the career break, the employee is entitled to return to work either on a part time or full time basis with no loss of status. Once again, this is a benefit which is growing in popularity and is likely to develop significantly in the near future.

Other benefits In addition to the above personal benefits, there are a substantial number of other benefits which companies can provide for employees which could be categorized as personal benefits. Such benefits include:

- personal counselling;
- career counselling;
- retirement counselling;
- compassionate leave;
- medical services/health screening (for example, doctor, dentist, optician, chiropodist);
- sabbaticals;
- long service awards;
- child care (for example, crèche, nurseries, child care payments or vouchers);

- sports and social facilities;
- subsidized catering/luncheon vouchers;
- mobile phones/telephone costs;
- clothing allowance/company uniform;
- funding for training/studies;
- credit card facilities.

Cafeteria Benefits

Within the United Kingdom, when organizations offer employees a certain number of remunerative benefits, the individual employee rarely has a choice regarding the content of their benefits package. This position may change, however, and reflect recent developments in the USA and Australia where more and more employees are being given a flexible benefits package – cafeteria benefits. The Institute of Personnel Management (1990) describes cafeteria benefits as 'flexible remuneration systems which allow employees to decide which elements they want in their compensation package and in what amounts'. The basic principle behind cafeteria benefits is that organizations can offer employees a range, or menu, of benefits with each benefit having an 'option price'. The employee is then given a 'credit amount' (monetary value, points allocation, or credits) to spend on benefits and they can tailor their own benefits package to suit their individual needs or desires. The credit amount available to each employee is likely to be dependent on such factors as status, length of service and salary level. It is important to emphasize that whilst the term cafeteria benefits tends to focus attention on the provision of a choice of benefits, in practice the concept usually involves the total remuneration package allowing individuals to alter the balance of benefits and cash pay as they wish. In addition, when an organization introduces a system of cafeteria benefits, it can decide either to allow choice over the whole range of benefits, or to provide a core of benefits with an element of choice over an additional number of benefits.

There are two main reasons behind the introduction of cafeteria benefits into organizations. Firstly, it is believed that allowing employees an element of choice over the content of their benefits package has a positive effect on the recruitment and retention of employees. In addition, as part of a wider strategy dealing with the motivation of employees, allowing employees the opportunity to select the benefits they desire can have a positive effect on employee motivation. Whilst there may be benefits regarding the use of a system of cafeteria benefits, it should be noted that such systems require both careful administration and full consideration of any taxation implications.

Conclusion

Whilst it is evident that there are a substantial number of remunerative benefits available to employers for inclusion within their total remuneration strategy, all of which may provide positive results, there are a number of key issues to be addressed when developing a benefits strategy:

- the benefits package should be designed to meet the needs of both the organization and the employees, and should be an integral part of the total remuneration strategy;
- the benefits package should assist in the achievement of business objectives and should support the culture of the organization;
- to be effective in terms of recruitment, retention, employee commitment and motivation, the benefits package should hold a value for the employee;
- the benefits package should not ignore, but instead complement, the effect of non-tangible benefits such as recognition, praise and encouragement;
- the benefits package should be competitive within the employment market, although it should also be creative and not merely reflect the policies of competing organizations;
- the total remuneration strategy, including the benefits policy, should be systematically reviewed, evaluated and 'repaired'.

10
Pension Schemes

Introduction

The issue of pension schemes is perhaps the most complicated aspect of the modern remuneration package. In recent years, the legislation governing the provision and management of pension schemes has become immense and increasingly complex. As a result, it is rare for employers to tackle the 'pension maze' alone; indeed, it is common for employers and human resource managers to consult pension scheme experts when considering the introduction or revision of pension schemes within their organization. The aim of this chapter is to give a brief introduction to the topic of pension schemes and provide a snapshot of the current position of pension provision within the United Kingdom.

A pension can be defined as a regular payment made by the state, employer or other body to individuals once they retire or reach a certain pensionable age. The primary purpose of such pension payments is to enable individuals to subsist without having to work. Whilst most employees within the United Kingdom are entitled to the payment of social security benefits on retirement, the level of such benefits tends to be rather low and generally only allows a fairly low standard of living. In order to enhance the quality of life following retirement, it is common for both employers and employees to make contributions to some form of pension scheme in order to provide additional benefits for the employee in their retirement years.

Historical Background

Whilst the main purpose of this chapter is to examine the current position regarding the provision of pension benefits within the

United Kingdom, it is useful to briefly examine the major historical developments in pension provision over the past century. The provision of pension benefits within the UK is not a new concept, with the first national pension scheme being devised in 1908. Although the development of pension provision has been constant throughout the past century, perhaps the most significant developments have taken place since 1975. On examining the major developments in pension provision, it is clear that there is a strong correlation between such developments and the introduction of various Acts of Parliament which regulate the operation and administration of pension schemes.

Main items of pension legislation 1918–1993

1918	Finance Act
1946	National Insurance Act
1975	Social Security Pensions Act
1986	Social Security Act
1988	Income and Corporation Taxes Act
1989	Social Security Act
1989	Finance Act
1990	Social Security Act
1992	Social Security Contributions and Benefits Act
1992	Social Security Administration Act
1992	Social Security (Consequential Provisions) Act
1993	Pension Schemes Act

During the early years of the twentieth century, there were increasing demands on employers from their employees to provide some level of pension benefit at the end of their employment lifetime. As a result, the Government introduced the 1918 Finance Act which provided attractive fiscal benefits to employers who made pension provision for employees or their dependants on retirement or death or if they become unable to work through ill-health. These fiscal benefits available to employers resulted in a substantial increase in the level of pension provision since many employers began to include pension benefits within the total remuneration package.

The next major development in pension provision occurred after the Second World War. Through the 1946 National Insurance Act, the Government announced the formation of the current national pension scheme. This pension scheme, which operates within a social security framework, came into effect in 1948. Graduated

Retirement Pensions were introduced in 1961. The next major development in pension provision resulted from the 1975 Social Security Pensions Act. This Act incorporated into the existing national pension scheme a provision for additional pension benefits via the State Earnings Related Pension Scheme (SERPS). SERPS came into operation on 6 April 1978. Under this system, employees became entitled to higher levels of pension benefits through additional earnings related National Insurance contributions to SERPS. In addition, the 1975 Act made it possible for employers to 'contract-out' of the State Earnings Related Pension Scheme and instead provide employees with additional pension benefits via an occupational pension scheme.

The 1986 Social Security Act widened the scope of 'contracting-out' further by allowing individual employees to contract-out of SERPS if they made alternative pension provision via a personal pension plan (PPP). This practice of allowing individuals to contract-out came into effect in July 1988. Another important development resulting from the 1986 Social Security Act was that from 6 April 1988 all occupational pension schemes had to operate purely on a basis of voluntary membership. Before this date, employers could make membership of their occupational pension scheme compulsory for all employees. From 6 April 1988, therefore, employees were free to decide what, if any, pension provision they made for themselves in addition to their potential right to a basic national pension, brought about by the 1946 National Insurance Act. As a result of the vast amount of pension legislation in existence, and the increasing complexity of pension provision, an attempt was made in 1992 to make the minefield of pension legislation more accessible and easier to understand. From 1992, all items of social security legislation which affected occupational and personal pension provision were consolidated into three Acts: The Social Security Contributions and Benefits Act 1992, The Social Security Administration Act 1992 and The Social Security (Consequential Provisions) Act 1992. It is likely that the topic of pension provision will continue to have a high profile, with a high probability of additional pension legislation being introduced in the 1994–5 session of Parliament.

State Pension

The existing State or National Pension consists of two components:

1   a basic retirement pension, and
2   an additional earnings related pension available via the State Earnings
     Related Pension Scheme (SERPS).

Basic retirement pension

On retirement, most employees, depending on their National Insurance (NI) contributions, are entitled to a basic retirement
pension from the state. Whilst the amount of benefit provided by the
basic retirement pension is low and generally only allows a sub-
sistence standard of living, it is a pension provision which the
employee can add to through additional contributions to the State
Earning Related Pension Scheme, an occupational pension scheme
or a personal pension plan. Within the basic retirement pension,
there are four categories of pension, two of which are dependent
on NI contributions (categories A and B) and the other two being
non-contributory (categories C and D).

Category A pensions are payable to men aged 65 or over and
women aged 60 or over irrespective of whether or not they have
retired or how much they earn, providing they satisfy the contribution requirements outlined below. The amount currently payable is
£57.60 per week (1 March 1995).

Category B pensions make provision for several payments which
may be made to widowers, widows, and married women claiming
pension benefits based on their spouse's NI contributions. Firstly,
there is a payment to widowers over the age of 65 or widows over the
age of 60 amounting to £57.60 per week (1 March 1995). Secondly,
in addition to the basic retirement pension for a retired man, there is
a payment for a dependent wife or 'person having care of child' of
£34.50 per week (1 March 1995). Thirdly, there is also a payment
for any dependent children of £9.80 per week for the first or eldest
child and £11.00 per week for each additional child (1 March 1995).
It should be noted, however, that the payment to dependent wives
and children is not payable where the dependent person earns more
than £45.45 per week (1 March 1995).

The entitlement to category A or category B pensions is based
mainly on the level of NI contributions of the 'appropriate person'
(the claimant, or person on whom the claim is based). The important criteria is whether or not the appropriate person has a sufficient
number of 'qualifying years', a qualifying year being a tax year in
which the individual has paid or been credited with NI contributions
on at least 52 times the weekly lower earnings limit for that year,

currently £57.00 (1 March 1995). To be eligible for the full rate of category A or category B pensions, the appropriate person must have a sufficient number of qualifying years amounting to at least nine-tenths of the years of his/her working life. For a man who started working at the age of 16 and retired at the age of 65, therefore, his working life is 49 years so he will require a minimum of 44 qualifying years. For a woman who started working at the age of 16 and retired at 60, her working life is 44 years so she will therefore require a minimum of 39 qualifying years. In summary, in order to be entitled to the full amount of category A or category B pensions, the appropriate person must have been making NI contributions for at least 90 per cent of their working life.

Should the claimant or their dependants not be entitled to the full amount of pension benefits, they may be entitled to a reduced amount, again based on the number of qualifying years. Depending on the ratio between the number of qualifying years and the number of years in the working life of the appropriate person, the claimant will be entitled to a percentage of the full basic pension. The table used for calculating the amount of pension entitlement is shown in table 10.1.

The non-contributory pensions, category C and category D, are paid to elderly claimants and are not dependent on NI contributions. The basic qualifying criteria for receipt of non-contributory pensions is the age of the claimant.

Category C pensions are payable to claimants who are not already receiving a National Insurance Retirement pension or whose NI retirement pension amounts to less that £34.50 per week (1 March 1995). The current levels of payment for category C pensions are as follows (1 March 1995):

Lower rate (married women)	£20.65
Higher rate (all others)	£34.50
Adult dependant	£20.65
Dependent children:	
first or eldest	£9.80
all other	£11.00

In order to be eligible for category C pensions, claimants must have satisfied the following entitlement criteria on 5 July 1970:

1 men aged 87 or over;
2 women aged 82 or over;

Table 10.1 *Calculating pension entitlement – entitlement is shown as a percentage of the full basic pension*

Number of qualifying years	Number of years in working life																		
	31	32	33	34	35	36	37	38	39	40	41	42	43	44	45	46	47	48	49
6	Nil	Nil	Nil	Nil	Nil	Nil	Nil	Nil	Nil	Nil	Nil	Nil	Nil	Nil	Nil	Nil	Nil	Nil	Nil
7	26	25	25	Nil	Nil	Nil	Nil	Nil	Nil	Nil	Nil	Nil	Nil	Nil	Nil	Nil	Nil	Nil	Nil
8	30	29	28	27	26	25	25	Nil	Nil	Nil	Nil	Nil	Nil	Nil	Nil	Nil	Nil	Nil	Nil
9	34	33	32	30	30	29	28	27	26	25	25	25	Nil	Nil	Nil	Nil	Nil	Nil	Nil
10	38	36	35	34	33	32	31	30	29	28	28	28	27	26	25	25	Nil	Nil	Nil
11	41	40	38	37	36	35	34	33	32	31	31	30	29	29	28	27	27	26	25
12	45	43	42	40	39	38	37	36	35	34	34	33	32	31	30	30	29	28	28
13	49	47	45	44	42	41	40	39	38	37	37	36	35	34	33	32	31	31	30
14	52	50	49	47	46	44	43	42	40	39	39	38	37	36	35	35	34	33	32
15	56	54	52	50	49	47	46	45	43	42	42	41	40	39	38	37	36	35	35
16	60	58	56	54	52	50	49	48	46	45	45	44	43	42	40	40	39	38	37
17	63	61	59	57	55	54	52	50	49	48	48	46	45	44	43	42	41	40	39
18	67	65	63	60	59	57	55	53	52	50	50	49	48	47	45	44	43	42	41
19	71	68	66	64	62	60	58	56	55	53	53	52	50	49	48	47	46	45	44
20	75	72	69	67	65	63	61	59	58	56	56	55	53	52	50	49	48	47	46
21	78	75	73	70	68	66	64	62	60	59	59	57	56	54	53	52	50	49	48
22	82	79	76	74	71	69	67	65	63	62	62	60	58	57	55	54	53	52	50
23	86	83	80	77	75	72	70	68	66	64	64	63	61	59	58	57	55	54	53
24	89	86	83	80	78	75	73	71	69	67	67	65	64	62	60	59	58	56	55

25	57	59	60	61	63	65	66	68	70	70	72	74	76	79	81	84	87	90	93
26	60	61	62	64	65	67	69	71	73	73	75	77	79	82	84	87	90	93	97
27	62	63	65	66	68	70	72	73	75	75	78	80	82	85	88	90	94	97	100
28	64	66	67	69	70	72	74	76	78	78	80	83	85	88	91	94	97	100	100
29	66	68	70	71	73	76	77	79	81	81	83	86	88	91	94	97	100	100	100
30	69	70	72	74	75	77	79	82	84	84	86	89	91	94	97	100	100	100	100
31	71	73	74	76	78	80	82	84	87	87	89	92	94	97	100	100	100	100	100
32	73	75	77	79	80	83	85	87	89	89	92	95	97	100	100	100	100		
33	75	77	79	81	83	85	87	90	92	92	95	98	100	100	100	100			
34	78	80	81	83	85	88	90	92	95	95	98	100	100	100	100				
35	80	82	84	86	88	90	93	95	98	98	100	100	100	100					
36	82	84	86	88	90	93	95	98	100	100	100	100	100						
37	85	87	89	91	93	95	98	100	100	100	100	100							
38	87	89	91	93	95	98	100	100	100	100	100								
39	89	91	93	96	98	100	100	100	100	100	100								
40	91	94	96	98	100	100	100	100	100	100									
41	94	96	98	100	100	100	100	100	100										
42	96	98	100	100	100	100	100												
43	98	100	100	100	100	100													
44	100	100	100	100	100	100													

3   married women under the age of 82 (but not less than 60 on 2 November 1970) whose husbands qualify for a category C pension;

4   a widow under the age of 82 whose husband was alive and 65 or over on 5 July 1948, providing that the woman was aged 40 or over when the . husband died;

5   a woman under the age of 82 whose marriage to a man who was alive and 65 or over on 5 July 1948 ended in divorce or annulment after the woman was 60.

Category D pensions are payable to people over the age of 80 who are not in receipt of a National Insurance pension or who are in receipt of a NI pension which is less than the higher rate of category C pension (£34.50 at 1 March 1995). The current level of payment of a category D pension is £34.50 (1 March 1995). In order to be eligible for a category D pension, the claimant must satisfy the following criteria:

1   be 80 years of age or over
2   at the time of claiming, normally live in England, Scotland or Wales, and
3   have lived in the United Kingdom for at least 10 years in any continuous period of 20 years which included the day before their 80th birthday or any day after that.

All of the above components of the basic retirement pension are increased each April in line with the rise in the Retail Price Index (RPI) of the preceding September.

State Earnings Related Pension Scheme

Because the level of the basic retirement pension is rather low, as mentioned above, employees can make additional contributions into the State Earnings Related Pension Scheme (SERPS) in order to provide additional pension benefits on retirement. The level of additional pension benefits available via SERPS is dependent on the individual's NI contributions throughout a large part of their employment lifetime. Currently, the calculation of SERPS pension entitlement is based on the individual's earnings since 6 April 1978, although after 1998, the calculation will be based on an average of their lifetime earnings.

The amount of SERPS pension to which an individual is entitled is calculated using the following steps:

1 The amount of earnings on which Class 1 National Insurance contributions have been paid in each tax year since April 1978 is calculated.

2 The figure for each tax year is then adjusted in line with the rise in national average earnings using figures approved by Parliament each year. The latest figures showing the percentage increase for annual earnings since 1978 are given in the list below. The figures used for these calculations should be those in force at the end of the tax year before the one on which the individual's 65th (men) or 60th (women) birthday falls.

3 The level of earnings required for the tax year in which the claimant is 64 (men) or 59 (women) to count as a qualifying year for a category A basic retirement pension is calculated: 52 times the weekly lower earnings limit for NI contributions (currently 52 × £57 = £2,964 (1 March 1995)).

Tax year	Percentage adjustment
1978–79	+291.0
1979–80	+244.8
1980–81	+188.2
1981–82	+141.6
1982–83	+119.3
1983–84	+103.3
1984–85	+88.2
1985–86	+76.6
1986–87	+62.2
1987–88	+51.1
1988–89	+38.9
1989–90	+25.8
1990–91	+17.3
1991–92	+6.5

4 This figure (£2,694) is then deducted from the adjusted earnings level for each tax year leaving a net amount for each year which counts for additional pension benefits.

5 Finally, the annual rate of additional pension is calculated by dividing the sum total of the net amounts for each tax year by one-eightieth (to calculate a weekly amount, the annual rate of pension is divided by 52).

As a result of the 1986 Social Security Act, now incorporated into the 1992 Social Security Contributions and Benefits Act, from the year 2010, the annual rate of additional pension will be calculated by dividing the sum total of the net amounts for each tax year by one-hundredth instead of one-eightieth. The reduction from one-eightieth to one-hundredth will be phased in over ten years commencing in the year 2000. When calculating the entitlement to a SERPS pension, consideration must also be given to the regulations governing widow's pension, widowed mother's allowance, double entitlements, deferred retirement, and other benefits or payments which may affect any pension benefits provided via SERPS.

It should be noted that as a result of subsequent legislation, the additional pension entitlement provided via SERPS can be replaced by an approved occupational pension scheme or personal pension plan. This procedure is known as 'contracting-out'. Alternatively, an employer can provide an occupational pension scheme in addition to any benefits available via SERPS. Similarly, the individual employee may decide to make contributions to a personal pension plan and continue to make contributions to SERPS. Either way, this procedure is known as 'contracting-in'.

Contracting-out

An occupational pension scheme can contract-out of SERPS if it can be established that it satisfies a minimum benefit test or a minimum contributions test. Contracting-out by either of these methods is governed by legislation and employers wishing to do so must obtain a contracting-out certificate from the Occupational Pensions Board (OPB). Should all the necessary requirements be satisfied, the OPB will issue a certificate although it will continue to supervise the scheme and may withdraw the contracting-out certificate if at any stage it fails to conform to the necessary requirements. As mentioned above, it is also possible for individuals to contract-out of SERPS by making alternative arrangements for additional pension benefits via an approved personal pension plan.

Where an occupational pension scheme is contracted-out of SERPS, both the employee and the employer receive a National Insurance rebate by paying reduced levels of National Insurance contributions. Currently, the NI contribution rate for employees under a contracted-out occupational pension scheme is reduced by 1.8 per cent whilst the contribution rate for the employer is reduced by 3.0 per cent (1 March 1995). For individual employees who contract-out of SERPS by making alternative arrangements via a personal pension plan, the arrangements regarding reduced NI contributions are slightly more complicated and bureaucratic. Whilst the individual will pay reduced NI contributions as described above, the employer continues to pay the full amount of NI contributions as if the employee was not contracted-out. On receiving the NI contributions from the employer, the Department of Social Security (DSS) passes on an appropriate proportion of the contributions (equivalent to the employer's rebate outlined above) to the employee's personal pension plan.

One major condition that contracted-out pension provision must fulfil is that the occupational pension scheme, or personal pension plan must pay at least the Guaranteed Minimum Pension (GMP). The GMP is equivalent to the amount the individual would have been entitled to if they had not contracted-out of SERPS but had continued to pay contributions to SERPS. Should an individual leave a contracted-out pension scheme within the first two years of membership, they are entitled to a refund of their contributions, less tax. If they have more than two years membership, however, and decide to leave, they are not entitled to a refund but may preserve or transfer their pension rights.

Occupational Pension Schemes

On retirement, occupational pension schemes normally provide two main benefits, an annual pension and a lump sum payment. The calculation of the amount of annual pension will largely depend on whether the occupational pension scheme is a salary related scheme or a money purchase scheme. With a salary related pension scheme, the pension entitlement is normally determined by an arithmetical formula which incorporates the salary or earnings of the individual. With the majority of salary related schemes, the arithmetical formula also incorporates the length of service of the individual or length of membership of the pension scheme. For example, on retirement, the employee may be entitled to one-sixtieth of the final year's salary for each year of service. Should the individual have a final year's salary of £18,000 with 40 years service, the pension entitlement will therefore be $1/60 \times £18,000 \times 40 = £12,000$. With a money purchase scheme, the contributions of all the members of the scheme are invested. Since the level of pension benefits are dependent on the return on the investments, the actual benefits likely to be payable are unknown.

An important aspect of occupational pension schemes are the limits on benefits imposed by the Inland Revenue. The main limits are set out below:

Benefit	Limit
Members pension	two-thirds of final year's salary
Widow's pension	two-thirds of member's pension entitlement
Dependant's pension	two-thirds of member's pension entitlement
NB: if both widow's and dependant's pensions are provided, the maximum amount payable is equivalent to the member's pension entitlement.	
Lump sum	one and a half times final salary
Life insurance lump sum	four times final annual salary plus a refund of contributions plus in terest

Additional voluntary contributions (AVCs)

From 6 April 1988, all occupational pension schemes are required to make provision for the payment of additional voluntary contributions (AVCs) by pension scheme members. The objective of AVCs is to allow individuals to pay more into the pension scheme in order to be eligible for the maximum level of pension benefits outlined above. Whilst AVCs attract the same tax relief as normal pension payments, it should be noted that the maximum amount which an individual can contribute to an occupational pension scheme is 15 per cent of earnings, including normal and voluntary contributions. This maximum level is set by the Inland Revenue. From 6 April 1989, the maximum limit of 15 per cent of earnings is also subject to an earnings cap which is currently set at £76,800 (1 March 1995). In addition, the Inland Revenue do not allow the benefits provided by AVCs when added to other pension benefits to exceed the maximum level of pension benefits set out above.

Free standing additional voluntary contributions (FSAVCs)

Instead of paying additional voluntary contributions (AVCs) to the occupational pension scheme of the employer, individuals can pay free standing additional voluntary contributions into a pension scheme administered by a third party unconnected with the employer. FSAVCs carry the same tax relief as normal pension payments and AVCs, although such tax relief is not obtained via the Pay as You Earn (PAYE) taxation system as would happen with normal pension payments and AVCs. As with occupational pension schemes and AVCs, the benefits available as a result of FSAVCs are subject to the maximum limits set out above.

Personal Pension Plans

As a result of the 1986 Social Security Act which introduced a provision allowing individuals to contract-out of SERPS by making alternative arrangements via a personal pension plan, there has been a substantial increase in the marketing of personal pension packages from a wide range of organizations in the finance sector. Whilst employees now have this option, it should be noted that an employee who does contract-out of SERPS via a personal pension plan cannot in addition be a member of an occupational pension scheme *unless* the occupational pension scheme is contracted-in and the personal pension plan is restricted to receiving the NI 'minimum contributions' from the Department of Social Security and is not therefore subject to contributions from the employee. It should also be remembered that the employee also has the option of contracting-in by continuing to pay contributions to SERPS and in addition taking out a personal pension plan.

As mentioned above, when an employee contracts-out of SERPS via a personal pension plan, the employer should treat them as a contracted-in employee for National Insurance contributions purposes. On receiving the NI contribution from the employer, the Department of Social Security will pass on the appropriate NI 'minimum contribution' to each individual's personal pension plan. The minimum contribution comprises two components:

1 the contracted-out rebate, and
2 tax relief at the basic rate on the employee's share of the contracted-out rebate.

Should an employee or employer wish to contribute more than the minimum contribution, they must make appropriate arrangements to do so, the Department of Social Security will only pass on the minimum contribution.

In addition to setting a maximum contribution level for occupational pension schemes, the Inland Revenue also places certain limits on the amount an employee may contribute to a personal pension plan. Such contribution levels are based on the salary of the individual and are set on an increasing scale related to the age of the employee. The current maximum contribution levels are as follows:

Age range	Maximum contribution level as a percentage of relevant earnings in tax year
35 or under	17.5
36–45	20
46–50	25
51–55	30
56–60	35
61 and over	40

Equal Rights

Whilst the topic of equal pay, which includes the payment of pensions to employees, is discussed fully in chapter 8, it should be emphasized that under the terms of the 1993 Pension Schemes Act, men and women must have equal access to occupational pension schemes, and any other pension benefits provided by the employer. This right is embedded in the 1970 Equal Pay Act and Article 119 of the Treaty of Rome. When providing an occupational pension scheme for employees, the rules of such pension provision, and any terms and conditions of employment relating to pensions, must be equally applied to both men and women. For example, the age requirement or length of service requirement for membership of an occupational pension scheme must be the same for both male and female employees. Similarly, the pensionable age for men and women must be the same. The actual pensionable age can be set by the employer, be it 58, 60, 65 or any other age, but whatever age is decided, it must be the same for both men and women. It is interesting to note that autonomy regarding legislative control over pension schemes was relinquished by the British Government when it became a signatory of the Treaty of Rome. As a result, any British legislation governing the management of pension schemes must conform to the appropriate laws detailed in the Treaty of Rome. In particular, whilst the Pension Schemes Act 1993 does provide men and women with equal access to occupational pensions schemes, there is no similar UK provision regarding the payment of pension benefits. The European Court of Justice, however, has ruled (as a result of the case of *Barber* v. *Guardian Royal Exchange Assurance Group* (1990)) that, since Article 119 of the Treaty of Rome states that men and women should receive equal pay for equal work, any pension benefits should count as part of pay. As a result, any pension benefits relating to service after 17 May 1990 (the date of the *Barber* judgement) must apply equally to men and women. It should be noted, however, that all equal pay pension cases to date have related to final pay schemes and the position regarding money purchase schemes remains uncertain. It is expected that in the near future new UK legislation will be produced to consolidate the issues highlighted by the *Barber* and other European Court of Justice judgements.

Conclusion

From this brief discussion regarding the provision of pension benefits to employees, it is clear that the topic of pension provision and corresponding legislation is very complex and subject to regular change. As a result, it is probably sensible that any employer considering the introduction of new pension provision, or revision of existing pension provision, should take appropriate advice from experts specializing in the subject area. It is important, however, that employers and managers have at least a basic knowledge of the different types of pension provision in existence, how each is funded, and the potential benefits to employees.

In summary, the majority of employees are eligible on retirement to receive a basic retirement pension provided by the state via National Insurance (NI) contributions from the employer and employee. Since the level of such benefits is rather low, additional benefits are now provided by the State Earnings Related Pension Scheme (SERPS) funded via additional NI contributions from the employer and employee. In addition to SERPS, or as an alternative, the employer and employee can make provision for additional pension benefits via an occupational pension scheme and/or a personal pension plan. Should such provision be made in addition to SERPS, this procedure is known as 'contracting-in'. Should the provision of an occupational pension scheme and/or personal pension plan be made as an alternative to SERPS, this procedure is known as 'contracting-out'. Should the employer and employee decide to contract-

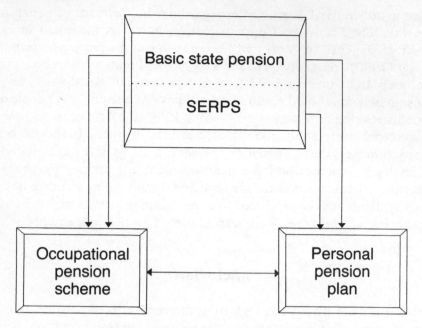

Figure 10.1 *Pension provision – options*

out by either method, both the employer and employee receive a contracting-out rebate by paying reduced levels of NI contributions. Employers and employees therefore have a variety of options regarding the method and level of additional pension provision. The options available to employers and employees can be illustrated as in figure 10.1.

11

Systems of Performance Related Remuneration

Introduction

In addition to selecting the correct salary structure and benefits package for employees, organizations may decide that the introduction of a system of performance related remuneration (PRR) into the total remuneration package will assist with the achievement of organizational objectives. In the same way that the salary structure and benefits package should be tailored to meet the needs and objectives of the organization and employees, the selection of a system of PRR should be carefully considered. The choice, implementation and administration of a system of PRR are all important factors which will influence how effective the use of PRR will be. The basic purpose of any system of performance related remuneration is to establish a correlation between the work performance of the individual employee, or group of employees, and their subsequent level of remuneration. By doing so, the intention is that the employee will be motivated to behave in such a manner that high levels of performance will be given in return for an enhanced level of remuneration. The main types of performance related remuneration include:

• Payment by results (PBR);
• Bonus schemes;
• Profit sharing;
• Profit related pay;
• Sales incentives;
• Employee share ownership plans (ESOP);
• Merit pay.

Payment by Results

Payment by results systems are based on the belief that a relationship can be established between effort and reward. It assumes that the attraction of a reward (money) will motivate individuals to behave in a certain manner (work productively). The underlying assumption therefore is that more effort will result in more money. Systems of payment by results are perhaps best suited for production orientated jobs where there is a quantifiable output. In such a situation, a direct correlation will be developed between the output of the employee and their subsequent remuneration – the more they produce, the more they get paid. There are various different systems of PBR which can be utilized by organizations.

(1)   Straight piecework. With this system, employees are paid a flat rate (piece rate) for each item/operation completed. The piece rates may be determined by method study and work measurement to determine standard times and corresponding rates for jobs. A straight piecework system can be illustrated as in figure 11.1.

(2)   Differential piecework. Differential piecework is a variation of straight piecework and involves the adjustment of the piece rate as production rate increases. Once production reaches a predetermined level, the cash rate for every additional piece produced/task completed starts to decline. With differential piecework, therefore, whilst

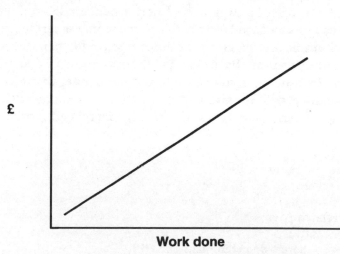

Figure 11.1   *Straight piecework*

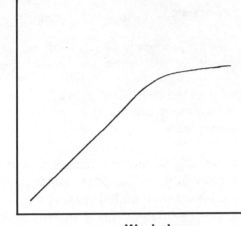

Work done

Figure 11.2 *Differential piecework*

the employee's earnings continue to increase as production in-creases, the rate at which earnings increase declines after a specified production level. A differential piecework system might be illus-trated as in figure 11.2.

(3) Measured daywork. The objective behind measured daywork is to guarantee, for the organization, a specified level of production from each employee each day by providing a reward (cash) to those employees who achieve a prearranged and accepted daily production level. Measured daywork therefore relies on work measurement to ascertain the appropriate daily production level for each individual.

(4) Group incentive schemes. The base for group incentive schemes is the work performance of a work group or organizational area. If the production output of the work group or area reaches a predetermined and agreed level, then the employees within that work group or area receive a cash payment which can either be paid equally or proportionately to the individuals.

(5) Plant-wide schemes. These schemes are an extension of the group incentive schemes which, instead of applying to a specific work group or organizational area, apply to a whole plant or even the entire organization. Variations of the plant-wide schemes are value added schemes and gainsharing. In a plant-wide scheme, all em-ployees in a plant or organization share in a pool bonus which is

linked to the level of output or added value of the organization which Armstrong (1988) defines as:

(a) *income* from sales of the product or service (output); LESS
(b) *expenditure* on materials and other purchased services (input); LEAVES
(c) *added value* which is either distributed as wages, salaries, pensions, interest on loans, taxes and dividends, or retained in reserves for investment and depreciation.

One of the best known added value schemes was developed by Rucker and is used mainly in America. This system establishes, over a period of time, the proportion of added value which is represented by payroll costs (typically 40–50 per cent). Once the added value has been calculated, the amount to be distributed can be calculated as follows:

Added value	= £800,000
Typical payroll costs (40% of added value)	= £320,000
Actual payroll	= £280,000
Amount distributed	= £ 40,000

Whichever system of payment by results is utilized by an organization, it is essential that all the employees affected have a clear understanding of how the system operates and how their performance influences their subsequent remuneration. To have a highly effective system of payment by results, the managers of the organization must make some important decisions regarding how the system should operate. Such decisions include:

• Should the remuneration of employees be based entirely on payment by results, or should they be paid a basic wage with a payment by results element in addition?
• How should the productivity levels and corresponding payment levels be established?
• Should payment by results remuneration levels have a ceiling, or cut-off point, or should there be no limits placed upon potential remuneration levels?

The formulation and implementation of a system of payment by results therefore requires careful consideration and should be continually monitored, evaluated and amended if necessary.

Bonus Schemes

Bonus schemes are systems of PRR which give individuals or groups of employees a cash bonus in return for the achievement of predetermined performance targets. The principal aim of a bonus scheme is to provide an incentive for high levels of effort and performance, and since bonus payments can be clearly related to the quantitative and qualitative aspects of group or individual performance, they are often an effective remunerative approach to the motivation of employees. In their factsheet on performance related pay in 1990, the IPM concluded that bonus schemes are most common for senior executives, sales staff and shop floor employees involved in direct production. It is suggested that bonus schemes are common for these types of jobs because there are measurable outputs which can be used to calculate bonus payments.

Armstrong and Murlis (1991) describe individual bonuses as payments made in addition to base salary which are related to the achievement of specified targets, the completion of a project or a stage of a project to a specified standard, the receipt of an appropriate performance rating, or any combination of these. Where the bonus payment is related to a specific number of units/tasks, it is essentially a payment by results system. The advantages and disadvantages of individual bonus schemes can be summarized as follows:

Advantages:

- rewards employees for effort and high levels of performance;
- schemes can be simple enough to allow easy administration;
- usually simple enough for employees to understand;
- lump sum cash payments appeal to some people;
- time gap between performance and payment is usually minimal;
- bonuses can be linked to achievements and targets hence creating a reward and an incentive.

Disadvantages:

- sometimes difficult to create a consistent relationship between the performance and the reward;
- may engender an individualistic approach rather than a team or group effort;

- difficult to apply to employees who do not have an easily quantifiable output.

Turning to group bonus schemes, they essentially provide cash bonuses for groups of employees based on the achievement of group performance targets. These schemes tend to encourage teamwork and are useful for jobs or tasks which rely on joint effort. It is also suggested by Armstrong and Murlis (1991) that group bonuses cause less ill feeling and divisions than individual bonus schemes. On the negative side, group bonus schemes can only be used where it is possible to identify employees who are working together as a group on identifiable tasks. In addition, group bonus schemes can often cause ill-directed peer group pressure and cause the diffusion of individual motivation.

Profit Sharing

Profit sharing is a system of PRR where the employer gives to employees, in addition to their normal remuneration, a proportion of the pre-tax profits of the organization. The profits can be distributed in several ways, and the various methods of distribution are examined below. The proportion of profits set aside and the actual method of distribution are at the discretion of management but may be determined by an established and published formula. A system of profit sharing must apply to all employees within an organization although there are a few classes of employee who are ineligible to participate in an approved scheme. Within most profit sharing systems, employees only become eligible to participate once they have satisfied a qualifying length of service. Whilst there are no rules regarding the length of the qualifying period, it would normally be long enough to exclude those employees with short lengths of service where staff turnover is occasionally very high. A typical qualifying period may be one or two years but should not exceed five years. Many reasons are given for the introduction of profit sharing, such as:

- to improve employee attitudes towards the organization;
- to provide a means of encouraging employees to become more involved with, and identify more closely with, company objectives;

- to encourage positive relationships between management and employees;
- to enable employees to share in the financial prosperity of the organization;
- to act as a self-financing method of increasing levels of employee remuneration;
- to provide a remuneration package which is comparable to that of competitors.

Amount distributed

There are several methods by which the organization can calculate the amount of profit to be distributed as profit shares. Firstly, the company can decide to allocate a predetermined percentage of pre-tax profits for profit sharing. Such an allocation would normally be dependent on the achievement of a minimum monetary profit. This method does have the advantage that the employees are made aware of the basis of distribution and the corresponding commitment of management. The second approach utilizes a system whereby the amount of profit to be distributed is calculated using a percentage of profit where profitability is measured by return on capital, return on investment, etc. Once again, this system may also involve a defined minimum profit level. The third approach deviates from the use of a predetermined or published formula but is instead based on the discretion of management. Within such a system, the amount of profit to be distributed amongst employees is decided by management with due consideration for factors such as profit levels, the expectations of employees, a subjective judgement of what would be a reasonable amount, and perhaps the industrial relations climate within the organization. The main disadvantage of this system is the secretive nature of the decision on the amount of allocation – this would appear to contradict the basic ethos behind the concept of profit sharing.

Methods of distributing profit shares

There are four main methods of distributing profits through a profit sharing scheme, these are:

1   as cash
2   as shares
3   as shares via an Approved Deferred Share Trust (ADST)
4   as a mixture of cash, shares and ADST

(1)   Cash. Under this system, a proportion of profit is set aside and distributed to employees as a cash bonus. The payment made to each employee is subject to PAYE income tax and National Insurance deductions.

(2)   Shares. Instead of employees receiving a cash bonus, the total amount put aside from profits is used to buy shares in the company and these shares are then distributed to employees. Again, each employee is liable for PAYE income tax and National Insurance on the value of the shares.

(3)   Approved Deferred Share Trusts (ADST). Approved Deferred Share Trusts were set up by the 1978 Finance Act and subsequent amendments. Before a company can operate an ADST, it must gain the approval of the Inland Revenue. Under an ADST, the company allocates a proportion of profit to a trust fund which acquires shares on behalf of the employees. It should be noted that the total market value of ADST shares allocated to any employee in any tax year is limited to £13,000 or 10 per cent of income, whichever is greater, subject to a ceiling of £8,000 – anything over this limit must be paid as cash or shares to individual employees. The employee cannot normally sell the shares during the first two years they are held by the trustees, unless the employee ceases employment with the company because of injury, disability, redundancy or reaching an age specified by the company which must be between 60 and 75. In such circumstances, should this happen before the fifth anniversary of the issue of the shares, income tax will be charged at the rate of 50 per cent. Tax on the value of the shares is only payable when they are sold, the employee paying tax on either the 'locked-in' price or the final selling price, whichever is the lower. The rate of taxation reduces the longer the shares are held, as follows:

Year in which shares are sold	Percentage of selling price subject to tax
3rd and 4th years	100
5th year	75
6th year and on	0

(4)   Mixed schemes. In a mixed scheme, the proportion of profit allocated to an employee may be taken as cash, as shares, as cash and ADST, or even part cash and part shares.

Calculating the allocation to individuals

Once the company has decided the amount which it is willing to distribute within the organization and the method of distribution, there are four main methods by which the company can decide how much of the allocation each individual employee will receive:

1 distribute the profit allocation on a pro-rata basis according to remuneration – this can be simply arranged by awarding each employee a percentage of basic pay;
2 distribute the profit allocation according to length of service, therefore providing high rewards to those employees with long periods of service;
3 distribute the profit allocation according to individual performance level;
4 distribute the profit element in equal amounts to all eligible employees – whilst being equitable, this method is rare.

Occasionally, some companies opt for a system of allocation to individuals which is based partly on the remuneration of the individual and partly on their length of service. Such a system would appear to recognize and reward loyalty to the organization. In addition, this system of allocation provides encouragement to those employees who have served the organization for many years but have not progressed to senior positions.

Whilst a system of profit sharing may result in higher levels of employee commitment, and therefore performance, to the organization through financial participation, the main disadvantage is that it is very difficult to establish a direct correlation between the work performance of individuals or groups, the financial performance of the organization, and the subsequent remunerative reward. An organization which utilizes a system of profit sharing based on organizational profit levels is likely to equally reward employees of the same grade even though their work performance differs significantly. A system of profit sharing is likely to more effective when profit sharing is associated with the financial performance of a department or other work group. In such a situation, the employees are fully aware that the performance of their department or group has a direct influence on profit, which has a corresponding effect on the amount of profit shared amongst the members of that department or work group. This situation would also encourage *all* members of the work group to work as a collective team since each employee is likely to have a direct influence on not only their own remunerative rewards, but also the rewards of the other team members.

Profit Related Pay

The Finance (No. 2) Act 1987 introduced income tax relief for employees who receive part of their pay in the form of profit related pay (PRP). As a method of performance related remuneration, PRP is unique in that it offers tax relief on cash payments which would be fully taxed under any other cash PRR system. Profit related pay can generally be defined as being part of an employee's pay formally linked to the profits of the organization or part of the organization in which they work. When the profits of the organization increase, the PRP part of pay also increases. When the profits fall, so does the PRP part of pay. Once again, if an employer wishes to operate a system of PRP, they must be registered with the Inland Revenue.

One half of any PRP payments which an employee gets under a registered PRP scheme can be free of tax up to the point where PRP is 20 per cent of pay or £4,000 per year, whichever is the lower. Thus up to 10 per cent of an employee's total pay or £2,000, whichever is the lower, could be exempt from tax in any one year. The tax relief on PRP payments is given by employers through the PAYE system. It should be noted that although income from PRP attracts tax benefits, it is subject to National Insurance contributions in the same way as other earnings.

The tax concessions relating to PRP are available to all private sector employees, and whilst employers are free to design their own schemes, they must:

1   Identify the employment unit – the organization or part of the organization which the scheme covers. The employer may have different schemes for different parts of the organization but in such circumstances they must make clear the rules of each scheme and the parts of the organization covered.
2   Define the employees within the employment unit to whom the scheme relates. This must represent at least 80 per cent of those employees within the employment unit, not counting excluded groups. Employees or directors with a 25 per cent or more

interest in the organization throughout the whole of the profit period should be excluded and the regulations permit the exclusion of part time workers (less than 20 hours per week) and those employees with less than a specified minimum period of service (must not be more than three years).

3 Identify the profit period – the 12 month accounting period for the calculation of PRP.
4 Determine how the profits of the employment unit are to be calculated. Profits must be those on the ordinary activities of the unit after taxation (as defined in the Companies Act 1985).
5 State the length of the scheme (at least 12 months).
6 Specify the method by which the 'distributable pool', that is, the total amount of PRP to be paid in respect of a profit period, is to be determined.

There are two ways in which the distributable pool can be calculated: *Method A*, where the pool is equal to a fixed percentage of the profits of the unit in the profit period, or *Method B*, where the pool is a sum which varies in line with year-on-year changes in profit. In either case, the scheme may contain certain rules which modify the effect of large changes in profits, in order to avoid large fluctuation in the amount of PRP or to safeguard a minimum level of profit. Full details on the registration and operation of profit related pay schemes are available from: The Profit Related Pay Office, Inland Revenue, St Mungo's Road, Cumbernauld, Glasgow.

The main disadvantage of profit related pay is similar to the problem of profit sharing – it is extremely difficult to identify a correlation between the performance of an individual, the profits of the organization, and the potential profit related element of pay. To be fully effective, the profit related pay system should be scaled down in such a manner that the individual can perceive a link between their individual or group performance and the potential increases in remuneration.

Sales Incentives

In contrast to the systems of PRR mentioned above, which can apply to most categories of staff, sales incentives are unique in the sense that they apply to only one category of staff – sales staff. The basis for all sales incentive schemes is a relationship between the level of sales value (performance) and the remuneration, or part of the remuneration, of the employee – as sales levels increase, so should the level of remuneration. The assumption is that sales staff will be motivated to achieve their sales targets by the attraction of increased remuneration. In order to be successful, sales incentive schemes should satisfy a few conditions:

1 the scheme should provide an adequate basic salary to provide security;
2 the level of total compensation should be competitive in the marketplace;
3 the scheme should be easily understood;
4 the effect of the scheme should support organizational objectives;
5 the scheme should be flexible enough to cope with changes in the marketplace, economy, etc.;
6 it should not be possible for management or employees to manipulate the scheme;
7 the sales targets should be challenging but achievable and should support consistent levels of performance;
8 sales targets/territories/areas/regions should be equalized;
9 feedback on performance (rewards) should be given at regular intervals.

Sales incentive schemes take many forms but two main groups can be identified: cash based schemes and non-cash based schemes. The principal types of cash based schemes are commission only, salary plus bonus, salary plus commission, and salary plus commission and bonus:

• *Commission only* In this type of incentive scheme, the entire salary is dependent on earnings related to sales performance – there is no basic salary to fall back on. These schemes put considerable pressure upon the sales staff but generally provide high rewards.
• *Salary plus bonus* Such schemes are based on a basic salary which can be enhanced with a cash bonus providing certain sales targets are met. The sales targets could be linked to the performance of either an individual or group or team.
• *Salary plus commission* These schemes, like the salary plus bonus schemes, are based on a basic salary which can be enhanced, in this case by a commission payment which is normally based on a percentage of the sales value.
• *Salary plus bonus and commission* This type of scheme is really a mixture of those schemes mentioned above – the sales person receives a basic salary which can be enhanced by a performance related bonus *and* a commission payment.

In sales jobs which are not suitable for incentive schemes, either because of the type of product being sold, or for other reasons, the sales people are normally paid high basic salaries which are competitive with sales jobs involving some form of incentive payment. Occasionally, non-cash based incentives are given to sales staff in addition to, or instead of, cash based incentives. Such non-cash based incentives can take many forms, from specially produced badges to holidays in the Bahamas. One example of a non-cash sales incentive is operated by a small company selling insurance packages. The company has six sales representatives and six company cars, and the cars are allocated on a monthly cycle depending on the sales performance of the sales representatives. Each representative is given a monthly sales target, their performance being assessed by monitoring actual sales against the predetermined targets. The top sales representative gets allocated the high specification executive car, the next four representatives get allocated a typical sales fleet vehicle, whilst the representative at the bottom of the league gets allocated a car from the lower end of the car market. Whilst all representatives get a company car, the incentive is at least to avoid the bottom of the league, although there may be an added incentive of being allocated the high specification executive car. Whatever non-cash based sales incentives are used, however, it is essential that their use is very carefully considered to achieve the best motivational effect.

Employee Share Ownership Plans (ESOP)

An employee share ownership plan is a method by which a private sector organization can distribute shares in the organization to employees either at full share value or at a discounted rate. An ESOP normally starts with a loan from a financial institution, guaranteed by the organization, to an Employee Benefit Trust. The loan is then used by the trust, sometimes with a contribution from the organization, to buy existing shares from the organization or its shareholders. If employees wish to buy shares at full market value, they may do so from this trust. In order to enable free or subsidized shares to be distributed, a second trust is formed, the Profit Sharing Trust, operating with money from the organization's pre-tax profits. The money in this trust is used to buy packages of shares from the Employee Benefit Trust for allocation to employees.

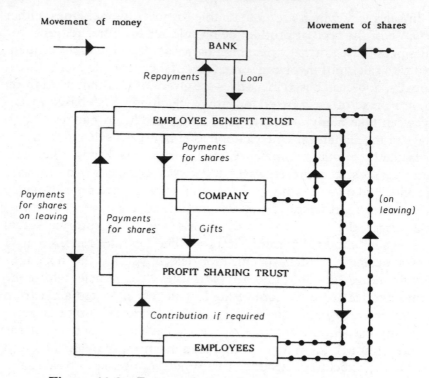

Figure 11.3   *Framework of employee share ownership plans*

The Employee Benefit Trust pays off its bank loan from the dividends of the shares it holds and from the money received from the Profit Sharing Trust, which is essentially an Approved Deferred Share Trust as described above. The Profit Sharing Trust holds the shares allocated to employees until they can be distributed free of tax. The framework of ESOPs is illustrated in figure 11.3 which is taken from Income Data Services Study No. 438, *Employee Share Ownership Plans.*

At this point, it is important to mention two other types of share option schemes: executive share option schemes and savings related share option schemes (SRSOS).

Executive share option schemes

Consequential to the 1984 Finance Act, the ruling Conservative Government introduced an approved share option scheme which allows employers to choose who participates. These provisions have subsequently been incorporated as Schedule 9 to the Income and Corporation Taxes Act (ICTA) 1988. Such schemes are now commonly referred to as executive share option schemes and have generally been introduced by companies as an incentive for senior and top management. Whereas other systems of PRR (for example, profit related pay and profit sharing) must be open to participation by the majority of employees, participation in an executive share option scheme can be restricted to those employees selected by the board of directors. The schemes must again be approved by the Inland Revenue. Executive share option schemes give the 'executives' the option of acquiring company shares on a stated future date at a share price fixed at the time of being granted the option. To gain the tax benefits associated with executive share option schemes, the shares must be held for at least three years and must be exercised within ten years. Providing these conditions are met, any gains made from the disposal of the shares will be subject only to capital gains tax and not income tax. Within executive share option schemes, a high level of financial participation is possible – the market value of the option can be up to four times the participant's annual taxable emoluments or £100,000, whichever is the greater. In an approved scheme, options cannot be granted at a discount on the market value of the shares unless the employer also operates an approved all-employee profit sharing scheme or savings related share option scheme. In such circumstances, a discount of up to 15 per cent on the market value of the shares can be granted.

Savings related share option scheme (SRSOS)

A savings related share option scheme is designed to give employees the option of buying ordinary shares in their company at a future date (between five and seven years) at a price fixed at the date the option is granted. The fixed price may incorporate a discount of up to 20 per cent of the market value of the shares at that time but such a discount is at the discretion of the company. At the end of the predetermined period, the employee can buy the shares at the agreed price using savings deducted from their salary under an Inland Revenue 'save as you earn' (SAYE) contract which the employee opens with either a building society, bank or the Department for National Savings. The maximum amount which an employee can contribute to their SAYE contract is £250 per month for five years. In addition, the amount payable upon exercise of the option may not exceed the amount available from the SAYE contract. If the employee elects for a five year contract, at the end of that period they will not only receive their savings with which they can buy shares but will also receive a single bonus equivalent to 12 months' savings. If, however, the employee elects for a seven year contract, at the end of the period they will receive their savings *and* a double bonus equivalent to 24 months' savings.

Merit Pay

Merit payment systems were defined by the IPM/IDS (1985) as methods of performance related remuneration which provide for periodic increases in pay which are incorporated into basic salary or wages and which result from assessments of individual performance and personal value to the organization. Such increases may determine the rate of progression through pay scales or ranges. They are expressed either as percentages of basic pay, as predetermined cash increments or as unconsolidated one-off lump sums. This definition *includes* all those incremental systems where increases are discretionary and not automatic and are based on individual assessment; it *excludes* productivity or other cash bonuses, incentive payments, piecework payments, fixed service increments, sales commissions and share option schemes.

The central feature of any merit payment system is the reward of remuneration in return for the achievement of a predetermined level of performance, or merit level. Crucial to the success of any merit payment system therefore is an effective method of assessing the performance of individuals. This assessment can then be used to determine whether or not the employee has satisfied the necessary 'merit criteria' and is eligible for a remunerative reward. Whilst performance appraisal is a common method of assessing the performance of employees, only 40 per cent of those organizations participating in the IPM/IDS 1985 survey, *The Merit Factor*, reported the use of performance appraisal when allocating merit pay. There are several methods by which merit pay can be allocated and some of these are examined below:

(1)   Fixed incremental scales. In this type of merit pay system, employees who satisfy the appropriate merit criteria are allowed to

progress up a fixed incremental scale at an accelerated rate, perhaps receiving a merit related incremental rise in addition to their service related incremental rise. In some cases, those employees who have poor levels of performance may have their service related increments withheld.

(2) Percentage increases. In this type of system, employees are given a percentage increase on their salary depending on their level of performance. A simple percentage rise system may look as follows:

Performance level	Percentage increase
unsatisfactory	0
satisfactory	2
above average	4
excellent	6

Occasionally, organizations base their percentage increases on a 'merit matrix'. Such a matrix gives different percentage increases to employees depending on both their performance level and their position in the salary band. An example of a merit matrix is given in table 13.6, p. 232.

(3) Parallel scales. This system of merit pay allows for individuals in the same job to progress up the salary range at different rates of progression depending on their performance assessment. To enable these different rates of progression, the system has a few salary scales for each particular job to which the individual is assigned depending on their performance level. Over a period of time, therefore, different employees will progress up the salary range, and have different salary limits, according to their performance rating. An example of a parallel scales system of merit pay might be illustrated as in figure 11.4 which is based on four performance ratings, A–D.

(4) Variable progression. This system of merit pay normally has few or no guidelines and permits variable rates of progression to individuals within a given salary range. Normally, the only constraint on the rates of progression are the budget limits for the department/division/company.

(5) Merit bars/control points. In a salary system which incorporates a merit bar/control point, an individual can progress up their

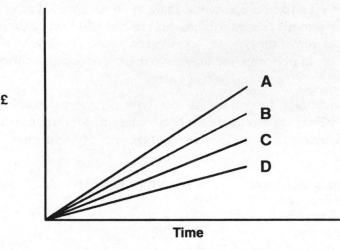

Figure 11.4   *Parallel scalles*

salary range by fixed or variable increments up to a defined limit. Progression beyond this limit (merit bar/control point) is subject purely to performance.

(6)   Merit bonuses. This system provides individuals with a cash bonus in addition to their salary, provided they meet a predefined performance or merit level.

Overall, the advantages and disadvantages of merit pay can be summarized as follows:

Advantages:

- can provide a direct correlation between individual performance and salary level;
- allows individuals an element of control over their salary level;
- designed, implemented and managed correctly, merit pay can motivate individuals to behave in a manner which supports the business objectives of the organization.

Disadvantages:

- relies heavily upon an assessment of individual performance which is liable to be subjective and inconsistent – the effect of personalities and relationships, and the fact that different managers are likely to give the same employee different performance ratings;

- any merit payment is a permanent increase in salary, even though performance levels may vary enormously on a year by year basis – one year of exceptional performance may result in a very high salary increase and even if this is followed by years of very poor performance, the individual will retain the initial salary increase;
- whilst merit payments may motivate the high performers, they may have a negative effect on average employees who, whilst not delivering high levels of performance, remain vital to the smooth running of all organizations;
- merit payments will result in additional salary costs for the organization on an ongoing basis and must therefore be carefully incorporated into the salary budget;
- to remain effective, merit payments must be based on an identifiable correlation between performance and remuneration – if this link is not clear, the effectiveness of the merit payment system is likely to be minimal.

Summary

In this chapter, we have examined various systems of PRR which attempt to establish a correlation between the performance level of employees and their subsequent remuneration. When designing or selecting a reward structure, the organization must ensure that it is appropriate to the needs of the organization and that it will be flexible enough to respond to internal and external pressures. An effective remuneration system should also be fair and consistent in rewarding employees at a level that is commensurate with their performance – this is where systems of PRR become effective.

In addition to giving adequate consideration to the salary structure and the use of systems of PRR, organizations must evaluate the total remuneration package which may involve the provision of various remunerative benefits. Such benefits may include the provision of company cars, pension schemes, mortgage assistance, relocation assistance, child care/crèche, subsidized catering, social and recreational facilities and so on. In order to be effective, each organization should design, administer and communicate their package of benefits carefully to ensure that it reflects the needs and objectives of the organization.

When selecting a system of PRR, organizations have a variety of systems to choose from, each system establishing a different correlation between performance and remuneration. The various systems of PRR available include:

- Payment by results – establishing a direct correlation between the level of production and remuneration;
- Bonus schemes – providing a cash bonus for the achievement of predetermined targets;
- Profit sharing – allocating to employees a proportion of the profits of the organization either as cash or shares;
- Profit related pay – establishing a correlation between part of an employee's remuneration and the profits of the organization or part of the organization in which they work;
- Sales incentives – a system of PRR which applies only to sales staff whereby a correlation is established between volume or value of sales and the salesperson's remuneration;
- Employee share ownership plans – a system of PRR whereby employees are given the opportunity to purchase shares in the company at a discounted price;
- Merit pay – establishing a correlation between the remuneration of an individual and their achievement of a predetermined 'merit' level of performance.

It is clear from the above evidence that the possibilities when designing a remuneration package are wide and varied and therefore need careful consideration. Ultimately, the organization must consider (a) the objectives of the organization, (b) the characteristics of the workforce, (c) external pressures and (d) the objectives of the remuneration package.

12

Remuneration in an International Context

Introduction

In recent years, human resource managers within many UK organizations have become increasingly involved in the management of the remuneration packages of employees working outside the UK. As the activities of organizations have expanded beyond the UK, it has become necessary to send employees abroad and/or employ foreign workers in their home country (local nationals). Under such circumstances, human resource managers are required to incorporate into the overall remuneration policy a specific policy on the remuneration of expatriate employees and local national employees. Whilst local nationals are likely to be employed under terms and conditions appropriate to the host country, the payment of expatriate employees can be very complex and result in burdensome administrative procedures. As with many areas of human resource management, assistance in the development of a policy on expatriate remuneration is available from a selection of consultants, including Employment Conditions Abroad Ltd, PE International, The Wyatt Company (UK) Ltd, and Business International Ltd. This chapter, however, will discuss many of the key issues to be considered when developing a policy on the remuneration of expatriate employees and provide a checklist to which employers can refer when devising such a policy.

In the modern business world, it is common for organizations to expand their markets and commence and sustain trading on a multinational basis. Within Europe, for example, the past decade has given rise to a significant increase in the level of international trade and the establishment of multinational operations. In such circumstances, it becomes necessary for organizations to send employees to work abroad on either a short-term or a long-term basis. Among the main reasons for such expatriate assignments are the following:

- to overcome the shortage of particular skills and/or experience in particular locations;
- to set up new operations/developments in foreign locations;
- to market the products or services of the organization in other countries;
- to provide employees with opportunities for career development;
- to undertake an analysis and troubleshooting exercise in foreign locations;
- to ensure the transfer of organizational culture/methods to international operations;
- to pass on skills and knowledge to local employees.

Types of Employment Abroad

The main factor differentiating between the types of employment abroad is the length of the assignment. Whilst some overseas assignments can be as short as a few weeks or months, other assignments can have a duration of many years. Essentially, there are six categories into which overseas assignments can be placed:

- extended business trip (two to six months);
- temporary overseas assignment (three months to a year);
- short-term assignment (up to two years);
- long-term assignment (typically three years);
- indefinite transfer;
- multi-mobile expatriation (the employee moves from one country to another);
- secondment (for the duration of the assignment, the secondee is employed by a foreign subsidiary and not the parent company).

When faced with the need to send an employee on an international assignment, the organization must carefully assess the particular requirements of each project before deciding upon the type of assignment to be given to each employee. The type of assignment selected has important implications for the subsequent remuneration package given to the individual, and for the corresponding cost to the organization.

Principles of the International Remuneration Package

Whatever policy the organization adopts regarding the remuneration of expatriate employees, the international remuneration package should be consistent and appropriate to the overall needs of the organization, the particular needs of the assignment and the needs of the individual employee. There are, however, a number of issues which must be addressed when establishing or reviewing an international remuneration package. For example, it is important that the remuneration package is competitive when compared with that of other expatriate employees in similar appointments in the same location. The package should also be perceived to be of an appropriate value in the eyes of the individual employee and should reflect both the responsibilities of the position and the demands of the particular type of assignment. Whilst the formation of any international remuneration package is likely to be a very complicated exercise and involve not only pay but a series of other remunerative benefits, the principles of the package and operational details must be easily understood by the employee. Sending an employee to work abroad on particular projects can involve considerable costs for the organization, so it is essential that each remuneration package is carefully designed to be as cost-effective as possible for the employer.

Overall, whatever type of assignment the employee is given, and whatever the content of the international remuneration package, the underlying objective should be to ensure that the individual employee's standard of living in the foreign country is maintained at a broadly comparable level to that which they experienced in their home country. The package should therefore aim to ensure that the employee is neither better nor worse off as a result of working abroad. In reality, however, it is common to find that the individual is likely to receive more than adequate compensation for accepting a placement abroad.

Determining Payment Levels

Depending on the type of assignment involved, there are several methods of determining the payment level for the expatriate employee. The method selected is primarily based on the length of the assignment, since some methods of determining payment levels are more appropriate where short periods abroad are involved whilst other methods are more appropriate for establishing payment levels for a long-term assignment. The four main methods of determining payment levels are:

- per diem allowances;
- market rates;
- budget system;
- build-up method.

Per diem allowances

A per diem allowance, or payment for daily expenses, is normally only suitable for short-term assignments, perhaps up to six months. This method of payment is relatively straightforward and does not result in an administrative burden for the organization. Essentially, an employee on a short-term assignment abroad will be paid their UK salary and in addition will be given a daily allowance to cover items of expenditure such as travel, entertainment, laundry, food and accommodation. The payment of a per diem allowance for longer assignments could prove very costly to the organization, and therefore the payment levels for employees on longer term assignments tend to be calculated using one of the methods outlined below.

Market rates

The market rate, or host country salary, method of establishing payment levels is primarily based on the payment of market rates for particular jobs in the host country. Irrespective of the salary level of the individual in the home country, the employee is paid the market rate for their job, in the currency of the host country. Under this system, the employee is treated as a local national and takes on the corresponding responsibilities such as paying local social security payments and local income tax, and joining the local company pension scheme, where appropriate. In addition to an annual salary, the market rate system may incorporate a number of benefits such as free accommodation, the payment of school fees, trips home, and perhaps a foreign service premium expressed as a percentage of salary.

The payment of employees using the market rate system tends to be most appropriate when the assignment is for an indefinite period of time or where the duration of the assignment is for a specified long period in excess of three years. Where an employee is moving from a low paying country to a higher paying country, for example, from Greece to Switzerland, the market rate method of payment is especially appropriate since it ensures that the employee can maintain a standard of living comparable to that experienced in the home country.

Budget system

The basis of the budget system of establishing payment levels is an assessment of two factors:

1 the salary of the individual, and
2 all costs associated with the transfer abroad, both in the home country and the host country.

Once the salary level and costs have been established, the total amount is translated into a single currency, normally that of the host country, and grossed up for tax. Whilst this system may appear to be relatively straightforward, it is not suitable for countries with volatile exchange rates since the amounts allocated require constant adjustment resulting in excessive amounts of administration and corresponding costs.

Build-up method

Whilst the build-up, or balance sheet, method of establishing levels of expatriate remuneration can be rather complex, it is the most common method used to assess the level of remuneration for employees working abroad, particularly for assignments of around three years. Using the level of home salary as a base for calculations, this method determines a salary level in the host country currency which takes account of any difference in the cost of living. The level of remuneration is calculated using a series of factors; a hypothetical example is illustrated in figure 12.1.

From the this figure, it can be seen that the first stage in assessing a build-up remuneration level is to determine the net salary level of the individual prior to the assignment. Once this salary level is determined, it is divided into two components:

Job title: Director of human resources
Personal status: Married, no children
Home country: UK
Host country: Switzerland
Social security: Contracted-in
Cost of living: UK (100); Switzerland (130)
Exchange rate: UK £1.00 = Swiss Franc 1.98 (6 September 1994)

Home salary (pre-assignment):

Gross salary		£45,000
Deductions:		
Tax	£13,429	
National Insurance (UK)	£2,007	£15,436
Net salary		£29,564
Housing and savings (37% of net salary)		£10,939
Spendable income (63% of net salary)		£18,625
		£29,564

Host country salary:

Housing and savings (10,939 × F1.98)	F21,659
Spendable income (18,625 × 1.30 × F1.98)	F47,941
Expatriate allowance (15% of home gross salary × F1.98)	F8,910
Total net salary	F78,510
Estimated tax (inc. UK National Insurance)	F19,627
Gross salary	F98,137

Figure 12.1 *Example calculation a build-up remuneration level*

- housing and savings – a notional figure representing the individual's obligations for items such as housing costs and savings;
- spendable income – an amount representing the proportion of salary typically used for day-to-day expenditure on items such as food and drink, entertainment, clothing and miscellaneous goods and services.

The next stage focuses on calculating the host country salary which will be paid to the employee for the duration of their period abroad. The host country salary comprises three components:

- housing and savings – the notional figure representing expenditure in the home country on items such as housing and savings is translated into the host country currency by applying the current exchange rate;
- spendable income – the amount representing expenditure on day-to-day items is adjusted via a cost of living index and the current exchange rate

to give a spendable income with an equivalent purchasing power in the currency of the host country;
- expatriate allowance – occasionally, some organizations include, as part of the build-up remuneration level, an allowance to compensate for the disruption involved in moving overseas, typically this sum will represent 10–15 per cent of gross home salary.

Totalled together, the above three factors represent the total net salary of the individual, in the foreign currency, for the duration of their assignment. This amount may be adjusted to take account of such factors as inflation and significant changes in exchange rates. Added to the net amount, to give a figure for gross salary, is an element representing deductions for taxation, including payments for UK National Insurance. In addition to the monetary elements of the remuneration package, the build-up method, like most of the other methods of establishing international payment levels, is likely to include the provision of a number of remunerative benefits. Examples of such benefits are discussed later in this chapter.

Method of Payment

Whilst an organization may choose any one, or a selection, of the above methods of establishing international remuneration levels, it must also decide whether such remuneration is to be paid in the currency of the home country or in the currency of the host country. Whilst some methods of establishing international remuneration levels may suggest payment in a particular currency, the key issue should be the needs of the individual employee together with the needs of the organization. Whether the organization decides to provide remuneration in the currency of the home or host country, or any combination of the two, such a decision should only be taken once all the variables have been given careful consideration.

Remunerative Benefits

In addition to establishing remuneration levels for employees working abroad, it is necessary for organizations to consider the entire remuneration package, including the provision of remunerative benefits. Whilst the organization may have a package of remunerative benefits applicable to employees in the home country, the content of the benefits package for expatriate workers is likely to differ somewhat, and requires careful consideration. Since each country in the world has a particular economic climate and culture, there is unlikely to be a single benefits package which is appropriate to all expatriate employees. As a result, the needs of the individual employee and the particular circumstances of each assignment must be carefully assessed before a benefits package is put together. Below is a brief description of the types of benefits which are likely to be considered when designing an international remunerative benefits package.

Accommodation

Next to the establishment of salary levels, the issue of accommodation is likely to be the most important for the employee working abroad. Whilst most employers will either provide free accommodation, or an accommodation allowance, there are two main problems to be faced by the expatriate employee – where to stay in the host country, and what to do with property in the home country.

When the assignment is for a short period, the employee is most likely to stay in a hotel which will either be paid directly by the organization or be paid by the employee through a per diem allowance. When the assignment is for a longer period, however, it is most likely that the employee will stay in rented accommodation, or perhaps in a flat or house bought by the organization for use by expatriate employees.

On the issue of property in the home country, if the employee is accompanied abroad by his/her family, there are a number of options regarding any property left in the home country. If the assignment abroad is for a period of three years or less, it is unlikely that the employee will sell the property in the home country, although this is an option if the assignment is for a long or indefinite period. Whilst the sale of the property will release capital which can be invested in other ways, the danger of selling the home property is the risk that the employee may have to re-enter the property market during a property boom. A more common situation is where the employee rents out the home property during the period abroad. Whilst this option will guarantee an income from the property, which will perhaps cover any mortgage and associated costs, there is a risk of having bad tenants. There are, however, a number of housing agents who, for an appropriate fee, will take care of any rented properties, dealing with any problems and any required maintenance. The third option is simply to leave the property vacant, although with such an option there is no income and, in addition, there is a risk of squatters.

Company car

Whilst most managerial grades will expect the provision of a company car in the host country, there are four main factors to consider when deciding whether or not to provide expatriate employees with a company car:

- *The situation of the employee pre-assignment* If the organization provided the employee with a company car in the home country pre-assignment, it is most likely that a similar provision will be made in the host country.
- *The situation of employees of a similar status in the host country* In the same way that remuneration packages in the home country require to be equitable and comparable to that of competing employers, it is important that similar comparisons are made in the host country. Where an employee of a similar status in the host country is provided with a company car, for example, it is highly probable that the expatriate employee will be given similar provision.
- *The duration and nature of the assignment* Where an assignment is for a short period, or is based in a city with adequate public transport and taxis, it may be that the provision of a company car is not required, or indeed is not desired. However, should the assignment be for a longer period, perhaps six months or more, or involve travel to and from work, the provision of a company car will be more likely.
- *Job requirement* For some expatriate assignments, the provision of a company car may be a job requirement. For example, a sales representative involved in travelling throughout the host country will require the provision of transport such as a company car.

Should the organization decide to provide the expatriate employee with a company car, there are two further issues which must be considered regarding such provision. Firstly, should the driving of the car be restricted to the employee only, or should other members of the family also be allowed to drive? And secondly, should the organization, in addition to providing the car, also provide a chauffeur/guard?

Medical insurance

Since very few countries in the world have national health provision as generous as that of the National Health Service in the UK, the issue of medical insurance is a very important issue for the expatriate employee. As medical facilities and corresponding costs vary greatly, depending on the host country, it is common for employers to arrange adequate medical insurance to cover the provision of private treatment in the host country or repatriation for health care in the home country. There are a number of companies within the UK which provide a range of health care insurance packages, the premiums for which are likely to vary depending on the host country.

Children's education

On the issue of education provision for the children of expatriate employees, there are essentially two choices:

• the children continue their education in the home country attending a UK boarding school, or
• the children also move abroad and attend a school in the host country.

Whilst the organization may wish to give the employee's family a choice regarding whether the children will attend school in the home or host country, there may be financial implications for the organization which will restrict such choice. Whilst the organization will normally meet the full costs of education in the host country, it is generally recognized that the costs for UK boarding schools are normally much higher. As a result, it is common for organizations to pay part of the UK boarding school fees, perhaps 75 per cent, and place a ceiling on the overall education assistance. It is also unlikely that the organization will pay for additional items such as sports equipment, music lessons or tap dancing classes.

Servants

In some countries, the employment of servants is still commonplace and is considered to represent affluence, status and power. Should an employee be assigned to a country with such a culture, it is likely that the employing organization will provide servants for the employee. Whilst one of the main reasons for employing servants is to conform with local practices, the employment of servants will also provide a source of income for the local economy. In addition to servants, in countries where security poses a threat to those perceived as being affluent, it is common for organizations to provide security guards as part of the benefits package.

Pensions

The most important issue regarding occupational pensions and expatriate assignments is to ensure that the employee's final pension is not adversely affected by a period of service overseas. Normally, the organization will encourage the employee to remain a member of the occupational pension scheme during the period of assignment. In addition, the organization is likely to maintain appropriate contribution levels based on the employee's home gross salary (pre-assignment) with notional adjustments to take account of inflation and salary reviews throughout the period of the assignment.

Annual leave

The general position on annual leave is to provide the employee with one month's leave after twelve months' service. In such circumstances, the organization will pay for return transport to and from the home country for the employee and his/her family. The frequency of such leave, however, is likely to increase if the employee is based in a country with high levels of danger or hardship. In addition, it is normal for the frequency of visits home to be greater if the employee is single or is unaccompanied abroad since the cost of transporting one person is less than that of transporting a family. Where the host country is characterized by low hardship or where return travel would involve prohibitive air fares, the frequency of visits to the home country is likely to be reduced, particularly if it would involve travel for the whole family.

Other remunerative benefits

Club membership It is common for organizations to pay for membership of a number of sports and social clubs.

Kit allowance where the climate of the host country is radically different to that of the home country, it is usual for organizations to provide an allowance for the purchase of suitable clothing.

Personal accident insurance it is essential that the employee and his/her family have adequate personal accident cover whilst travelling to and staying in the host country.

Utilities where the cost of utilities such as gas, water, electricity and telephone are excessive, it is usual for the organization to make a contribution towards such costs.

Relocation when an employee has an assignment abroad, there are a number of relocation costs which should be met by the employer, such as the security and maintenance of property in the home country, the storage of furniture and the shipment of personal effects.

Taxation Implications

Under certain circumstances, employees working abroad are not required to pay UK income tax on their earnings overseas, unless their salary is actually paid in the UK. The two occasions when expatriate employees gain exemption from UK income tax are outlined below.

(1) Assignments consisting of a period of at least one whole tax year. To gain exemption from UK income tax under this heading, the employee must be able to demonstrate to the Inland Revenue that they are neither resident nor ordinarily resident in the UK. In order to gain such status, the following conditions must be met:

* the period overseas must be to work full time under a contract of employment where the duties will be carried out overseas, and
* the period of absence *and* the period of employment must extend for a complete tax year or more, and
* any interim visits to the UK must not last for more than six months in any one tax year or average three months per tax year over a three year period.

(2) Assignments of 365 days, whether or not this covers a complete tax year. To gain exemption from UK income tax under this heading, the employee must satisfy the following conditions:

* the period overseas must be to work full time under a contract of employment where the duties will be carried out overseas, and

- the period of employment overseas must extend to at least 365 days, and
- the employee does not return to the UK for a visit which exceeds 62 days, and
- the total number of days spent in the UK must not be more than one-sixth of the total number of days spent overseas.

In both of the situations outlined above, the qualifying period for gaining exemption from UK income tax starts with the first day of non-residence and ends with the last day of non-residence. Whilst the employee may gain exemption from income tax liability for payments abroad, they will still remain liable for UK tax on any UK source of income. In addition to the above provisions, there are separate provisions covering aeroplane and ship crews, divers and others working on North Sea oil rigs, Foreign Office and other Crown employees working overseas and European Community (EC) employees.

When designing the remuneration packages for expatriate employees, organizations must carefully consider any taxation implications for the employee. Once again, the guiding principle is that the employee should be no worse off as a result of an assignment overseas. Since the taxation rates in the host country may be higher, as well as lower, than UK income tax rates, the design of the remuneration package and payment arrangements require careful consideration. In an attempt to ensure that the employee does not suffer any financial penalty, the organization can use one of the following methods of managing taxation.

Tax equalization

Using this method, the company calculates the amount of tax which the employee would have paid had they remained in the home country. This amount is then deducted from the gross pay of the individual whilst they are overseas. In return, the organization takes on any liability for tax payable on the remuneration package in the host country. This method therefore ensures that the package actually received in the host country is at least equivalent to, if not better than, the package to which the employee would have been entitled had they remained in the UK. This method of managing taxation is incorporated into the build-up method of establishing payment levels outlined above.

Tax protection

Under this system of managing taxation, the employee carries all liability for income tax in the host country, but there are two possible scenarios. Should the taxation rates of the host country be lower than that of the home country, the employing organization need take no action – the expatriate employee simply enjoys the benefit of low or even zero levels of taxation. On the other hand, should the income tax rates in the host country be higher than that of the home country, the organization will be required to compensate the employee for any difference in the amount of tax actually paid.

The above taxation implications for international remuneration have been greatly simplified to give the reader a basic understanding. In reality, they are very complex and any organization contemplating assignments abroad should seek the advice of a taxation specialist.

Third Country Nationals

Occasionally, organizations requiring workers for overseas assignments employ individuals whose home country is neither that of the employer nor the host country. As a result, a third nation is introduced into the employment relationship. Whilst a third country national (TCN) may be employed for various political and economic motives, a common reason for employing some TCNs is that such employees can often be a cheap source of labour. Employees from countries such as Pakistan and the Philippines, for example, may be willing to work in a foreign host country for a relatively low-cost remuneration package. In addition, it may be easier to persuade employees from such countries to work in host countries with poor living conditions.

When employing TCNs, perhaps the most important issue for the employing organization is the question of establishing payment levels. As discussed above, the payment levels for expatriate employees can be based either on the payment trends of the employee's home country or on the payment trends of the host country. When a TCN is involved, however, the payment levels can also be based on a third source, the payment trends in the employer's home country. The important issue is that whatever source is used for establishing payment levels, it must be acceptable to both the TCN and the employing organization. It is extremely difficult, however, to establish a feeling of equity when there are a number of TCNs employed who have different home countries. The payment of TCNs therefore requires careful consideration in light of the needs of the employee, the employer and the situation in the host country.

Conclusion

Whilst the aim of this chapter has been to provide a brief discussion of the main issues surrounding the remuneration of expatriate workers, it is clear that the design, implementation, administration and monitoring of international remuneration systems requires a considerable amount of expertise. Therefore, any organization contemplating the use of expatriate employees for international assignments should employ or consult an expert who specializes in this area of remuneration policy. It should be noted, however, that any policy on expatriate remuneration should consider the following key points:

* company policy on expatriate employment/TCNs;
* contracts of employment and the requirement to work overseas;
* policy on accompanied/unaccompanied assignments;
* work/residency permits;
* international driving licences;
* medical checks and medical insurance;
* language training/orientation briefings;
* pre-assignment visits;
* the basis on which payment is made, and where it is made;
* income tax liability;
* the provision of remunerative benefits;
* pet quarantine arrangements;
* repatriation procedures.

13
Managing the Reward System

Introduction

Once an organization has designed and implemented reward management practices which are appropriate to the needs of the organization, and will contribute to the achievement of organizational objectives, it is essential that the reward policy and corresponding reward systems are controlled, monitored and reviewed. Since the modern business world is continually changing as a result of market pressures, organizations are required to adapt and develop to maintain a competitive edge over rival companies. This requirement for organizations to adapt and develop has a corresponding impact on most management policies, including the reward policies. As the demands on an organization and its employees change, it is necessary to review how effective the remuneration policies of the organization are, and whether or not they continue to contribute to the corporate objectives. In addition, if reward policies are designed and implemented without an ongoing process of monitoring and evaluation, the reward systems are likely to become stagnant and develop a variety of inconsistencies and operational problems such as grade drift, excessive salary reviews, discriminatory reward packages, the incorporation of expensive and unnecessary remunerative benefits and unclear guidelines regarding the establishment and review of salary levels. Consequently, if the reward policies of an organization are to remain effective and an integral part of the corporate strategy, it is essential that the reward management practices are controlled, monitored, reviewed and if necessary amended accordingly. This chapter aims to examine some of the most important issues regarding the control of reward systems and in addition discusses the significance of computerization and communication within reward management.

Controlling the Reward Policies

There are a number of procedures which can be utilized by senior management in order to control the reward policies within organizations. For maximum effectiveness, these procedures should perhaps be used in a systematic and cyclical fashion. Together, the procedures should help to ensure that the reward policies of the organization remain effective, within the control of management and have a significant role within the overall strategy of the organization. The procedures which organizations may consider to assist with controlling their reward policies include:

- systems for monitoring the reward policy;
- systems for monitoring salary budgets;
- salary review systems;
- job grading systems;
- systems for determining salary levels on appointment or promotion.

Monitoring the Reward Policy

Any policy adopted by an organization should be an integral part of the corporate strategy aimed at achieving organizational, departmental and individual objectives. Since one of the highest costs in most businesses is the provision of remuneration packages in terms of basic salary, remunerative benefits and perhaps performance related pay, it is essential that the reward policies of the organization are monitored to ensure that they are operating effectively. Otherwise, the organization is likely to be spending a large amount of income on the payment of salaries and wages without getting the maximum return on such expenditure. The purpose of monitoring the reward policy of the organization is therefore to ensure that:

- The reward systems support the objectives of the organization. The effect which reward systems have on the behaviour of employees must be appropriate to the needs of the organization and should ultimately assist with the achievement of corporate objectives.

- Salary levels are comparable to that of competing employers. The managers must be confident that the remuneration packages which they offer to different categories of workers are at least equivalent to, or indeed better than, those of other organizations which require similar categories of workers.
- The salary structure is not being eroded by unjustifiable upgradings (grade drift). The reward policies must ensure that there are clear guidelines regarding the regrading of employees; it should be made impossible for managers to award unjustifiable upgradings.
- Internal differentials are appropriate and are being maintained. Since all organizations comprise a number of categories of employee, each one requiring different skills and abilities, it is important that there are differentials, where appropriate, between different categories of employee to ensure that there is fairness and equity in the provision of remuneration.
- The salary structures and salary progression are being managed properly and are effective. Even though an organization may have put considerable effort into designing and implementing remuneration policies, it is nevertheless essential that, after the system has been implemented, the organization makes sure that the salary structures and salary progression are operating effectively. If this is not the case, there will be a requirement for review and subsequent rectification.

. Salary Budgets

The provision of remuneration packages is a necessary cost within any business and can often represent a significant proportion of the turnover of the organization. To illustrate the high costs associated with remunerating employees, table 13.1 contains information on six

Table 13.1   *Remuneration costs as a percentage of turnover*

Company	Year	%
British Gas plc	1993	64.1
Forte plc	1993	32.0
Hanson plc	1994	49.4
Marks & Spencer plc	1994	35.2
Rolls Royce plc	1993	29.8
Royal Bank of Scotland	1994	28.3

high profile organizations, showing their remuneration costs as a percentage of turnover.

One method of controlling expenditure within organizations is through the use of a series of financial budgets. In addition to having budgets for areas of expenditure such as advertising, training, capital and so on, in order to control the expenditure relating to remuneration, it is essential that the managers of the organization establish, and operate within, a salary budget. The salary budget normally represents the sum of the salaries of all the employees, including any remunerative benefits, plus any additional projected costs such as general salary reviews and individual performance related reviews. Throughout the financial year, the human resource managers within the organization should monitor the actual expenditure on salaries and compare this against the budgeted figure. Table 13.2 shows a simple method by which the salary budget can be monitored on a month by month basis for different categories of employee.

Using such a method for checking the actual expenditure on salaries against budgeted expenditure, the managers of the organization can very quickly identify areas of concern regarding the overpayment or indeed underpayment of salaries for particular categories of employee, or for the organization as a whole. To retain control over the salary budget, it is essential that checks are carried out on a systematic basis in order that appropriate action can be taken to ensure that the actual expenditure on salaries remains close to the allocated budget. In addition to comparing actual expenditure against budgeted expenditure, salary budgets can also be monitored by measuring attrition and calculating comparative ratios.

Table 13.2   *Salary budget*

Month: May

Grade	Budget for year	Actual cost for month	Budgeted cost for month	%+/−	Actual cost for year to date	Budgeted cost for year to date	%+/−
1	480 000	39 000	40 000	−2.5	194 000	200 000	−3.0
2	504 000	44 500	42 000	+5.9	235 000	210 00	+11.9
3	900 000	78 750	75 000	+5.0	383 000	375 000	+2.1
4	1 800 000	175 000	150 000	+16.7	815 000	750 000	+8.7
5	600 000	46 500	50 000	−7.0	228 000	250 000	−8.8
6	204 000	18 150	17 000	+6.8	83 500	85 000	−1.8
Total	4 488 000	401 900	374 000	+7.5	1 938 500	1 870 000	+3.6

Measuring attrition

When an individual leaves an organization and is replaced by a new employee on a lower salary level, the salary costs for the budget period are likely to be lower than predicted, given a normal flow of leavers and starters within the organization. In reality, however, the net surplus arising from any reduced salary costs is often used to finance, or part finance, general salary reviews and individual merit increases within the organization. This procedure is known as attrition. In order to be able to accurately forecast salary budgets for future years, it is useful for organizations to estimate the real cost of general salary reviews and individual merit reviews, taking appropriate account of any attrition. A simple method of calculating attrition is to take the budgeted salary cost for each grade of employee and subtract from this figure the actual cost less the sum cost of any general salary review and individual merit reviews. The resulting figure represents the amount which has been contributed to the cost of any general salary review and individual merit reviews from any net surplus resulting from reduced salary costs. An example of calculating attrition is given in table 13.3.

Calculating comparative ratios

Comparative ratios involve making a comparison between the average salary for a particular grade and the salary mid-point for that grade. If the salary structure has been designed properly and is operating effectively, the average salary for the grade should be very similar to the mid-point. Comparative ratios are calculated by using the following formula:

Table 13.3 *Calculating attrition*

	Grade 1 (£)	Grade 2 (£)	Grade 3 (£)
A Budgeted salary costs for year	480 000	504 000	900 000
B Actual salary costs for year	475 000	545 000	956 000
C Cost of general salary review	28 800	30 240	54 000
D Cost of individual merit reviews	43 200	45 360	81 000
E Attrition [A-(B-C-D)]	77 000	34 600	79 000
F Net increase/decrease (B-A)	−5 000	41 000	56 000

$$\text{comparative ratio} = \left(\frac{\text{average of all salaries in grade} \times 100}{\text{mid-point of the grade}}\right)$$

Should the comparative ratio equal 100, this would indicate that the salary budget was on target and that the salary structure was appropriately designed and operating effectively. If, however, the comparative ratio was greater than 100, this would indicate either that the staff on the particular grade were being overpaid, or that the grade was characterized by employees who were at the top end of the salary range, perhaps those employees who had worked for the organization for many years. In contrast, should the comparative ratio be less than 100, this would suggest either that employees on the particular grade were being underpaid, or alternatively that the grade was characterized by employees at the lower end of the salary range, such as employees who had recently joined the organization.

Overall, the use of salary budgets can greatly assist with the management of the reward system by carefully monitoring actual expenditure on salaries against budgeted expenditure. In order to be most effective, salary budgets should be examined for each category of employee on a systematic basis in order that worrying trends can be identified and appropriate corrective action taken.

Salary Review Systems

Within any organization which employs staff, there is likely to be, at some stage, demands for a salary review. It is unlikely that employees will be willing to accept a static salary level for a prolonged period of time and will at least expect their salary levels to stay in line with the level of inflation. The employees may seek to establish a general annual salary review or, alternatively, may prefer an *ad hoc* approach to salary reviews whereby the issue of salary reviews can be raised whenever the need arises.

From the viewpoint of the managers of the organization, because of the very high ongoing costs associated with the remuneration of employees, there are a number of very important decisions to make regarding the issue of salary reviews. Firstly, the organization, and the employees, must be very clear about the type of salary review to be incorporated within the remuneration policy, and in addition must, where appropriate, establish an agreed procedure and timescale for negotiating and implementing salary reviews. It is also important that the management of the organization retain control over the salary reviews and the associated salary budget, and must therefore incorporate into the salary review procedure a number of control mechanisms.

Types of salary review

Within the modern organization, there are a number of types of salary review which can be adopted. Bearing in mind the high costs associated with the remuneration of employees, and the increasing level of competition in the business world, it is essential that the type(s) of salary review adopted by an organization is consistent with the needs of the organization and can be controlled by the management. The management must therefore carefully consider the characteristics and implications of each type of salary review and incorporate a salary review procedure which supports the remuneration strategy and business objectives of the organization.

A phenomenon common to many organizations is the concept of the annual general salary review which is generally associated with reviewing all salaries in line with inflation, and maintaining comparability with the external employment market. These general salary reviews are often negotiated with employee representatives, with the associated negotiation and collective bargaining procedures commonly being referred to as the 'pay round'. Such salary reviews become expected by employees irrespective of their own individual performance level and the overall performance of the organization; their expectation is to receive an increase in salary at a certain time each financial year. Should an organization decide to award a general salary increase to all employees, it is essential that an assessment is made of the effect that such an increase in salary levels would have on the salary budget. In addition, it is vital that the organization reviews the impact a general salary review would have on the salary structures, in particular, the minima, maxima and mid-points of each salary range.

Another type of salary review which has been commonly used within the United Kingdom, particularly in the public sector, is the concept of incremental payment systems. An incremental payment system is based on the premise that following each additional year of service with the organization the salary of each individual employee will be reviewed by moving the individual a predetermined number of steps up their salary structure. For example, had an employee joined an organization on 1 March 1995 on a salary of £14,000 on the salary structure shown in the list below, and was moved up one step for each additional year's service, on 1 March 1996 their salary would be reviewed and increased to £15,400. This process would be repeated for each additional year of service so that on 1 March 1997 the salary would be reviewed to £16,940, and so on.

Step	Salary(£)
1	14000
2	15400
3	16940
4	18634
5	20497
6	22547
7	24802
8	27282

The main concern with reviewing salaries through an incremental payment system relates once again to the expectations of the employees. Irrespective of the performance levels of the individual or the organization, each individual employee will look forward to a particular date in the calendar year, their anniversary of service, and expect their salary to increase by a predetermined and known amount. Whilst this situation makes it possible for the management of the organization to predict future salary budgets, it also results in a position whereby the management have little control over the increased expenditure. In order to regain some element of control over incremental increase, some organizations have introduced a condition whereby they will only award such increases if the performance level of the individual is of a satisfactory level. The issue of relating salary reviews to performance levels is discussed in more detail below.

A third method of reviewing salary levels can be achieved by establishing a correlation between pay and the performance of the individual – an individual salary review. Under such a system, the salary of an individual employee will only be reviewed, and possibly increased, if the performance of the employee reaches a predetermined performance or merit level. A variant of the individual salary review would be to establish a correlation between the performance of a group of employees, or the organization, and the salaries of the members of the group, or the organization. By using a system involving a correlation between performance and salary levels, the organization can be reasonably confident that salary increases will only be given to employees who deserve them and who are making a contribution to the objectives of the organization. Under such circumstances, therefore, the management of the organization retain an element of control over salary reviews and corresponding expenditure.

In summary therefore, there are three types of salary review which organizations can utilize – general salary reviews, incremental increases and individual salary reviews. It should be noted that there are organizations which utilize all three types of salary review and therefore make it possible for employees to have their salary reviewed on three occasions each year. Alternatively, organizations can elect to utilize only one system for reviewing salaries, or any combination of the three systems discussed. For example, an organization may decide to have a general salary review to take account of any increase in the cost of living, and offer in addition an individual salary review based on the performance of each individual employee. Another possibility is to only offer an individual salary review which, whilst incorporating a reward for high levels of performance and an element to take account of any increase in the cost of living, remains linked to the attainment of a predetermined performance level. Whatever system, or combination of systems, is utilized by an organization, the vital concern should be that the review policy is compatible with the overall remuneration strategy and supports the objectives of the organization.

Control of salary reviews

Control mechanisms   Whichever policy is adopted by an organization regarding the issue of salary reviews, it is important that appropriate control mechanisms are incorporated into the salary review procedure. These control mechanisms should give managers guidance regarding the operation of salary reviews and the constraints within which they operate. Factors which could be incorporated into control mechanisms include:

* guidance on who has authority to propose and authorize salary increases resulting from a salary review;
* the establishment and communication of budget limits for salary reviews;
* guidance on what factors should affect the salary review decision, and how the decision should be implemented;

- the allocation of responsibility to a manager, or group of managers, to co-ordinate and monitor the salary review procedure;
- the generation of data to assess whether or not the salary review procedure is consistent with the objectives and management strategy of the organization.

Guidelines for individual salary reviews   Should the managers of an organization decide to implement a system of individual salary reviews, it is only likely to operate successfully if the individuals involved with assessing individual performance levels and attaching an appropriate salary increase are given a number of guidelines regarding how the system should operate. Below are some examples of areas of guidance which managers should perhaps consider.

Before it is possible to undertake any review of salaries, including reviews associated with individual performance, it is essential that managers are fully aware of any budget restrictions relating to proposed increases in salaries. If there are no budget restrictions on salary reviews, which is extremely unlikely, then managers need not be highly concerned about the effect which their decisions will have on expenditure related to remuneration. If, however, there are certain budgetary restrictions on salary reviews, either in terms of an organizational or departmental salary budget, then detailed guidelines should be given to managers to enable them to make decisions which take account of any restrictions and help guarantee that expenditure on salaries remains within budget.

When making decisions regarding the work performance of individual employees and their future salary levels, it is important that managers have knowledge of the pay ranges for different categories of employee. At a basic level, each manager should be aware of the minimum, maximum and mid-point salary level for each grade of worker so that before salary reviews are awarded, the manager can consider the position of the employee in relation to the salary range and take account of this when making their decision. For example, if an employee was on the minimum salary for their grade and had demonstrated superior performance levels, the manager may be able to award a significant increase in salary, say 12 per cent. On the other hand, if the employee was near the maximum of the salary range and demonstrated superior performance, the level of increase which the manager could award would be constrained by the maximum salary level or ceiling of the grade.

Another form of guidance which can be given to managers when reviewing individual salary levels relates to the level of salary increase

Table 13.4   *Performance standards and salary increases*

Performance standard	Percentage salary increase
A Performance outstanding	12
B Performance significantly above requirements	9
C Performance above requirements	6
D Perfomance meets requirements	3
E Performance below requirements	0
F Performance unacceptable	0

which can be given in return for different standards of performance. Such guidelines tend to be fairly rigid and consist of a number of predetermined performance standards, each of which has an associated salary increase. An example of such guidelines is given in table 13.4.

Perhaps one of the most inflexible guidelines which can be given to managers concerning the review of individual salary levels relates to the concept of forced choice distribution salary reviews. The basic principle of forced choice distribution salary reviews relates once again to a number of defined performance standards, normally five. A simple example of the five standards could be high, above average, average, below average and low performance. Once the performance standards have been defined, and an appropriate salary increase attached to each standard, each manager is then required to place a given percentage of their employees in each standard. Table 13.5 gives an example of how this could operate in practice. The allo-

Table 13.5   *Forced choice distribution salary reviews*

Performance standard	Percentage of employees	Percentage salary increase
A High performance	10	12
B Above average performance	20	8
C Average performance	40	4
D Below average performance	20	0
E Low performance	10	0

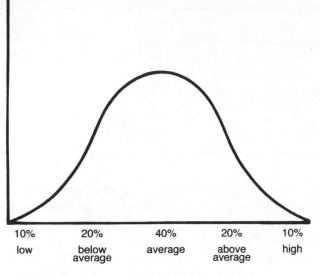

| 10% | 20% | 40% | 20% | 10% |
| low | below average | average | above average | high |

Figure 13.1 *Normal distribution curve*

cation of employees to each category should reflect a normal distribution curve as illustrated in figure 13.1.

Another guideline which managers can be given to assist with individual salary reviews is based on the concept of a merit matrix. The basic principle of a merit matrix is to award different salary increases, expressed as a percentage of salary, to employees depending on their performance level and their current position in the salary range. By reviewing salaries using a merit matrix, managers are not only given guidance regarding the level of salary increase to be allocated to different performance levels, but in addition have such increases related to the individual's position on their salary scale. This allows the level of salary increase to be tapered off as employees reach the maximum salary level for their grade. An example of a merit matrix is illustrated in table 13.6.

A simple guideline for managers regarding individual salary reviews could be to allocate salary increases to staff depending on their performance ranking amongst their peer group. For example, if a manager was responsible for a team of six Grade 3 employees, then he/she could rank the employees according to their performance level and attach a corresponding salary increase. For a small team of employees, a ranking procedure would be relatively straightforward since the manager should be fully aware of the performance level,

Table 13.6   *Merit matrix*

Performance standard	Position in salary range										
	95	96	97	98	99	100	101	102	103	104	105
Outstanding	9	8	8	7	78	6	6	6	5	3	2
Very effective	7	6	6	5	4	3	2	2	1	0	0
Satisfactory	5	4	3	2	1	1	0	0	0	0	0
Unsatisfactory	0	0	0	0	0	0	0	0	0	0	0

strengths and weaknesses of each member of staff. For a large team or department, however, such a process would be extremely complicated and open to inconsistencies. A salary review ranking procedure could operate as illustrated in table 13.7.

A final guideline which managers could use for individual salary reviews relates to the use of salary modelling. With the increasing complexity of computer programs and an associated trend towards simplified methods of operating such programs, remuneration specialists are now capable of recording, monitoring and predicting trends in salary budgets, including trends in salary reviews. As a result, organizations can now be in a position to accurately relate salary increases to the work performance of employees through the use of reward management software packages. In theory, once the assessment of an individual employee's work performance has been carried out, the manager should be able to input this data into a computer program which will then calculate an appropriate review of salary based on trends identified by the program and any limitations set by the management of the organization.

Table 13.7   *Salary review – ranking*

Grade 3 employees	Performance ranking	Percentage salary increase
Ronald Andrews	4	4.5
John Ballantyne	6	1.5
Joanne Carlyle	2	7.5
Tom Dryburgh	1	9.0
Colin Mainland	3	6.0
Moira Mitchell	5	3.0

Whichever method of salary review is utilized by an organization, it is a precondition for the successful operation of such systems that the managers responsible for implementing the system are given comprehensive guidelines regarding how the system should be operated. Overall, the individual manager should have no doubts regarding any constraints or limitations within which the individual salary reviews should operate. If no such guidance is given, the individual salary review system of the organization is likely to develop significant operational problems which could lead to serious implications for the organization, such as levels of expenditure on salaries which are greatly over budget.

Grading jobs   A further method of controlling salary reviews is to produce a number of guidelines relating to the regrading of jobs within organizations. In addition to being clear about the structure and operation of grading systems within an organization, it is important that managers are aware of and understand the procedures involved in dealing with requests or demands for regrading. For example, each manager should be aware of who within the organization is the authorized person to regrade jobs using an appropriate and agreed procedure. One method by which jobs can be regraded is by utilizing a job evaluation system as described in chapter 7. Within a job evaluation system, there are certain procedures for grading employees according to their value to the organization. The authorized body within a job evaluation system is often the Job Evaluation Team. When dealing with demands for regrading, it is essential that the authorized person resists pressures from managers and employees to regrade in line with market trends and instead relies on the agreed procedure. As with most aspects of remuneration policy, it is important that the policy on the regrading of employees is systematically monitored and evaluated to ensure that it is operating effectively.

Setting salaries on appointment   When employees join an organization, it is necessary to decide upon an appropriate starting salary level. Whilst this salary level should reflect such factors as qualifications and experience, it must also be consistent with internal relativities within the organization, including the policy of salary reviews. Therefore, it is important that the organization has a policy regarding the determination of salary levels on appointment. Whilst the starting salary of a new employee is likely to be towards the minimum salary for the grade, the policy regarding starting salaries should be flexible enough to allow the payment of higher starting salaries in certain circumstances, perhaps up to 25 per cent above the minimum salary or even higher for exceptional cases.

In addition to a policy for the determination of starting salaries for new employees, the organization should also have a similar policy relating to the determination of salary levels for promoted employees. Whatever policy the organization decides upon, it is important that promoted employees perceive a significant increase in salary on promotion which reflects the changes in responsibility and demands associated with the new grade.

Reward Management and Computerization

Since the 1980s, there have been significant technological advances in the design of computer hardware and software. The modern computer is now much smaller and yet substantially more powerful than the computers of even 15 years ago. Technology has progressed at such a rate that managers today can buy a battery operated portable laptop computer with a colour LCD screen which weighs 2.0 kg (4.4 lb) with a hard disk capacity of 250 MB. The software available enables managers to record and process data for a variety of management functions, including human resource management. Information stored on computer, which was previously manually recorded, can now be analysed and recalled in a matter of seconds. In addition to assisting the human resource manager with reward management, computerization can prove invaluable in other personnel operations such as absence control, manpower planning, training and development, performance appraisal and job evaluation.

The decision whether or not to utilize computerized systems to assist with reward management will depend on a number of factors within the organization. Overall, the managers must be confident that the expenditure, time and effort associated with installing, operating and maintaining computer systems is justified and will improve the efficiency of the organization and in turn assist with the achievement of organizational objectives. The factors likely to influence the decision whether or not to install a computer system include:

- the number of employees;
- the availability of staff and financial resources;
- the complexity of the pay structure;
- the types of analyses required.

In relation to reward management, the human resource manager can utilize computerization to assist with various forms of analyses to ensure that all aspects relating to the remuneration of employees are managed effectively. In particular, computerized reward packages can assist with:

- analysing internal equity;
- conducting external comparisons;
- forecasting future pay developments;
- managing salary budgets;
- developing remuneration packages;
- processing the payroll;
- transferring data.

The use of computerization within the human resource management function of reward management can therefore result in HRM managers having immediate access to any information relating to the remuneration of employees. Such access allows the managers to closely monitor the reward systems, identify any areas of concern and initiate future developments in the reward policy and practices of the organization.

Reward Management and Communication

An important factor to consider when seeking to manage the reward system is to ensure effective communication between the management and the employees regarding the reward policies. If the remuneration package offered to each employee is to be effective in establishing and maintaining high levels of individual and organizational performance, each employee must be clear about their own individual performance requirements and the resulting rewards. Only through effective communication regarding the reward policy and associated procedures will the expectations of employees be accurate and reflective of the reward strategy of the organization.

The type of information which should be given to employees regarding the reward system is often detailed and personal to the individual. It is therefore essential that such information is communicated effectively using the most appropriate method of communication. Aspects of the reward system which should be communicated to employees include details of:

- all components of their remuneration package, including their salary level, any benefits entitlement and any performance related aspects of pay;
- the salary and benefits structure for their grade, including information on any rules relating to salary progression;
- the salary policy of the organization;
- the benefits policy of the organization;
- the policy on the grading and regrading of employees;
- performance requirements, including information on how the performance of individual employees is assessed.

Depending on the nature of the information to be communicated, and whether it is for personal or general circulation, the choice of the method of communication is very important. Whilst there are a wide variety of methods of communication, the most important factor is that the method chosen is likely to be effective and is appropriate for the type of information being communicated. Methods of communication which are utilized to communicate information on reward systems include:

- job advertisements and recruitment literature;
- noticeboards;
- company magazines;
- employee handbooks;
- specific publications on certain aspects of the remuneration package;
- team briefings;
- company videos;
- letters and memorandums;
- contracts and statements of the terms and conditions of employment;
- interviews and meetings;
- management/staff committees.

Whilst there are a variety of communication methods available, each of the above methods is most appropriate for certain types of information, in particular circumstances. If, for example, an organization wishes to inform all staff about the reward and benefits policy of the organization, this is probably most effective when communicated via the staff handbook. In contrast, if it is necessary to inform employees of their new salary level, this information is most effectively conveyed in a personal letter or memorandum. Whichever methods of communication are used by an organization, it is vital that all managers are fully aware of the importance of effective communication and, in addition, the possible consequences of poor and ineffective communication. The Institute of Personnel Management in their 1985 study, *The Merit Factor – Rewarding Individual Performance*, identified 12 rules for internal communication which can be used as basic principles for effective communication. The 12 rules are detailed below.

1 There is no such thing as a stone cold certainty in business decisions and it is important everyone in a business realizes this.
2 If a Board cannot or will not clearly spell out its business strategy employees are entitled to assume it does not have one.
3 Assume that in an information vacuum, people will believe the worst.
4 Never take it for granted that people know what they are talking about.
5 Always take it for granted that people doing a job know more about it than you.
6 Telling people something once is not much better than not telling them at all.
7 Never assume that people will tell you anything that reflects unfavourably upon themselves.
8 Remember that employees read newspapers, magazines and books, listen to the radio and watch TV.
9 Do not be afraid to admit you were wrong; it gives people confidence that you know what you are doing.
10 Asking for help, taking advice, consulting and listening to others are signs of great strength.
11 Communicating good news is easy but even this is not done often by management; bad news is often left to rumours and grapevine.
12 Changing attitudes to change behaviour takes years – changing behaviour changes attitudes in weeks.

Conclusion

Since the payment of salaries and the provision of other remunerative benefits is a significant item of expenditure for most organizations, it is essential that such expenditure is carefully managed in order to guarantee the maximum level of return for the organization. Whilst the primary purpose of providing a remuneration package for an employee is to reward them for service to the organization, it is also important that such remuneration secures work performance of a high quality which supports the overall business strategy of the organization. It is therefore essential that the reward policy of any organization is not only carefully planned but is also monitored and controlled using a variety of control mechanisms and reward guidelines. This should help to ensure that the organization is providing the correct level of remuneration which motivates the employee to provide work of a high standard which contributes to business objectives. It should also be noted that the use of computerization within reward management can have important implications for the human resource manager. Computerized reward systems allow much of the reward management information to be recorded, analysed and recalled on computer, giving the human resource manager almost instant access to data and trends associated with the remuneration of employees. Another key element affecting the effectiveness of the reward system is communication with employees. If the reward system is to be effective in motivating employees to perform to a high standard, managers must ensure that employees are kept informed, using the most appropriate and effective communication methods, of all aspects of the reward policy which affects them.

Bibliography

ACAS 1987: *Labour Flexibility in Britain: The 1987 ACAS Survey*, ACAS, London.

ACAS 1988: *Developments in Payment Systems: The 1988 ACAS Survey*, ACAS, London.

ACAS 1989: *Job Evaluation – An Introduction*, ACAS Advisory Booklet No. 1, ACAS, London.

ACAS 1990: *Appraisal Related Pay*, ACAS Advisory Booklet No. 14, ACAS, London.

Alderfer, C. P. 1972: *Existence, Relatedness, and Growth*, Collier-Macmillan Limited, London.

Anderson, G. C. 1986: *Performance Appraisal*, University of Strathclyde Business School, Glasgow.

Argyle, M. 1989: *The Social Psychology of Work*, Penguin, Harmondsworth.

Armstrong, M. 1988: *A Handbook of Personnel Management Practice*, Kogan Page, London.

Armstrong, M. 1990: *A Handbook of Human Resource Management*, Kogan Page, London.

Armstrong, M. and Murlis, H. 1980: *A Handbook of Salary Administration*, Kogan Page, London.

Armstrong, M. and Murlis, H. 1991: *Reward Management: A Handbook of Remuneration Strategy and Practice*, Kogan Page, London.

Baird, L. S., Post, J. E. and Mahon, J. F. 1990: *Management: Functions and Responsibilities*, Harper and Row, New York.

Beardwell, I. and Holden, L. 1994: *Human Resource Management*, Pitman Publishing, London.

Bilton, T. *et al.* 1982: *Introductory Sociology*, The Macmillan Press Ltd, London.

Bindra, D. and Stewart, J. (eds) 1971: *Motivation*, Penguin Books, Harmondsworth.

Bowey, A. M. (ed.) 1982: *Handbook of Salary and Wage Systems*, Gower Publishing Company Limited, Aldershot, England.

Bowey, A. M. *et al.* 1982: Effects of incentive payment systems, United Kingdom 1977–1980. *Department of Employment Research Paper No. 36*, United Kingdom.

Bowey, A. M. and Thorpe, R. 1987: *Payment Systems and Productivity*, The Macmillan Press, London.

Brading, L. and Wright, V. 1990: 'Performance related pay', *Personnel Management Factsheet 30*, Institute of Personnel Management, London.

Brindle, D. 1987: 'Will performance pay work in Whitehall?' *Personnel Management*, August 1987, Institute of Personnel Management, London.

Buchanan, D. A. 1979: *The Development of Job Design Theories and Techniques*, Saxon House, Aldershot.

Buchanan, D. A. and Boddy, D. 1983: *Organisations in the Computer Age: Technological Imperatives and Strategic Choice*, Gower Publishing Company, Aldershot.

Buchanan, D. A. and Huczynski, A. A. 1991: *Organisational Behaviour*, Prentice-Hall International, Hemel Hempstead, England.

Buchanan, D. A. and McCalman, J. 1989: *High Performance Work Systems: The Digital Experience*, Routledge, London.

Burns, T. and Stalker, G. 1961: *The Management of Innovation*, Tavistock Press, London.

Cumming, M. W. 1986: *The Theory and practice of Personnel Management*, Heinemann, London.

Curnow, B. 1989: 'Recruit, retrain, retain: personnel management and the three Rs', *Personnel Management*, November 1989, Institute of Personnel Management, London.

Currie, R. M. 1963: *Financial Incentives*, British Institute of Management, London.

Dale, B. and Cooper, C. 1992: *Total Quality and Human Resources*, Blackwell Publishers, Oxford.

Davidson, J. P. *et al.* 1958: *Productivity and Economic Incentives*, Allen and Unwin, United Kingdom.

Department of Employment 1990: *Employment Gazette*, February 1990, HMSO, London.

Department of Employment 1973–1994: *The New Earnings Survey*, HMSO, London.

Dessler, G. 1983: *Improving Productivity at Work – Motivating Today's Employees*, Reston Publishing Company Inc. Virginia.

Easterby-Smith, M., Thorpe, R. and Lowe, A. 1991: *Management Research: An Introduction*, SAGE Publications, London.

Evans, D. 1990: *Supervisory Management – Principles and Practice*, Cassell Educational Limited, London.

Fowler, A. 1988: 'New directions in performance pay', *Personnel Management*, November 1988, Institute of Personnel Management, London.

Fowler, A. 1990: 'How to design a salary structure', *PM Plus*, December 1990, Institute of Personnel Management, London.

Geen, R. G., Beatty, W. W. and Arkin, R. M. 1984: *Human Motivation*, Allyn and Bacon Inc., Boston.

Gill, D. 1977: *Appraising Performance*, Institute of Personnel Management, London.

Gillham, B. (ed.) 1981: *Psychology for Today*, Hodder and Stoughton, London.

The Government Statistical Service 1987: *Report on the Census of Production*, 1987 Edition, HMSO, London.

The Government Statistical Service 1990a: *Annual Abstract of Statistics*, 1990 Edition, HMSO, London.

The Government Statistical Service 1990b: *Monthly Digest of Statistics No.529*, January 1990, HMSO, London.

Greenhill, R. T. 1990: *Performance Related Pay for the 1990s*, Director Books, Cambridge.

Guest, D. 1974: 'What's new in . . . motivation?' *Personnel Management*, May 1984, Institute of Personnel Management, London.

Herzberg, F. *et al.* 1959: *The Motivation to Work*, John Wiley, New York.

Hodgkinson, S. 1990: 'A note on postal surveys in management research', *Graduate Management Research*, vol. 5 no. 1, 1990, Cranfield Press, Bedford.

Hume, D. A. 1993: 'The application of systems of performance related remuneration in the UK food industry', Ph.D. thesis, University of Glasgow, Glasgow.

Income Data Services 1987: *PRP and Profit Sharing*, IDS Study 397, Income Data Services London.

Income Data Services 1988: *Paying for Performance*, Income Data Services, London.

Income Data Services 1989a: *Employee Share Ownership Plans*, IDS Study 438, Income Data Services, London.

Income Data Services, 1989b: *A Guide to Performance Related Pay*, Income Data Services Public Sector Unit, London.

Income Data Services 1990: *Putting Pay Philosophies into Practice*, IDS Research File 15, Income Data Services, London.

Income Data Services/Coopers and Lybrand 1989: *Paying for Performance in the Public Sector: A Progress Report*, Income Data Services, London.

Income Data Services/Institute of Personnel Management 1985: *The Merit Factor – Rewarding Individual Performance*, Income Data Services, London.

Inland Revenue 1989: *Tax Relief for Profit Related Pay: PRP2 Notes for Guidance*, Inland Revenue, Cumbernauld, Glasgow.

Institute of Personnel Management 1982: *Practical Participation and Involvement: Pay and Benefits*, Institute of Personnel Management, London.

Institute of Personnel Management 1990: *Incentive Payment Schemes (IPS): A Review of Settlements 1983–1990,* Institute of Personnel Management, London.

Institute of Personnel Management 1992: *Performance Management in the UK: An Analysis of the Issues,* Institute of Personnel Management, London.

Kellogg, M. S. 1965: *What To Do About Performance Appraisal,* American Management Association, New York.

Kinnie, N. and Lowe, D. 1990: 'Performance related pay on the shopfloor', *Personnel Management,* November 1990, Institute of Personnel Management, London.

Lawler, E. 1983: *Pay and Organisation Development,* Addison-Wesley, Massachusetts.

Leane, J. 1987: 'The value-added approach to sharing company wealth', *Personnel Management,* October 1987, Institute of Personnel Management, London.

Lewin, K. and Cartwright, D. (eds) 1951: *Field Theory in Social Science,* Harper and Row, New York.

Lindop, E. 1989: 'The turbulent birth of British profit sharing', *Personnel Management,* January 1989, Institute of Personnel Management, London.

Locke, E. and Latham, G. 1984: *Goal Setting: A Motivational Technique that Works,* Prentice-Hall, Englewood Cliffs, New Jersey.

Long, P. 1986: *Performance Appraisal Revisited,* Institute of Personnel Management, London.

Maslow, A. H. 1954: *Motivation and Personality,* Harper and Row, New York.

McBay, A. 1989: 'Share option schemes', *Personnel Management Factsheet 19,* Institute of Personnel Management, London.

McClelland, D. C. 1961: *The Achieving Society,* Van Nostrand Reinhold, New York.

McDougall, C. 1973: 'How well do you reward your managers?' *Personnel Management,* March 1973, Institute of Personnel Management, London.

McGregor, D. 1960: *The Human Side of Enterprise,* McGraw-Hill, New York.

Millward, N., Stevens, M., Smart, D. and Hawes, W. R. 1992: *Workplace Industrial Relations in Transition,* Aldershot, Dartmouth.

Mook, D. G. 1987: *Motivation: The Organization of Action,* W. W. Norton and Company, New York.

Nash, A. N. and Carroll, S. J. 1975: *The Management of Compensation,* Brooks/Cole Publishing Company, Monterey, California.

Neale, F. (ed.) 1991: *The Handbook of Performance Management,* Institute of Personnel Management, London.

Poole, M. and Jenkins, G. 1988: 'How employees respond to profit sharing', *Personnel Management*, July 1988, Institute of Personnel Management, London.

Pratt, K. J. 1985: *Effective Staff Appraisal: A Practical Guide*, Van Nostrand Reinhold (UK) Co. Ltd, Berkshire.

Rawlins, C. 1992: *Introduction of Management*, HarperCollins, New York.

Rees, D. G. 1989: *Essential Statistics*, Chapman and Hall, London.

Sargent, A. 1990: *Turning People On*, Institute of Personnel Management, London.

Simpson, W. A. 1983: *Motivation: A Manager's Guide*, The Industrial Society, London.

Sisson, K. 1994: *Personnel Management*, Blackwell Publishers, Oxford.

Smith, I. G. 1984: 'Matching the incentive to the performer', *Personnel Management*, January 1984, Institute of Personnel Management, London.

Smith, I. G. 1989: *Incentive Schemes: People and Profits*, Croner Publications Limited, London.

Stewart, V. and Stewart, A. 1982: *Managing the Poor Performer*, Gower Publishing Company Limited, Aldershot, England.

Strohmer, A. F. 1970: *The Skills of Managing*, Addison-Wesley Publishing Company, California.

Taylor, F. W. 1911: *Principles of Scientific Management*, Harper, New York.

Torrington, D. and Hall, L. 1987: *Personnel Management: A New Approach*, Prentice-Hall International, London.

Torrington, D., Hall, L., Haylor, I. and Myers, J. 1991: *Employee Resourcing*, Institute of Personnel Management, London.

Torrington, D., Weightman, J. and Johns, K. 1989: *Effective Management: People and Organisations*, Prentice-Hall International, London.

Trade Union Research Unit 1988: *The Growth of Merit Pay in the Private Sector*, Technical Note 105, Trade Union Research Unit, Oxford.

Vroom, V. 1964: *Work and Motivation*, John Wiley, New York.

Walker, C. R. 1950: 'The problem of the repetitive job', *Harvard Business Review*, 28.

Walpole, R. E. 1976: *Elementary Statistical Concepts*, Collier Macmillan Publishers, London.

Weightman, J. 1990: *Managing Human Resources*, Institute of Personnel Management, London.

Woodley, C. 1990: 'The cafeteria route to compensation', *Personnel Management*, May 1990, Institute of Personnel Management, London.

Index

ACAS, 77–84, 92–3, 144, 147
added value, 187–8
Agricultural Wages Board, 103
Alderfer, C. P., 10, 18–20, 22
approved deferred share trusts
    (ADST), 192
attracting employees, 62–4, 88, 91,
    96
attribution theory of motivation,
    25–6

bonus schemes, 189–90
Burns, T., 49–50

cafeteria benefits, 167–8
cognitive theories of motivation,
    10–11, 23–8, 32–4
    and remuneration, 27–38
collective bargaining, 65–6, 101–2
commission, 7, 81, 82, 195–7
communication and reward
    management, 70, 235–7
computerization and reward
    management, 234–5
consultants, 106–7

data on remuneration trends,
    103–10
dissatisfiers, 16–17, 52–3
dysfunctional effects of PRR, 67–
    71

employee commitment, 36
employee differentials, 66–7,
    100–1
employee motivation, 3, 5–6, 9–
    10, 15–18
employee performance, 3–5, 101
    and remuneration, 5–7
employee share ownership plans
    (ESOP), 77, 94, 197–200
    executive share ownership
        schemes, 198–9
    savings related share option
        schemes, 199–200
empowerment, 35
equal pay, 129–32, 135–50
Equal Pay Act 1970, 129–32,
    135–50
    definition of pay, 138–9
    employees protected, 137–8
    employer's defence, 145
    Industrial Tribunal procedure,
        146–9
    and job evaluation, 129–32,
        142–3
    like work, 140–2
    and pension provision, 182–3
    remedies, 149
    scope, 137
    selecting a comparator, 139
    work rated as equivalent, 142–3
equity, 57–8